IMAGES
of America

CEMETERIES OF THE EASTERN SIERRA

ON THE COVER: This early image is of one of the cemeteries at Bodie, now a state historic park. Gold was found there in 1859, and at its peak, Bodie had over 8,000 residents. As the mining discoveries faded, so too did the population in this isolated town. By about 1887, only 1,500 people remained. (Courtesy of University of Southern California, on behalf of the USC Specialized Libraries and Archival Collections.)

IMAGES
of America

CEMETERIES OF THE EASTERN SIERRA

Gena Philibert-Ortega

ARCADIA
PUBLISHING

ISBN 978-0-7385-4786-2

Published by Arcadia Publishing
Charleston, South Carolina

Printed in the United States of America

Library of Congress Catalog Card Number: 2007924273

For all general information contact Arcadia Publishing at:
Telephone 843-853-2070
Fax 843-853-0044
E-mail sales@arcadiapublishing.com
For customer service and orders:
Toll-Free 1-888-313-2665

Visit us on the Internet at www.arcadiapublishing.com

To David, Daniel, and Brandon,
whose support made all the difference.

Contents

ACKNOWLEDGMENTS

Like any work that evolves, this book is the result of much collaboration, help, and encouragement from various people living in the Eastern Sierra region and outside of it as well. My most heartfelt thank you goes to Jane Wehrey for her help, advice, knowledge of Independence and Manzanar history, and proofreading of this manuscript. Kent Stoddard and the Mono County Historical Society provided images, information, and proofreading assistance. Richard Potashin, park ranger at Manzanar, and Jerry Eskew provided historical knowledge and photographs. Maggie Wittenberg provided help and support. Thanks for photographs goes to Dace Taube from the University of Southern California digital archives and the staff at the California State Library in Sacramento. The Inyo County Eastern California Museum provided photographs and research assistance. The reference librarians at the San Bernardino County Public Library in Yucaipa provided interlibrary loan materials. Thank you to Judith Butler for information and the picture of her great-aunt, Nevada Belle Butler Hall, and to Arlene Pearce, who shared pictures and information about her family. Terri Dean of the Pioneer Cemetery District in Bishop and Virginia MacLeod from the Big Pine Cemetery District provided cemetery histories. Harv Galic provided pictures regarding the Rettenbachers. Cat House provided cemetery pictures. I want to thank the many people who provided insight, directions, local history, and resources. It would be almost impossible to acknowledge them each by name, but they are all important just the same. I wish to thank those in my own community who regularly asked about this book and reminded me how important it was going to be.

My family has been a big support through the research and writing of this book. My husband, David Ortega, took many of the pictures and drove around all parts of the Eastern Sierra looking for cemeteries. My children, Daniel and Brandon, helped and endured trips that involved libraries, museums, and "dead people." My cousin, Diana Draper, provided research assistance.

I also wish to thank my editor at Arcadia Publishing, John Poultney, for his enthusiasm and guidance through the process of making this book a reality.

INTRODUCTION

California's Eastern Sierra is a land of stunning contrasts and sparse population. Inyo and Mono Counties, two of the largest in California, make up this region but together have fewer than 32,000 people. Inyo County alone is home to Mount Whitney, the highest peak in the lower 48 states at an elevation of 14,496 feet, and the lowest point in the United States, Death Valley, at 282 feet below sea level. The Owens Valley, which lies within Inyo County, is a narrow, high desert land, shadowed by the eastern face of the Sierra Nevada on the west and the Inyo/White Mountains on the east. It is a dry landscape that has supplied Los Angeles with much of its water since 1913. Driving through this region, one sees natural wonders such as the ancient Bristlecone pine, the oldest life form on earth; the fascinating rocks of the Alabama Hills; and fields of hardened lava that flow visible from the highway that runs the length of the Eastern Sierra. Known for its backdrops for hundreds of Western movies, the region is also home to Bodie, a well-preserved real ghost town.

This area has been home to the Paiute and Shoshone Indians and to miners and pioneers who settled and established towns, farms, and cattle ranches. Opportunities to make a living and the promise of wealth brought most people in the late 19th century. As towns were established, more people arrived, with an eye to prospering in business from the growing influx of ranchers and miners. Much later, a whole population of uprooted people of Japanese ancestry would be forced to live out World War II behind barbed wire in the shadow of the Eastern Sierra. More recently, it is the ragged beauty and emptiness of the land that bring new residents to join others whose roots go back to pioneer times.

Two of our most uniquely American authors described this region. In his book *Roughing It,* Mark Twain wrote of Mono Lake, often called the Dead Sea of California:

> It is one of the strangest freaks of Nature to be found in any land, but it is hardly ever mentioned in print and very seldom visited, because it lies away off the usual routes of travel and besides is so difficult to get at that only men who are content to endure the roughest life will consent to take upon themselves the discomforts of such a trip.

Mary Hunter Austin (1868–1934), an early feminist writer who was known for defending the rights and way of life of Mexican Americans and Native Americans, lived in Independence. Her small brown house still stands off the highway that runs through the town. Austin described the region in her book, *Land of Little Rain* (pages 61–62):

> This valley is a narrow one, a mere trough between hills, a draught for storms, hardly a crow's flight from the sharp Sierras of the Snows to the curled, red, and ochre, uncomforted, bare ribs of Waban. Midway of the groove runs a burrowing, dull river, nearly a hundred miles from where it cuts the lava flats of the north to its widening in a thick, tideless pool of a lake.

The cemeteries in this region range from the "garden" style, with a more parklike setting, found in the town of Bishop, to the deserted, overgrown, nearly forgotten graveyards of mining towns like Keeler and Cerro Gordo. Many small towns in Inyo County have not one but two or more cemeteries. In and around Independence, for example, there is a large town cemetery, a Jewish cemetery, and a virtually unknown Chinese burial ground. Six miles south is the cemetery at the former Manzanar War Relocation Center. Three cemeteries are in Lone Pine, one of which is a mass grave for those killed during the 1872 earthquake. At Bodie, tourists usually do not leave without visiting its cemetery, which is not just one but three distinct burial areas.

Eastern Sierra cemeteries are often unusual. A small stream flows through some, with the occasional fish making his way along as well. Quail regularly run through another with their young. Surrounding older graves in many cemeteries are small wood or iron fences that protect them from the dangers of a bygone era when cattle trampled grave sites or even uncovered the contents within. Dirt mounds cover some graves as a way to ensure that the grave does not sink or become exposed. Western pioneers were all too familiar with what could happen to graves through exposure to harsh elements, animals, and uncaring people. These graves hold the early pioneers of this valley—prospectors, farmers, ranchers, newspapermen, service workers, and even the occasional prostitute—as well as those who came later.

Cemeteries are fragile windows into the past. Those of the Eastern Sierra trace the area's history back more than 100 years. Previous writings about the pioneer cemeteries show that time has not been kind, and vandals and environmental conditions have led to missing and unreadable tombstones. Even in the six months of researching and writing this book, I was able to document at least one instance of a headstone being vandalized.

This book is not meant to be an exhaustive guide to all cemeteries or grave sites in this region. More than one grave is located at high altitude in the Sierra Nevada where only experienced hikers can go. Others, familiar to those in an earlier time, are now places where only the unknown are buried. Although it is in Inyo County, Death Valley and its graves are not featured here. This book is but a small look at some of the many cemeteries in this region and the people who helped make its history. I hope this book will serve as a catalyst to better understanding our history and respecting those who came before us.

One

Land of Little Rain

Visiting the Owens Valley can lead one to easily imagine what the area must have been like over 100 years ago. Between the small towns that populate Inyo County, much of the land seems almost untouched. Homes from the late 19th century still stand in the valley's four main communities: Bishop, Big Pine, Independence, and Lone Pine. Similarly, some cemeteries that house the remains of the area's pioneers look as though they have not been visited since those times.

Writer Mary Austin called this the "Land of Little Rain." It is a place where there is little rainfall, only an average of 5 inches annually. Most of the moisture in this area comes in the form of snow at the higher elevations. The 19th-century pioneers of this area lived in a diverse community that included Native Americans, Mexicans, Chinese, and various European ethnic backgrounds. This diversity becomes obvious when visiting the local cemeteries.

In size, Inyo County, which includes Death Valley, is the second largest county in California but has only just under 20,000 residents. More than 12 cemeteries and various random grave sites are scattered throughout this vast area. These graves include those who died in rugged mountain terrain and local residents buried closer to where they lived. Numerous memorials are scattered along the landscape, honoring those who have died in mountain climbing accidents and plane crashes and those who have been killed in auto accidents along Highway 395, the highway that connects the Los Angeles basin with Nevada.

Early burials reflect the lack of resources available to a region that remained isolated from the rest of California. Writer Mary Austin describes helping local women prepare bodies for burial, including washing and dressing the dead. Specialty fences to be placed around a grave, to deter wandering cattle, were manufactured and shipped in from other areas. Grave markers range from those made with local stone and metals decorated with Victorian imagery and verse to simple wooden crosses.

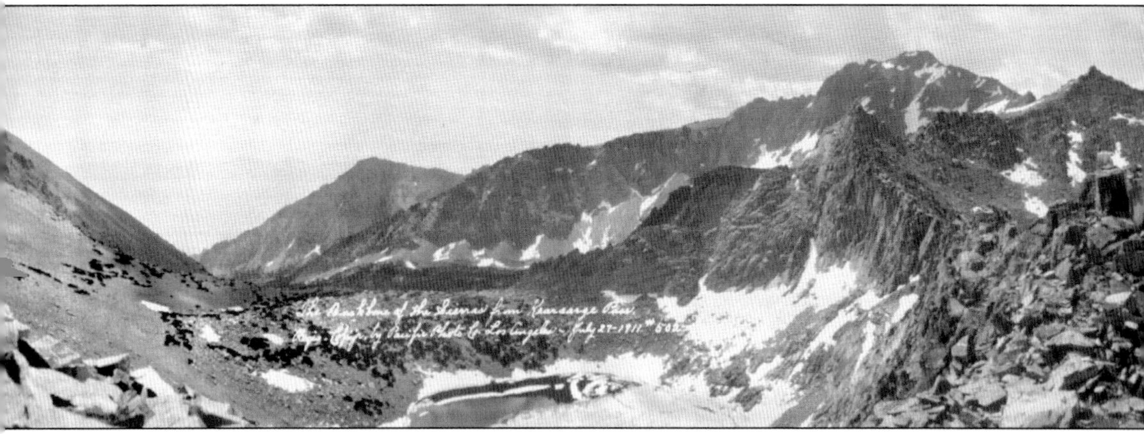

The Sierra mountain range is 400 miles long and approximately 45 miles wide. The heart of the eastern range stretches from Mount Whitney to Tioga Pass and includes Inyo and Mono Counties. Mount Whitney, the highest point in the contiguous United States, is part of the Eastern Sierra. The masses of rock that are the base of the Eastern Sierra range are believed to have been formed 65 to 225 million years ago. This range includes a volcanic chain, an active glacier, and the oldest

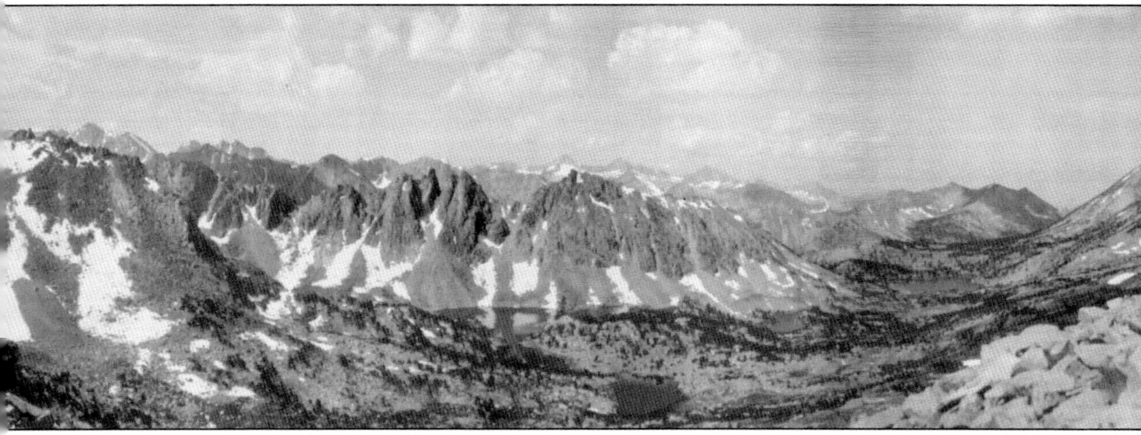

body of water in North America, Mono Lake. While ancient geological occurrences resulted in the forming of these mountains and nearby features, more modern events also have an effect. The 1872 Lone Pine earthquake resulted in an uplift of approximately 17 feet. (Courtesy of the Library of Congress, Prints and Photographs Division.)

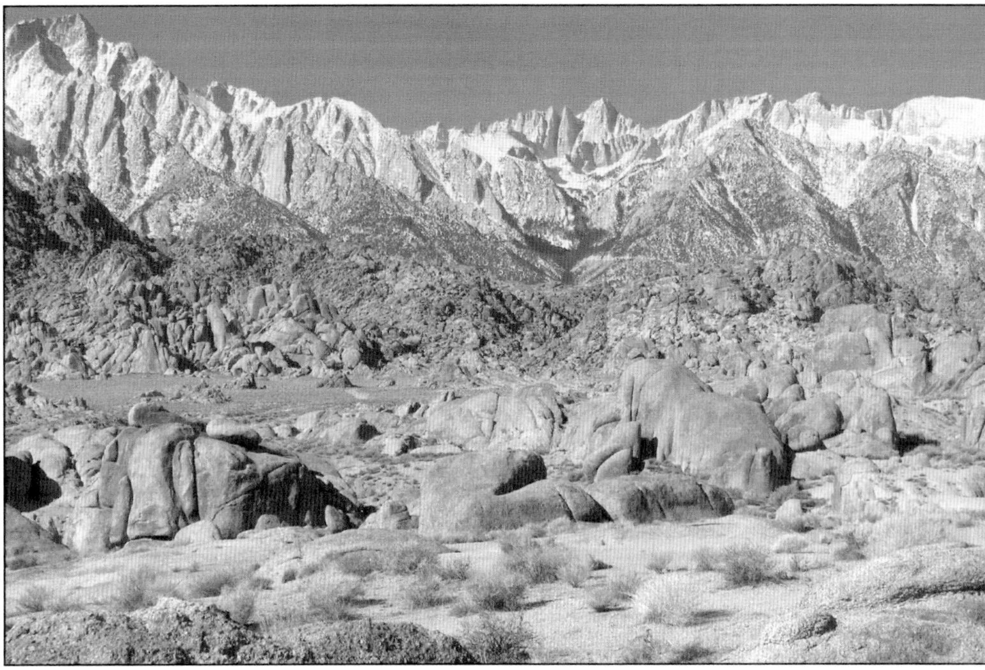

Mount Whitney, at 14,496 feet, is the highest point in the contiguous United States. Named after the chief geologist of California, Josiah Whitney, it is one of the most frequently climbed mountains in the United States. The main trail to Mount Whitney begins at Whitney Portal, near Lone Pine. (Courtesy of David Ortega.)

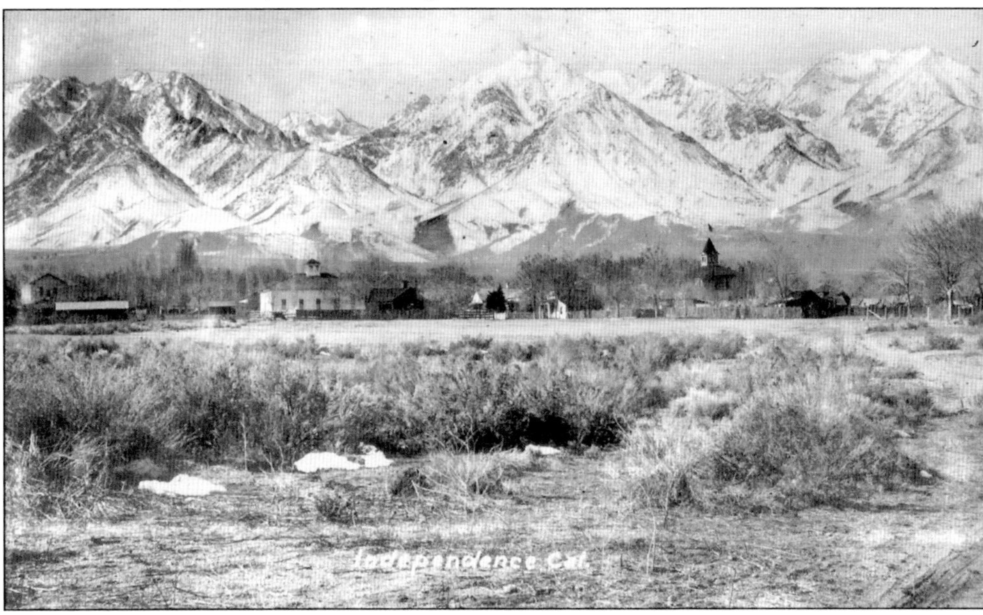

The county seat of Inyo County since 1866, Independence takes its name from the Civil War–era military fort Camp Independence, later renamed Fort Independence. The town was the home of writer Mary Austin, who refers to her home there in her book, *The Land of Little Rain*. This picture shows the Eastern Sierra mountain range in the background. (Courtesy of the California History Room, California State Library, Sacramento, California.)

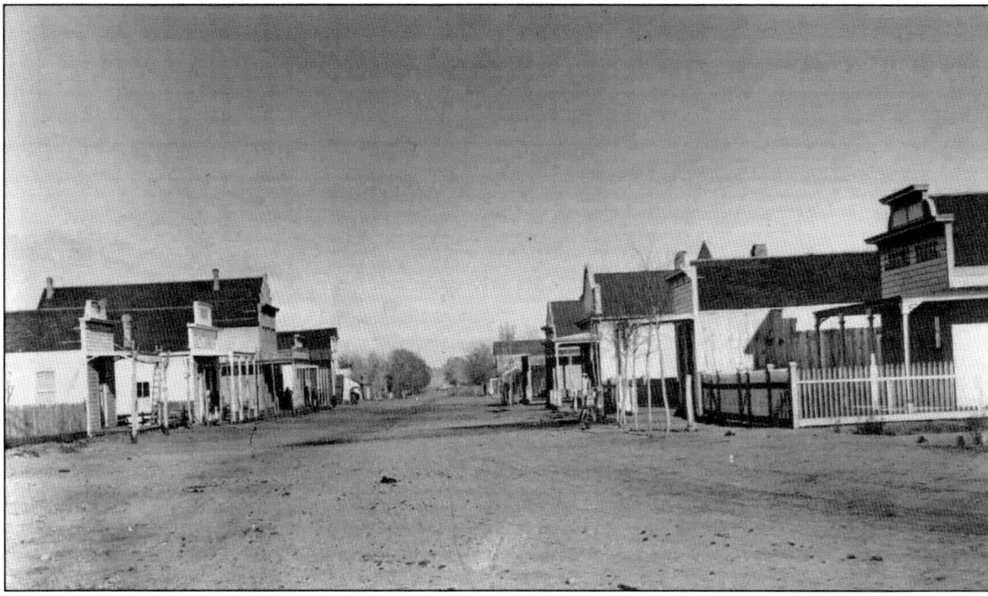

Located between the towns of Lone Pine and Big Pine, Independence has been the home of miners, merchants, and farmers, and during World War II, Manzanar War Relocation Center was to the south of the town. The Independence area is the home of four cemeteries, including a town cemetery, a Chinese cemetery, a Jewish cemetery, and the cemetery at Manzanar. (Courtesy of County of Inyo, Eastern California Museum.)

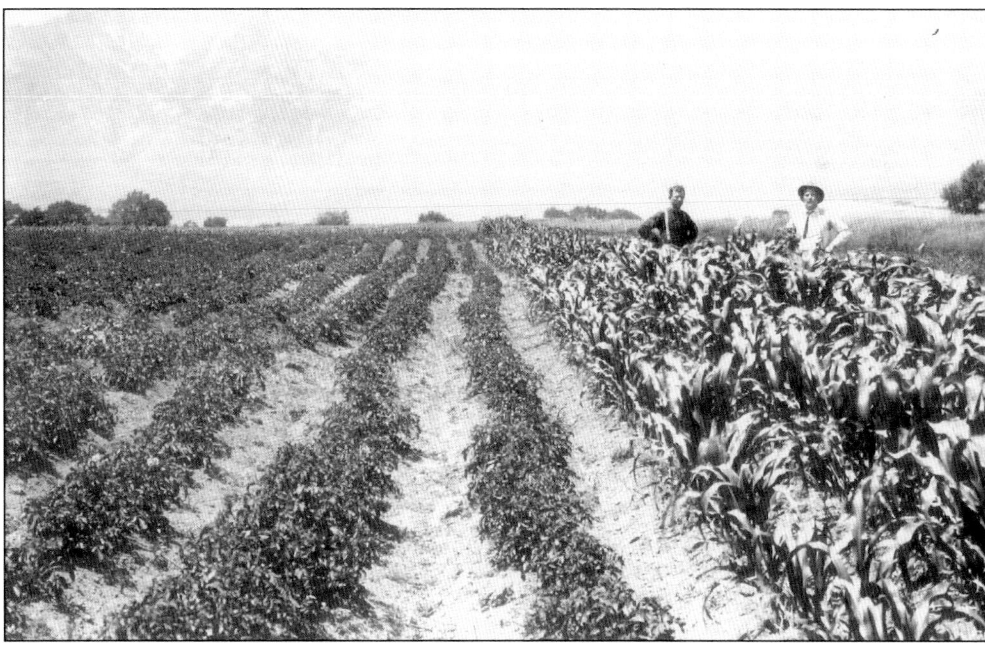

While people came to the Owens Valley region for many reasons, most who settled here were farmers or ranchers. One Independence settler, Jacob Vagt, was said to have had a successful farm that included vegetable crops, peaches, and even grapes. The local paper, the *Inyo Independent*, wrote of his skill and his ability to produce crops even in difficult conditions. (Courtesy of the California History Room, California State Library, Sacramento, California.)

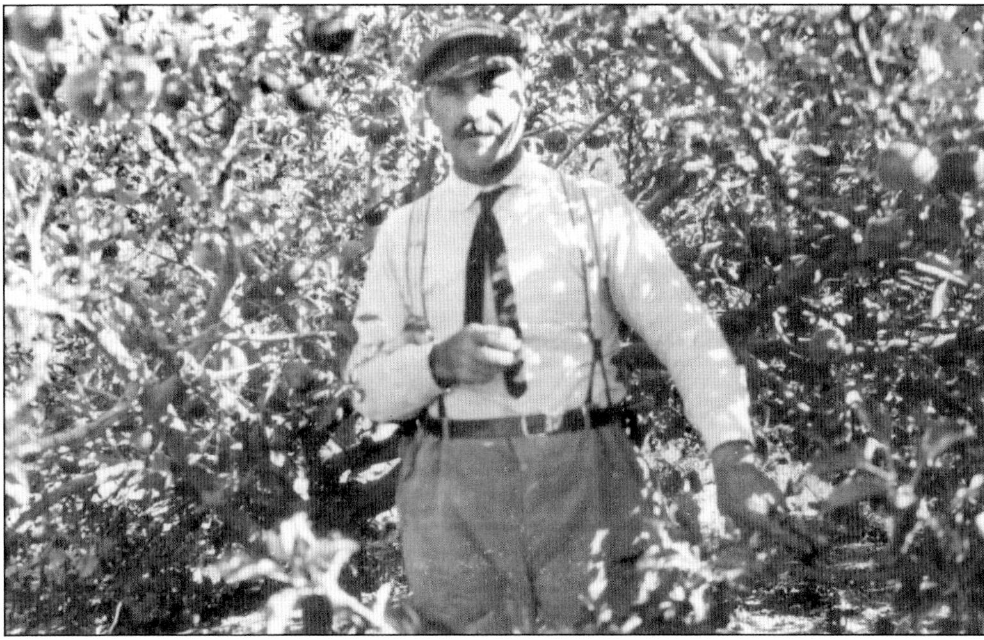

By 1926, there were approximately 595 farms in the valley. In 1911, some 22,000 apple trees were planted near the town of Manzanar (Spanish for "apple orchard"). A concrete and gravity-flow irrigation pipe system was constructed to help carry water to the farms and ranches at Manzanar. Later, during World War II, the abandoned orchards were tended by the Japanese interned at Manzanar. (Courtesy of the California History Room, California State Library, Sacramento, California.)

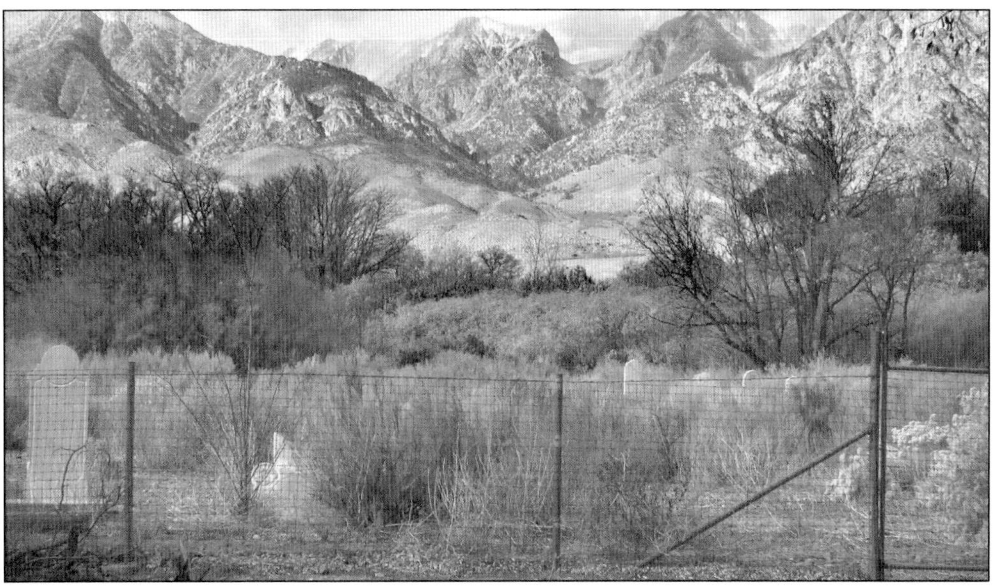

This Civil War–era post, two miles north of today's town of Independence, housed Union soldiers who had been sent to the Owens Valley to protect the pioneers and mediate the growing conflicts between the white settlers and the Native American population. The post included a cemetery. Originally a soldier's cemetery, it was entrusted to the local citizens when the fort was decommissioned in July 1877. (Courtesy of David Ortega.)

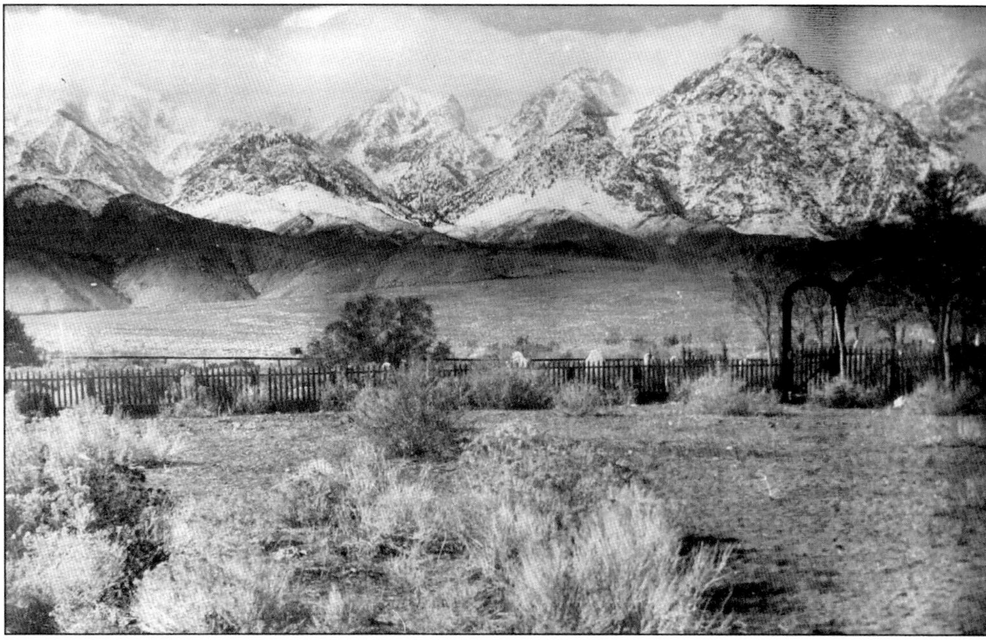

Because the military believed that the Fort Independence cemetery was not being cared for as they requested, the soldiers buried there were moved in 1898 to the Presidio in San Francisco. It is said that a Mrs. Lewis who ran the county hospital at the fort buried paupers in unmarked graves on the southwest side of the cemetery. Twenty-three gravestones remain in the cemetery today. (Courtesy of County of Inyo, Eastern California Museum.)

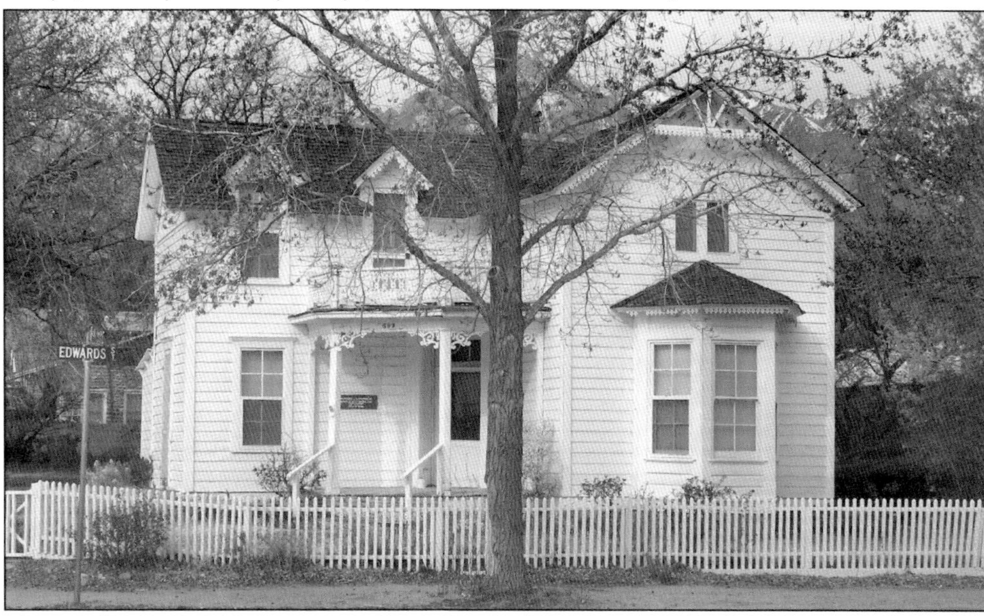

The residence of the last commander at Fort Independence, this home was built in 1872 to replace quarters destroyed by the Lone Pine earthquake. The fort was decommissioned in 1877, and its buildings remained there until 1883 when they were sold at public auction. This home was purchased by V. G. Thompson and moved to its current location at Highway 395 and Main Street in Independence. (Courtesy of David Ortega.)

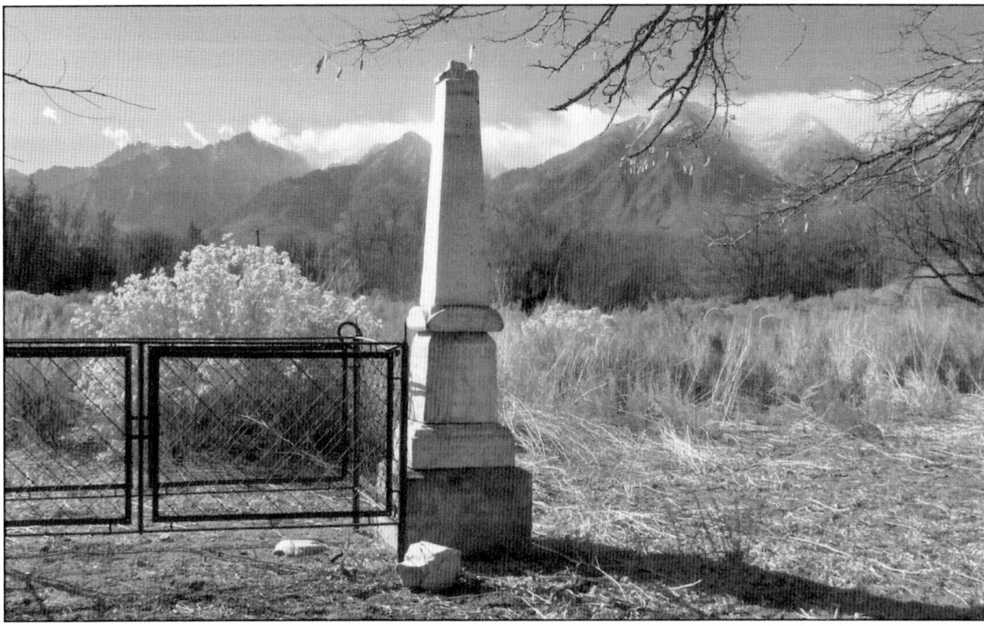

David Naylor was living in Inyo County by 1870 and was issued a patent for land in Big Pine in 1874. He died only five years later at the age of 50, leaving his wife, Ellen, and three children. His young daughter, Ellen J. Naylor, died in May 1870 and is buried at the fort cemetery. (Courtesy of David Ortega.)

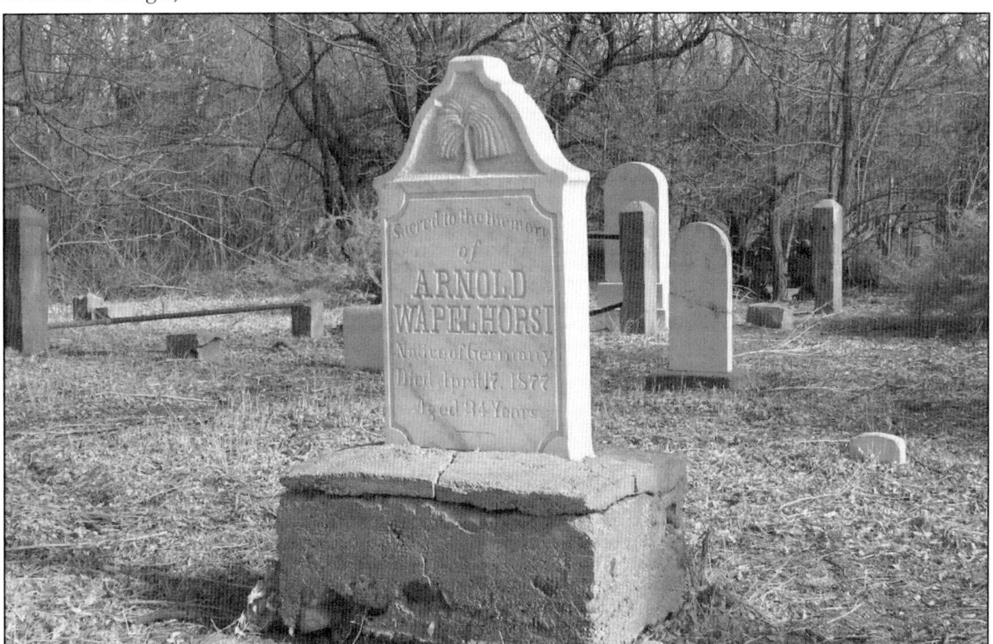

Arnold Wapelhorst, a German immigrant who resided in Independence and Cerro Gordo, came to the area with an interest in mining. He married the daughter of Margaret Louis, the proprietor of the American Hotel in Cerro Gordo. Residents of both towns attended his August 1875 wedding at the hotel. Arnold died on April 17, 1877, at the age of 34, leaving his wife, Lulu, and daughter, Marguerite. (Courtesy of David Ortega.)

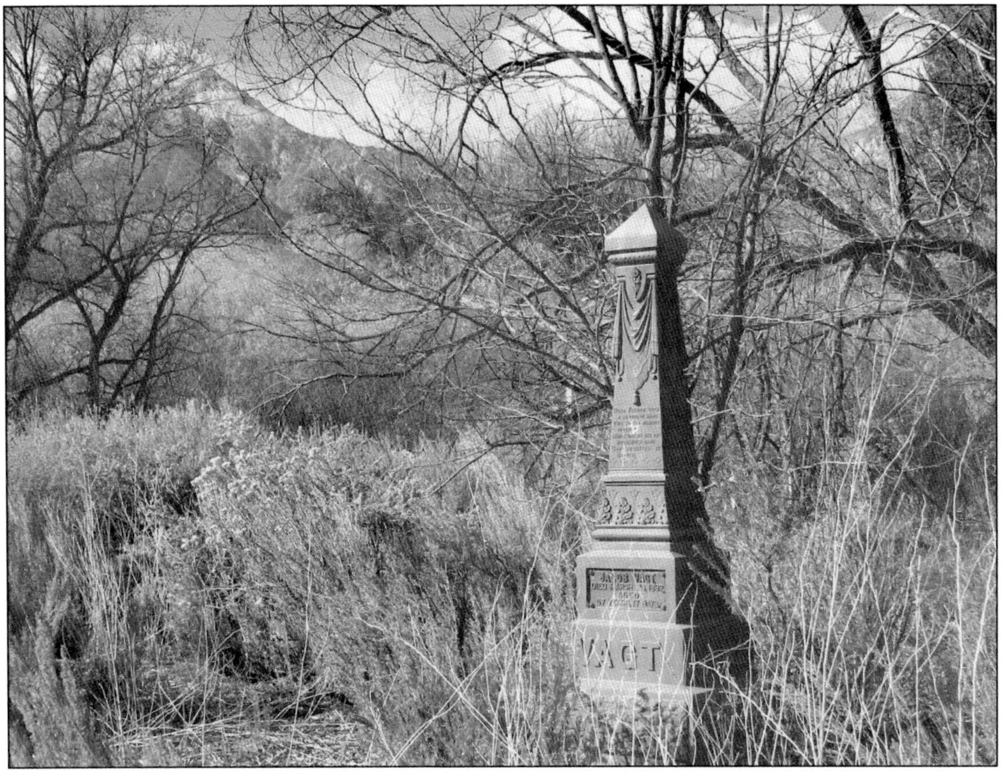

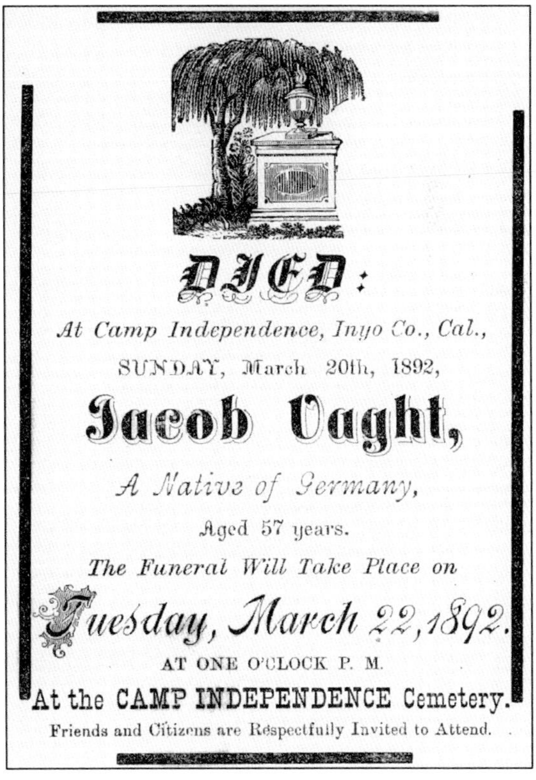

DIED:

At Camp Independence, Inyo Co., Cal.,

SUNDAY, March 20th, 1892,

Jacob Vaght,

A Native of Germany,

Aged 57 years.

The Funeral Will Take Place on

Tuesday, March 22, 1892.

AT ONE O'CLOCK P. M.

At the CAMP INDEPENDENCE Cemetery.

Friends and Citizens are Respectfully Invited to Attend.

Jacob Vagt was a successful farmer growing peaches, grapes, and corn near Fort Independence. He and his wife, Henriette, had emigrated from Germany. The 1872 earthquake demolished their adobe home, but they survived by breathing through an air hole that Jacob had dug with a tablespoon. Jacob Vagt died on March 20, 1892, and Henriette died just six days later, on March 26, 1872. Her refusal to eat or drink hastened her death, according to most accounts. (Above, courtesy of David Ortega; at right, courtesy of County of Inyo, Eastern California Museum.)

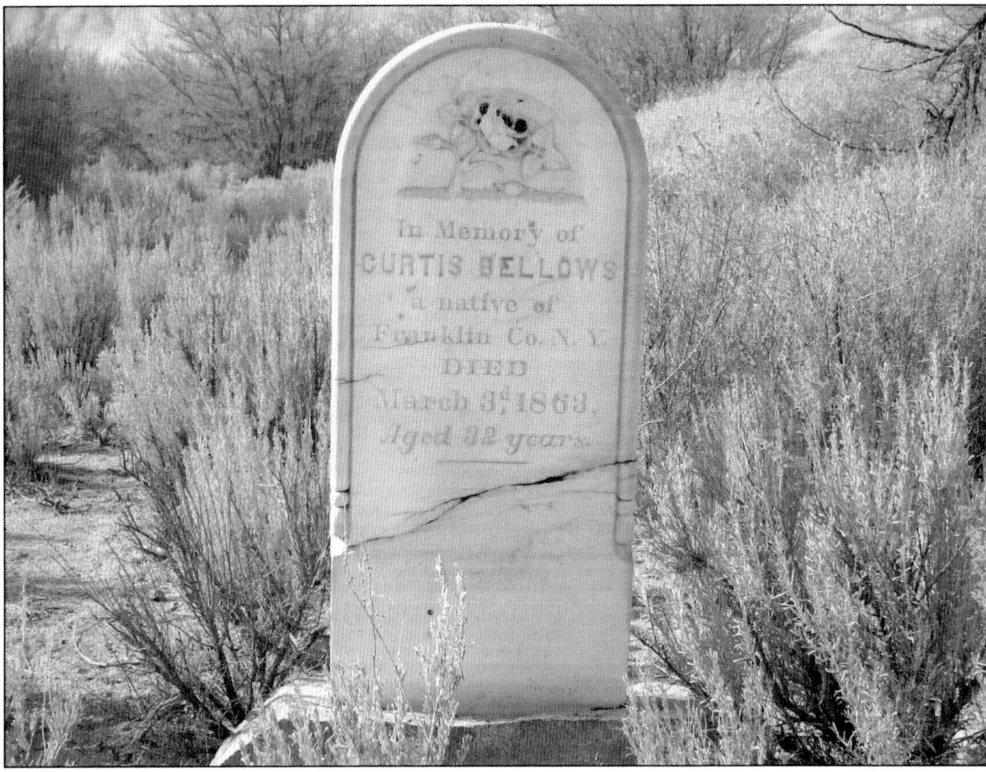

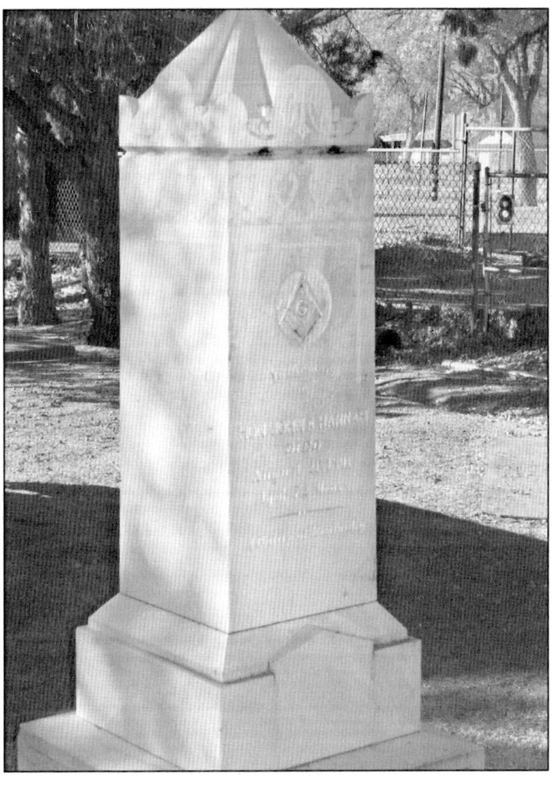

Curtis Bellows lived at the Ida mine east of present-day Manzanar. In March 1863, he was fetching water when Native Americans fatally shot him with an arrow. His mining partner ran home and escaped. Fifteen soldiers returned to recover the body, and he was buried in a ravine near Independence. This marker at the Fort Independence cemetery was later made into a permanent memorial. (Courtesy of David Ortega.)

Judge John A. Hannah was born in Kentucky in 1819. His career included stints as a soldier in the Seminole War, a dairyman in Napa, and a mining recorder in Cerro Gordo. He served as Cerro Gordo's justice of the peace and was elected judge in 1871. He served as a superior court judge for Inyo County from 1880 to 1890. Hannah died in Independence in 1891. (Courtesy of David Ortega.)

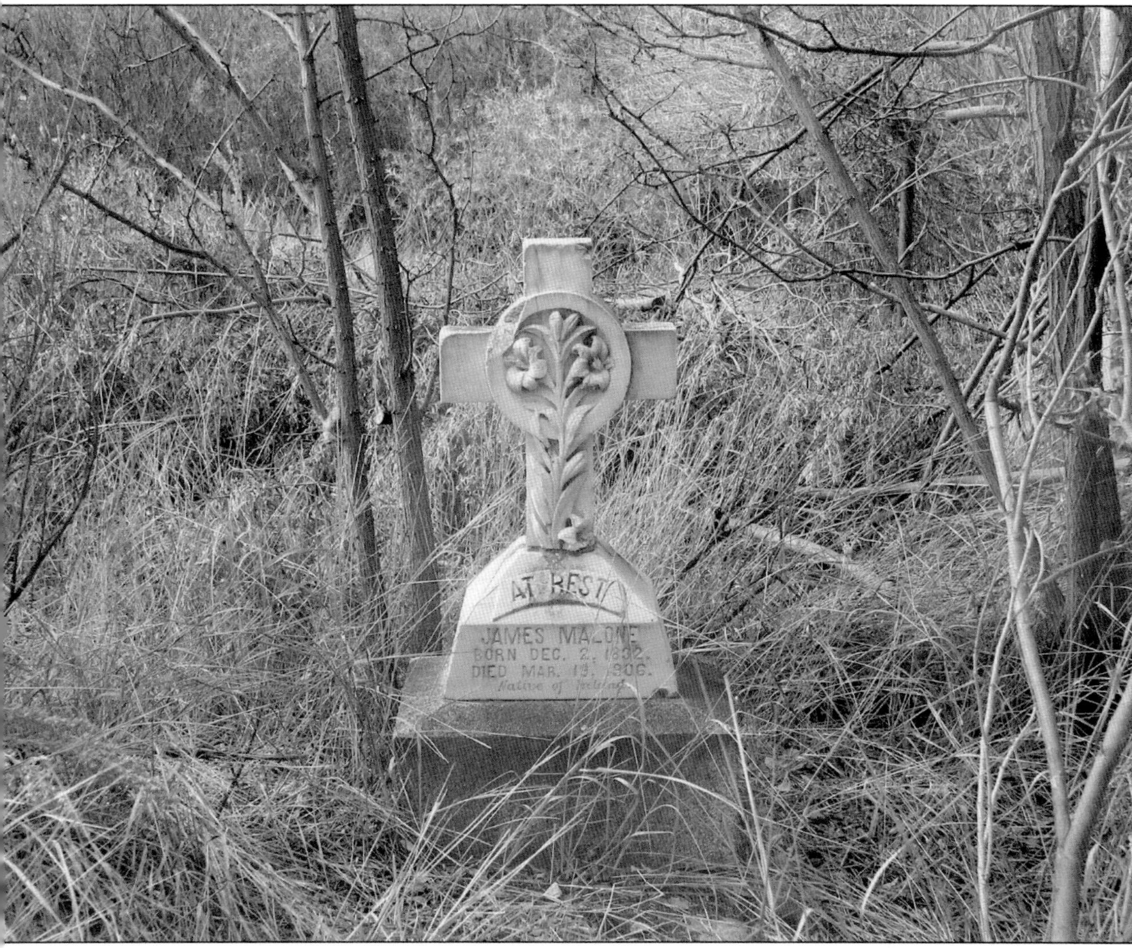

James Malone, an Irish immigrant, is buried in the Fort Independence Cemetery. He worked as a farmer in Independence and the surrounding area for approximately 30 years prior to his death in 1906. The calla lily on his tombstone symbolizes marriage. His daughter Mary, who died at 18 years of age, is buried a few feet away from her father. (Courtesy of David Ortega.)

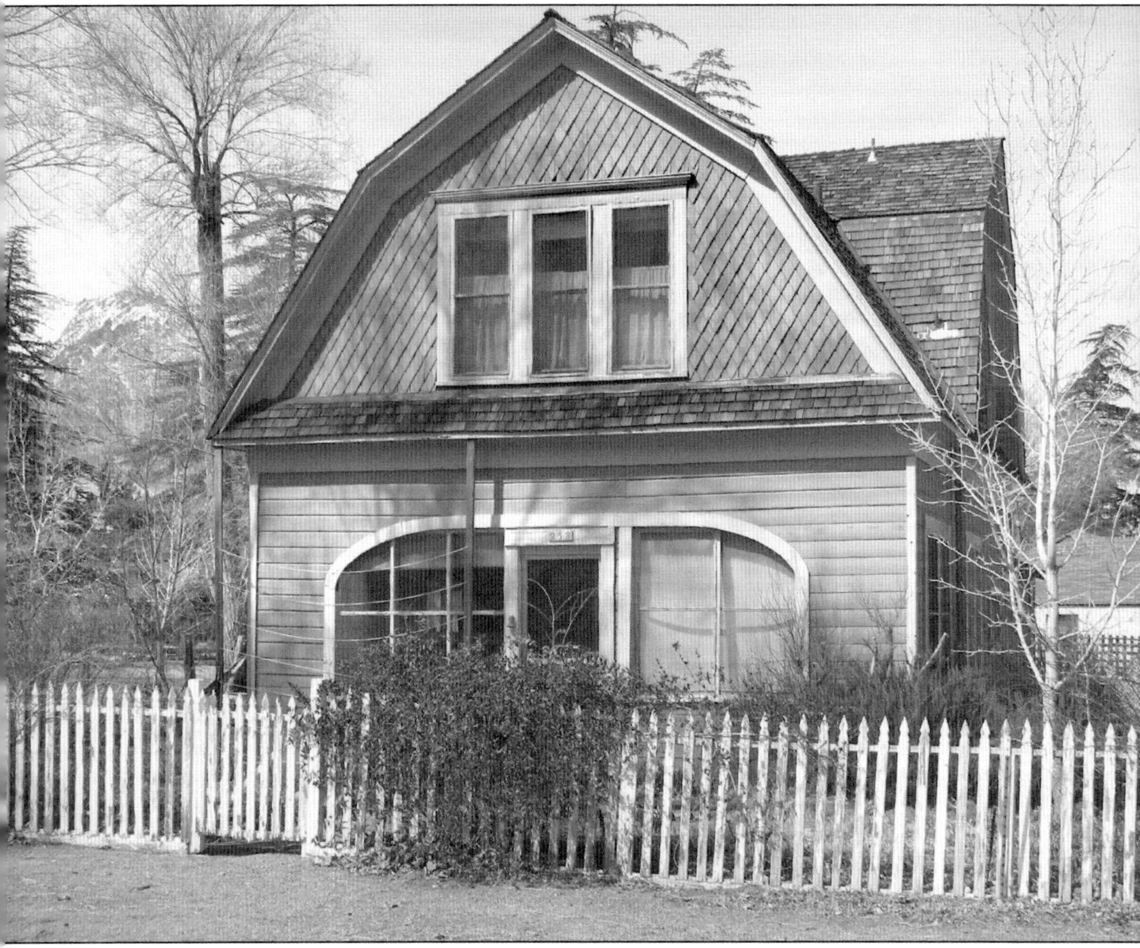

The writer Mary Hunter Austin (1868–1939) lived in the Owens Valley with her husband, Stafford Austin, and daughter, Ruth. She worked as a schoolteacher and wrote articles for the local paper before she gained fame as an author. Even after Mary left the valley to follow her literary pursuits, she remained passionate about the area and was outspoken in her opposition to the Los Angeles Aqueduct. (Courtesy of David Ortega.)

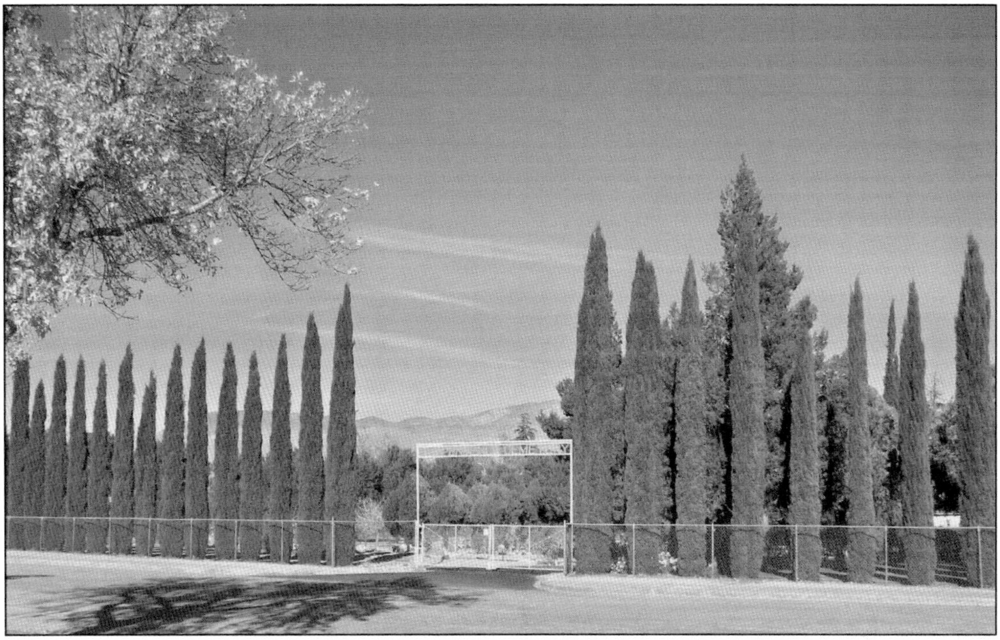

The Independence Cemetery, located on Clay Street, is the final resting place for the town's pioneers as well as people of the present day. Many who settled in neighboring areas such as George's Creek and the orchard town of Manzanar also are buried here. Originally a Masonic cemetery, it eventually became the burial ground for the entire community. (Courtesy of David Ortega.)

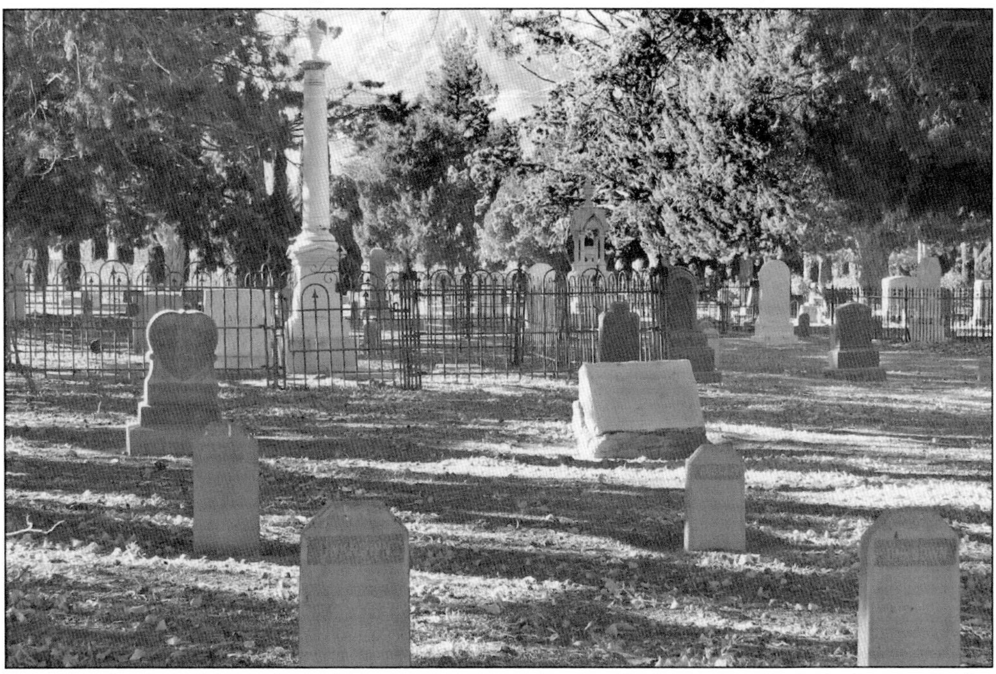

A unique feature of the Independence cemetery is that a small stream runs through the north edge of it. This stream, fed by Independence Creek, can possibly have trout swimming through it that are stocked by the Mount Whitney trout farms and other local hatcheries. The Fort Independence cemetery also has a small creek running along the side of it. (Courtesy of David Ortega.)

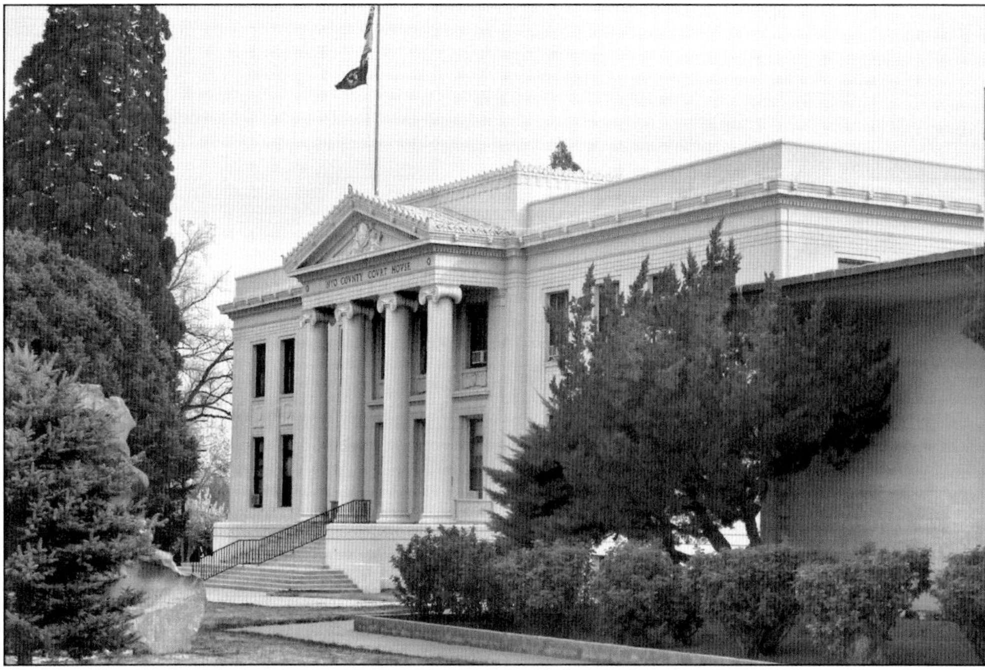

Inyo County, with Independence as its county seat, was formed in March 1866. Completed in 1921, the current courthouse, located on Highway 395, is the fourth courthouse built for the county. The first was destroyed in the 1872 Owens Valley earthquake centered near Lone Pine. An 1886 fire that destroyed 38 buildings in Independence leveled the second courthouse. (Courtesy of David Ortega.)

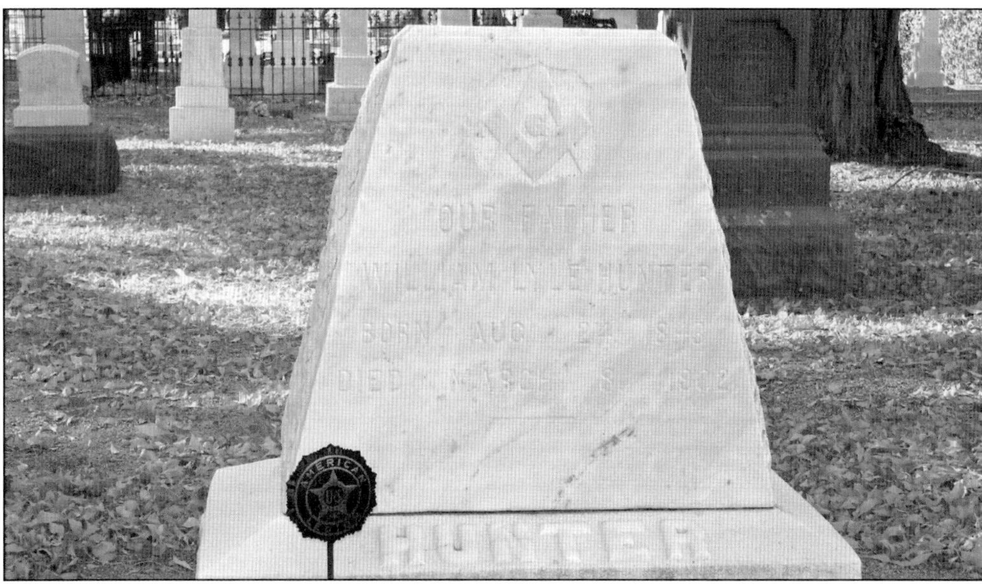

A Confederate soldier during the Civil War, William Lyle Hunter set his sights on California and its promises of gold. His career included mining and a stint as the Inyo County recorder. Of his funeral, the local newspaper wrote, "The coffin was draped in the American flag and the body followed to its last resting place by a large concourse of friends who loved and honored him in life." (Courtesy of David Ortega.)

Fred and Frederike Schabbell were some of the homesteaders that lived within a mile of Camp Independence. When their son Fred, named after his father, was born on February 8, 1877, he was given a large welcome by the soldiers at the camp. A party was held, and the soldiers brought gifts for the parents and the baby. (Courtesy of the author.)

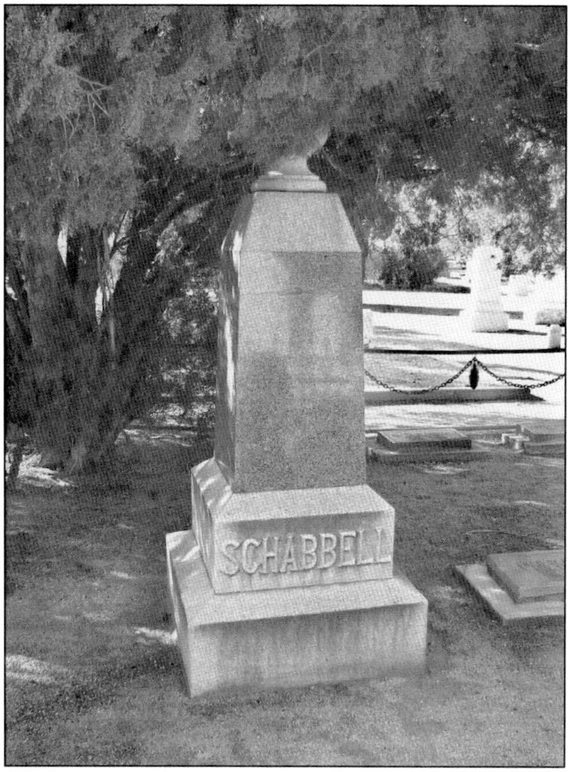

The compass and square on the top of William Lafayette Moore's tombstone in the Independence cemetery indicates that he was a member of the fraternal order known as the Masons. The Masons were an important leadership group in early western communities. Among the Masons in this area were many prominent ranchers and businessmen. (Courtesy of David Ortega.)

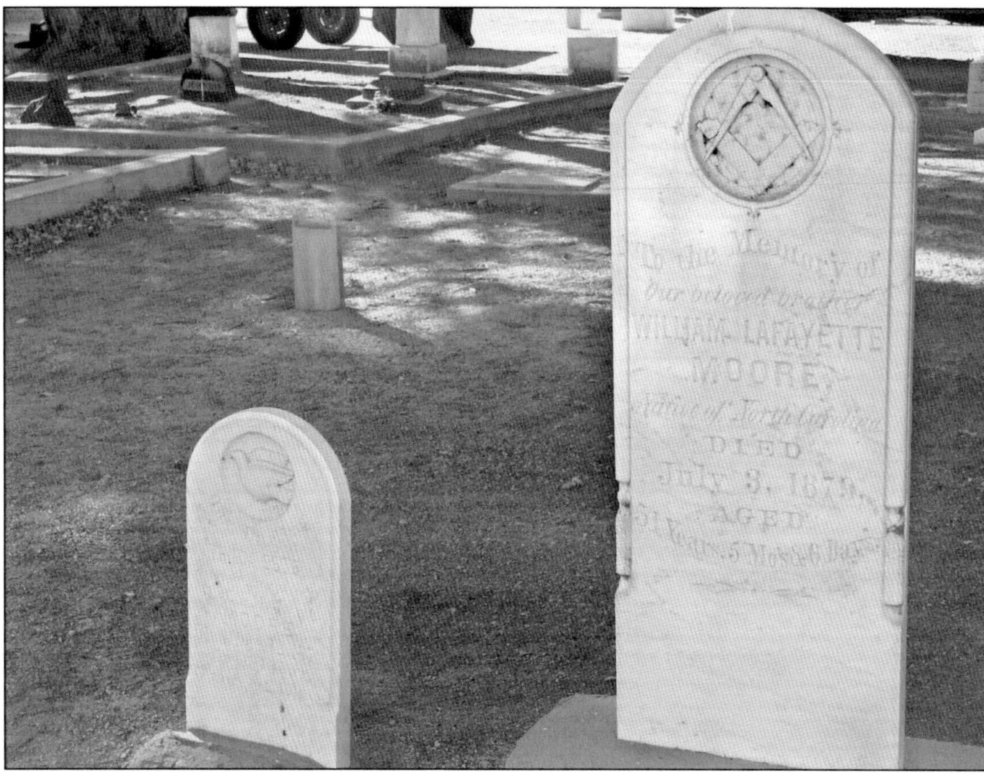

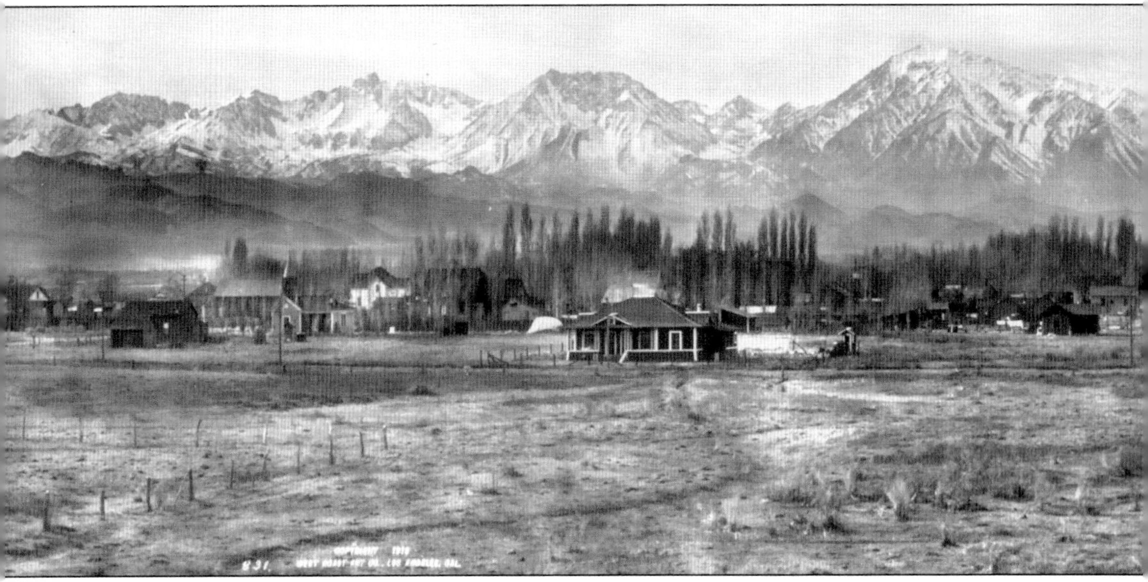

Bishop is named after Samuel Addison Bishop, one of the first white settlers in the Owens Valley. He drove 600 head of cattle into the valley from Fort Tejon in August 1861 and provided a much-needed commodity for the growing population of miners. The city was incorporated in

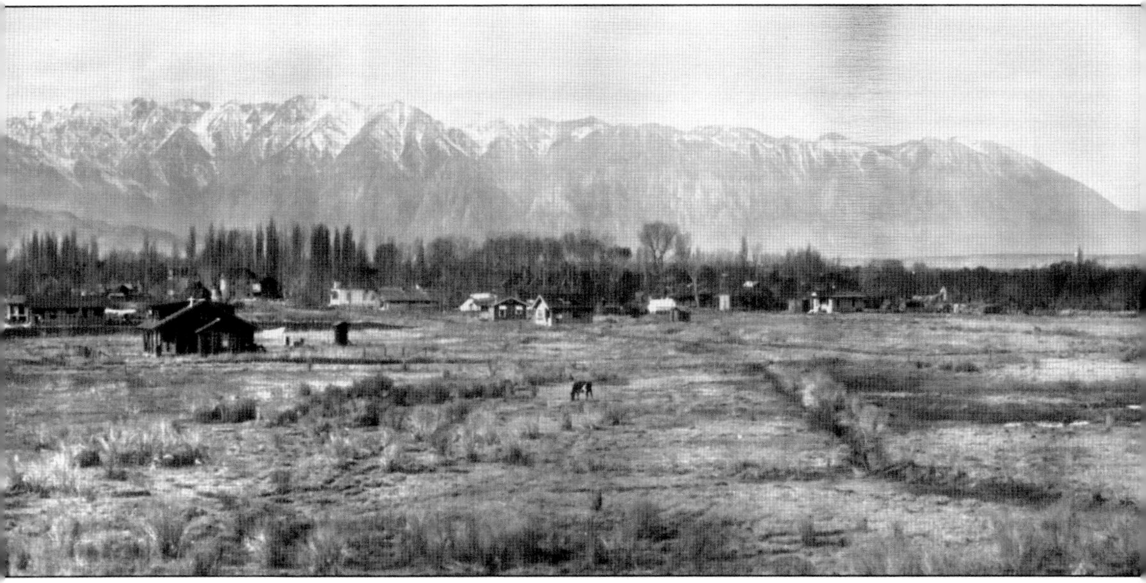

1903 and remains Inyo County's only incorporated town. (Courtesy of Library of Congress, Prints and Photographs Division, West Coast Art Company.)

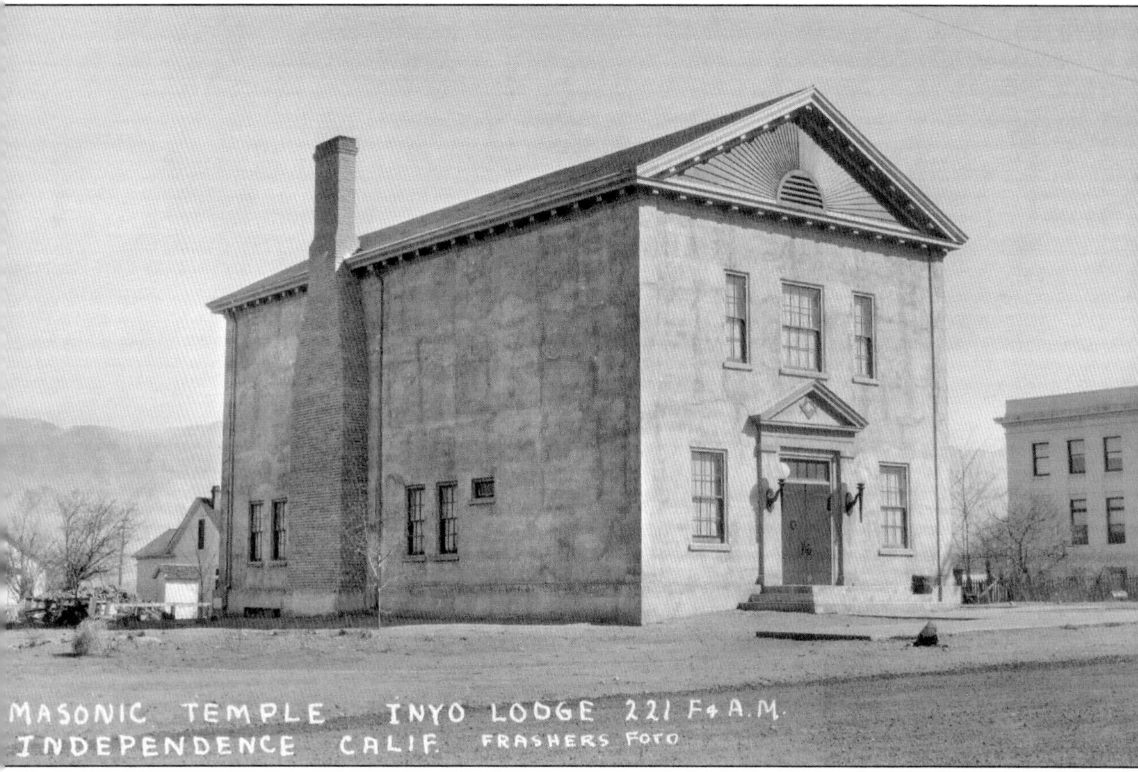

James Brady, superintendent of a smelting mill in Swansea, near Lone Pine, began recruiting Masons in southern Inyo County in 1870 to establish a lodge. By then, approximately 75 Masons lived in southern Inyo. The Inyo Lodge, founded in 1872, is located in Independence and is the oldest Masonic body in Eastern California. (Courtesy of Pomona Public Library, Pomona, California.)

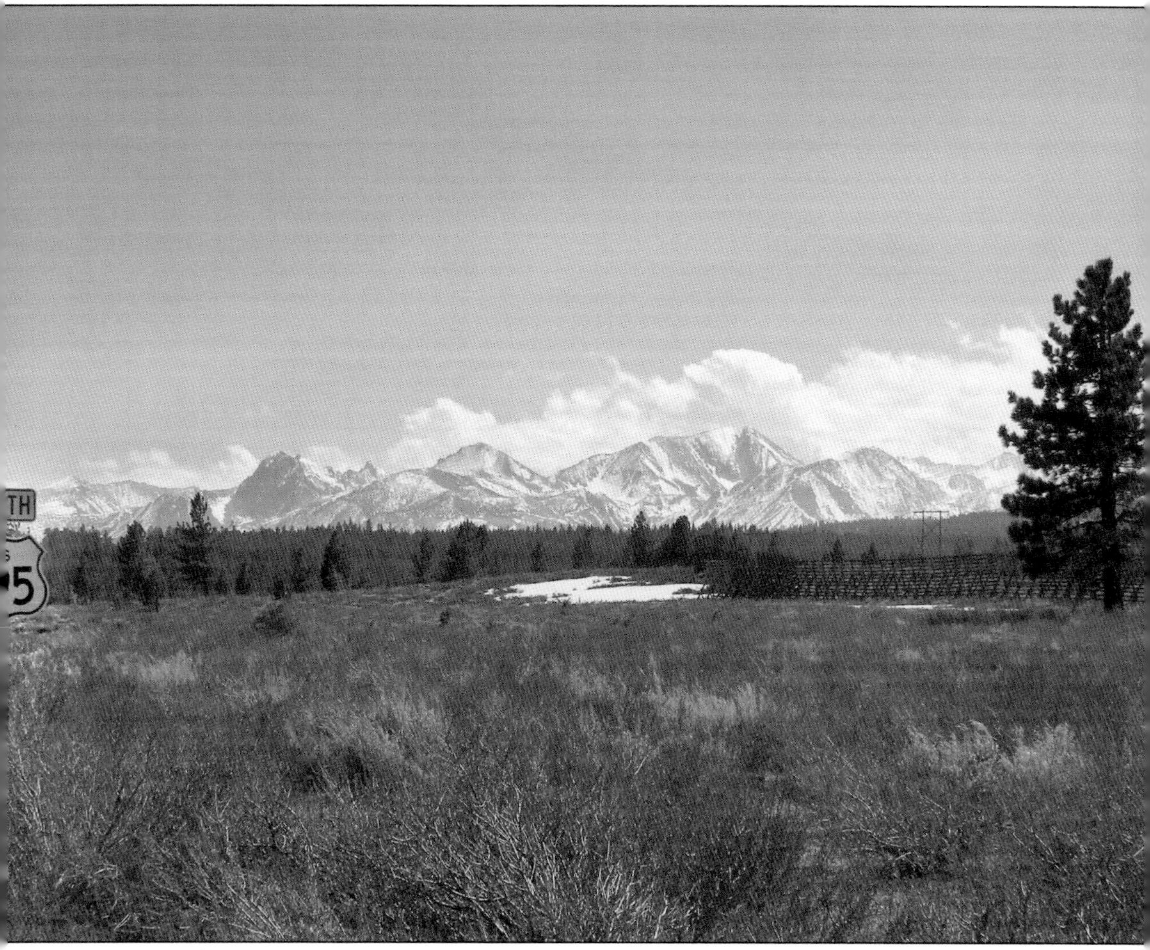

The Owens Valley is 100 miles in length and extends from the city of Bishop to the south. In 1845, the Owens Valley, River, and Lake were named for Richard Owens, who was an army captain in John C. Fremont's expedition to the area. It wasn't until about 1865 that a population boom occurred when gold was discovered north of Owens Lake. (Courtesy of David Ortega.)

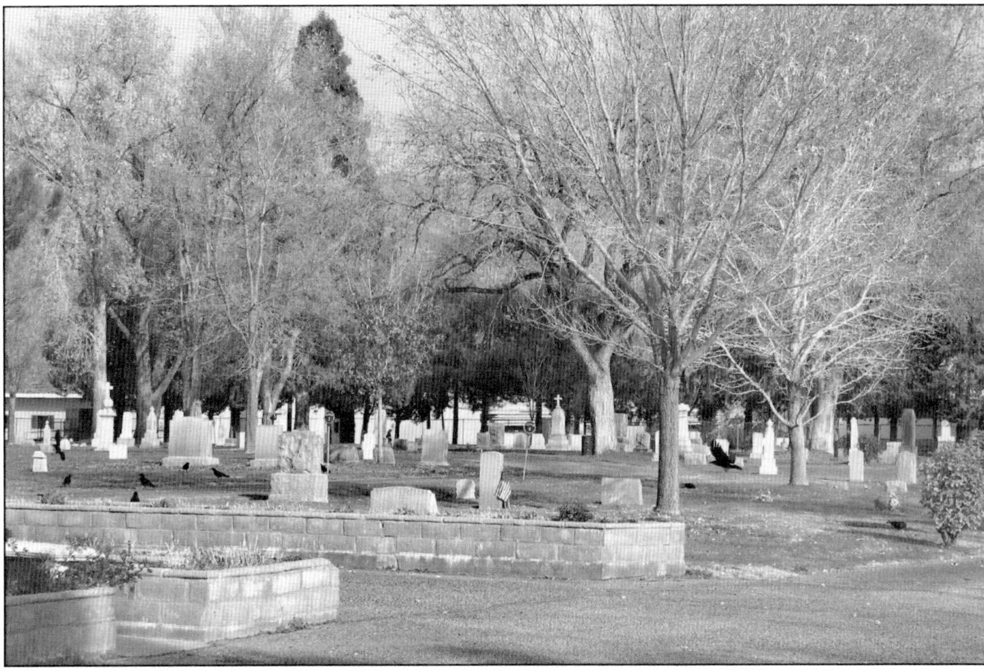

The Pioneer Cemetery District in Bishop was formed in 1927 and combined West Line Street Cemetery, established in 1868 (formerly known as Pioneer Cemetery), and East Line Street Cemetery, established in 1896 (formerly known as the Masonic and Odd Fellows Cemetery). The two contain over 5,000 graves in about 23 acres. The oldest burial in the Pioneer Cemetery District West is George Smith in 1863, and the oldest known burial for the East Line Street Cemetery is Franklin W. Hutchinson, a farmer from Bishop Creek who died in 1874. (Courtesy of David Ortega.)

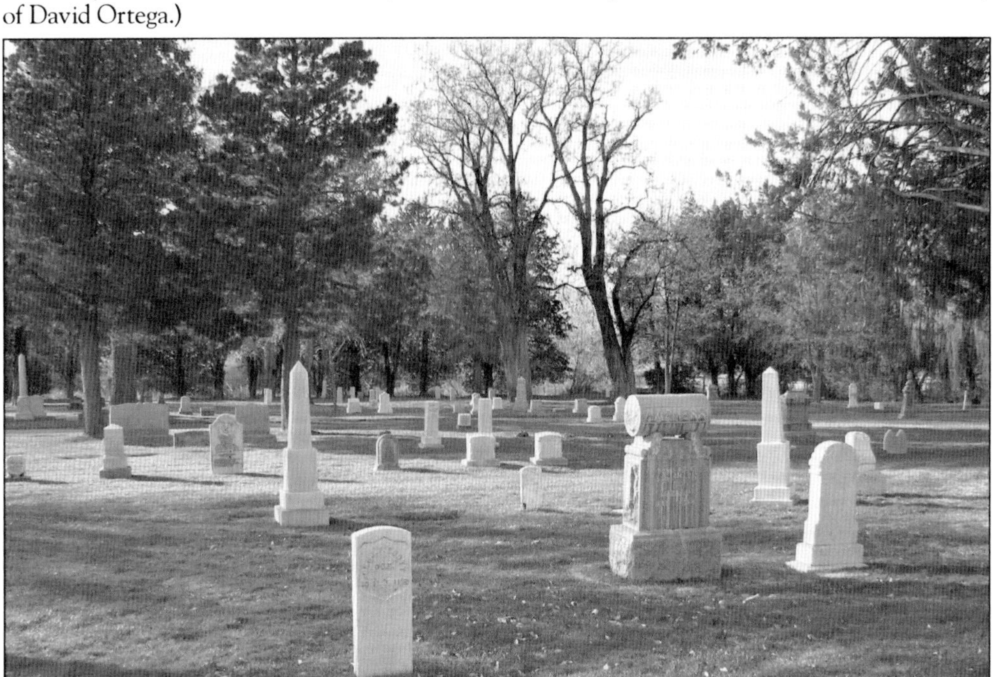

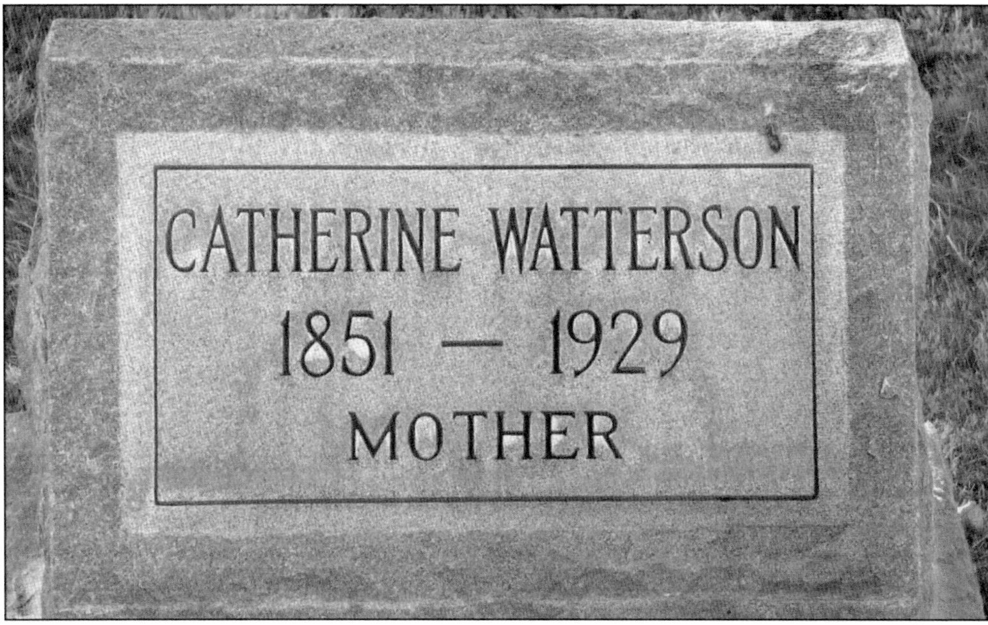

Catherine and James Watterson were immigrants from the Isle of Man, who initially settled in Virginia City, then moved to Benton, 40 miles north of Bishop. It was on a trip to Bodie in 1881, to negotiate opening a general store, that James caught pneumonia. Concerned that he needed to be present for the birth of his fourth child, he declined to stay in bed in Bodie and, heading back to Benton, died en route. James was temporarily buried in Benton. Later, in 1906, when the family moved to Bishop, Kate had James's body moved to the Bishop Pioneer Cemetery. (Courtesy of David Ortega.)

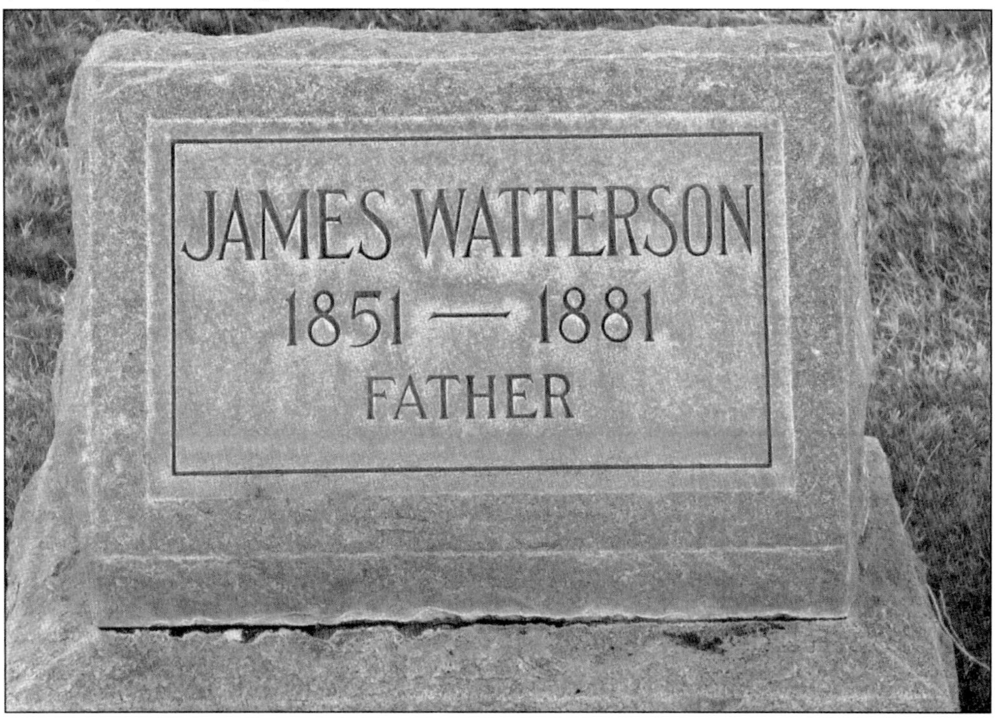

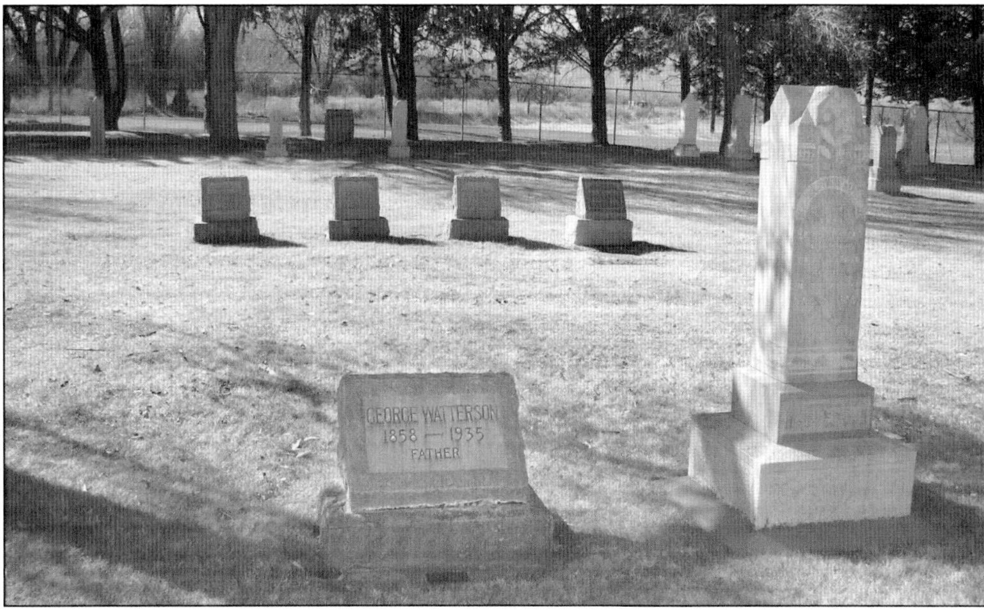

George Watterson was the uncle of Mark and Wilfred Watterson, who were key players in the aqueduct resistance. George favored an agreement being made with Los Angeles over the aqueduct that would favor landowners like himself. It was George Watterson's application to open a new bank that triggered a state audit of his nephews' bank, the Inyo County Bank, and led to their indictment and eventual prison sentence. (Courtesy of David Ortega.)

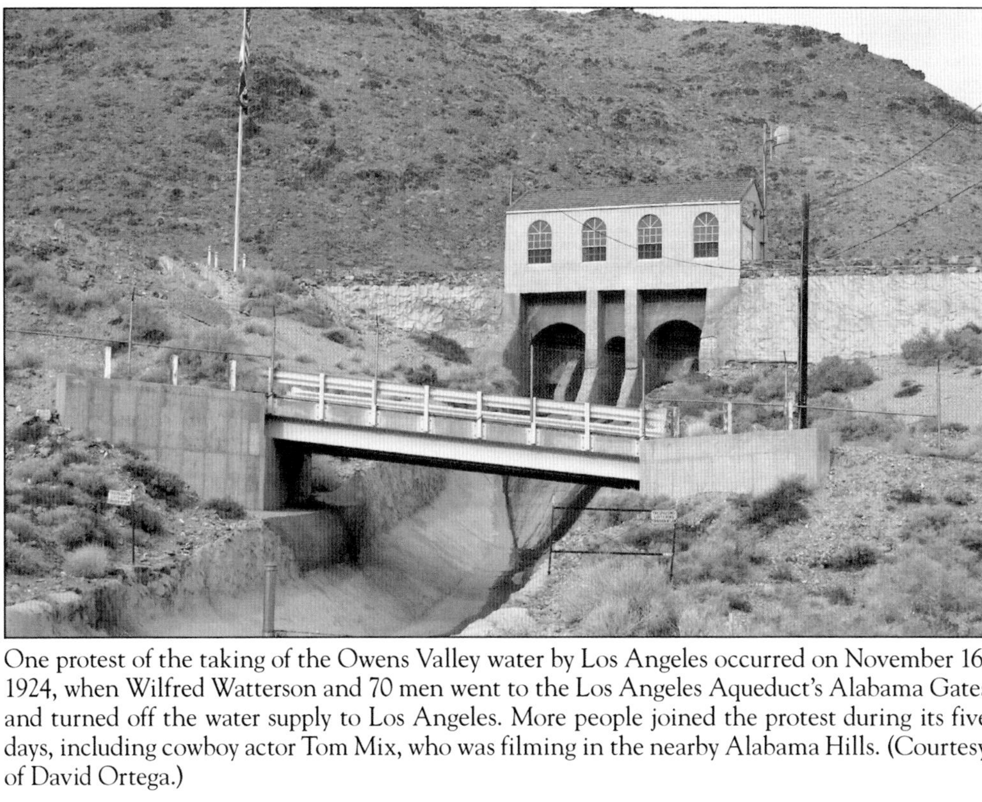

One protest of the taking of the Owens Valley water by Los Angeles occurred on November 16, 1924, when Wilfred Watterson and 70 men went to the Los Angeles Aqueduct's Alabama Gates and turned off the water supply to Los Angeles. More people joined the protest during its five days, including cowboy actor Tom Mix, who was filming in the nearby Alabama Hills. (Courtesy of David Ortega.)

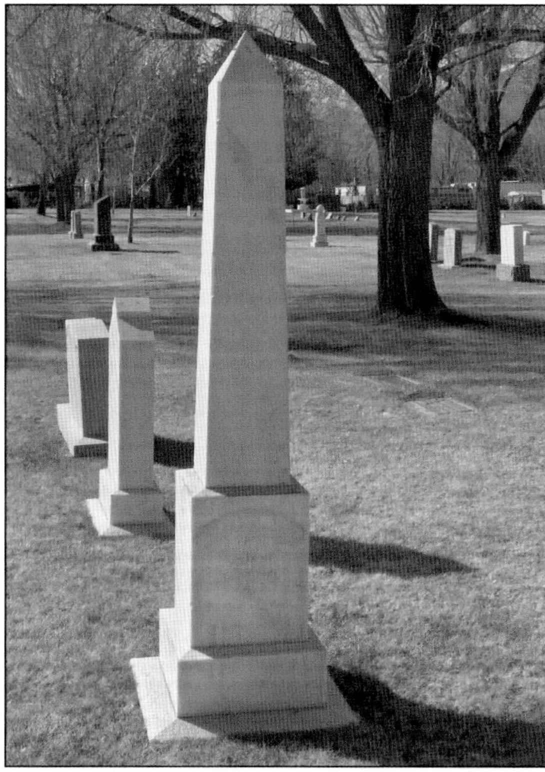

Founder of the *Inyo Independent* and *Inyo Register* newspapers, Pleasant A. Chalfant came to Independence about 1870 from Highland County, Ohio, where he was born in 1831. In 1885, Chalfant and his son Willie began the *Inyo Register.* The Chalfants and their son are buried in the East Line Cemetery in Bishop. (Courtesy of David Ortega.)

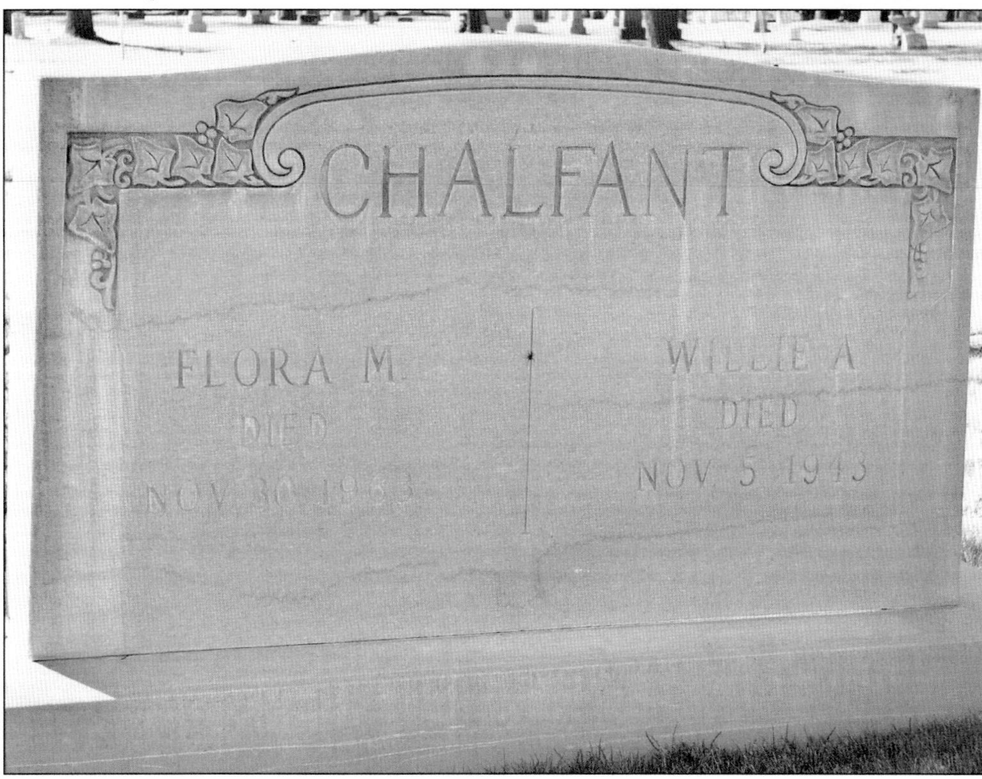

When his father, Pleasant, became the Inyo County assessor, William A. Chalfant took over for him at the *Inyo Register* and, until 1942, was owner of the Chalfant Press Company, which published four newspapers and numerous books about the Eastern Sierra. Bill Chalfant was a respected presence in the region for many decades. He wrote the first history of the area, *The Story of Inyo,* along with books on other local topics. (Courtesy of David Ortega.)

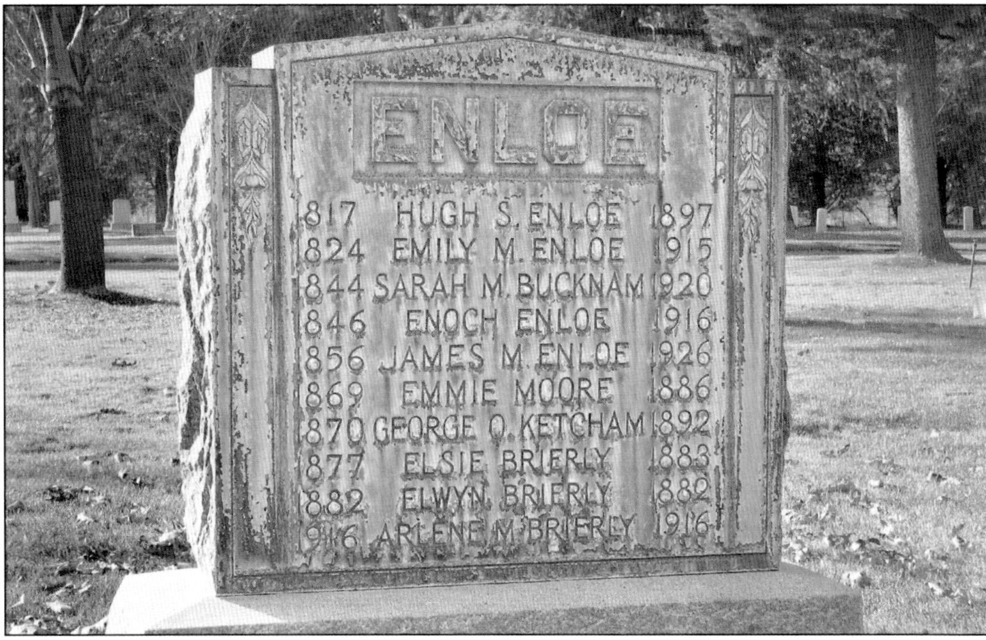

James Enloe came to Inyo County with his family in 1875, having spent his childhood in Visalia. He worked as a teamster while living in Bishop and then went on to Arizona and Tulare County. In 1893, he returned to the area to live with his elderly parents and worked as a gold miner and farmer. He is buried in the Bishop Pioneer Cemetery. (Courtesy of David Ortega.)

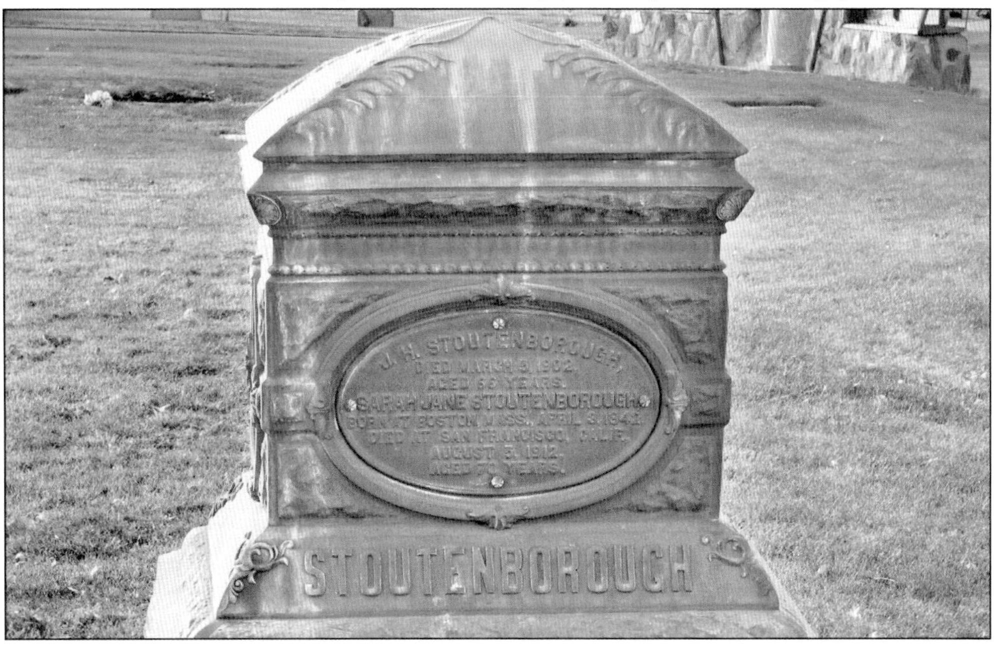

J. H. Stoutenborough was the owner of a general store located on the corner of East Line Street and Main Street in Bishop, California. General stores differed from present-day grocery stores, mainly in the variety of merchandise they carried. Stoutenborough, for example, kept a supply of dynamite in a shed behind the store. One day, the dynamite blew up, causing major damage to the store and a home. (Courtesy of David Ortega.)

Belle and Jim Butler, Nevada Belle Butler Hall's mother and stepfather, moved to the Owens Valley from Nevada about 1902 after a visit to the region. The family continued to reside there for the next four generations. The Butlers led a meager existence until Jim struck it big in May 1900. Working as a part-time prospector, he found a rich claim in the region they later named Tonopah. The Butlers went on to own both a ranch in the hills above Big Pine and the Big Pine Hotel. Nevada Belle, Belle's daughter, was beautiful, bright, and involved in local community affairs, election work, and helping her husband, Leicester Hall, run his law office. Her family was devastated when she suddenly took ill during the flu epidemic and died in November 1918. She is buried beneath her beloved White Mountains in the town of Bishop. (Courtesy of Philip Butler and Belle (Butler) Test family collection.)

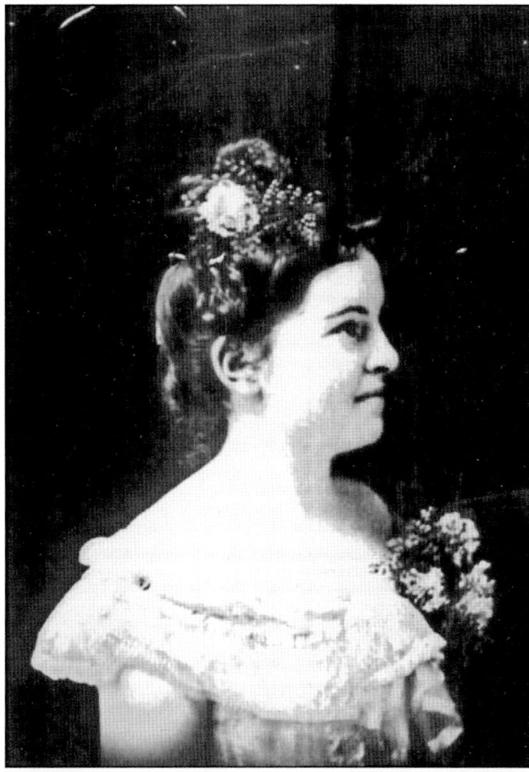

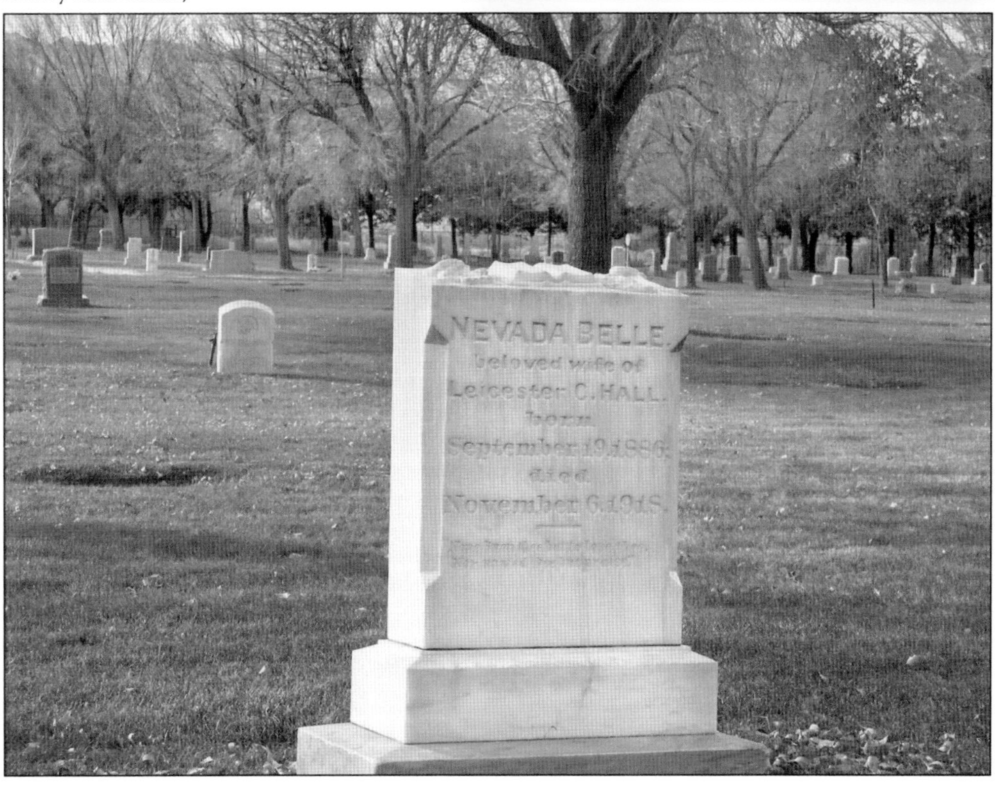

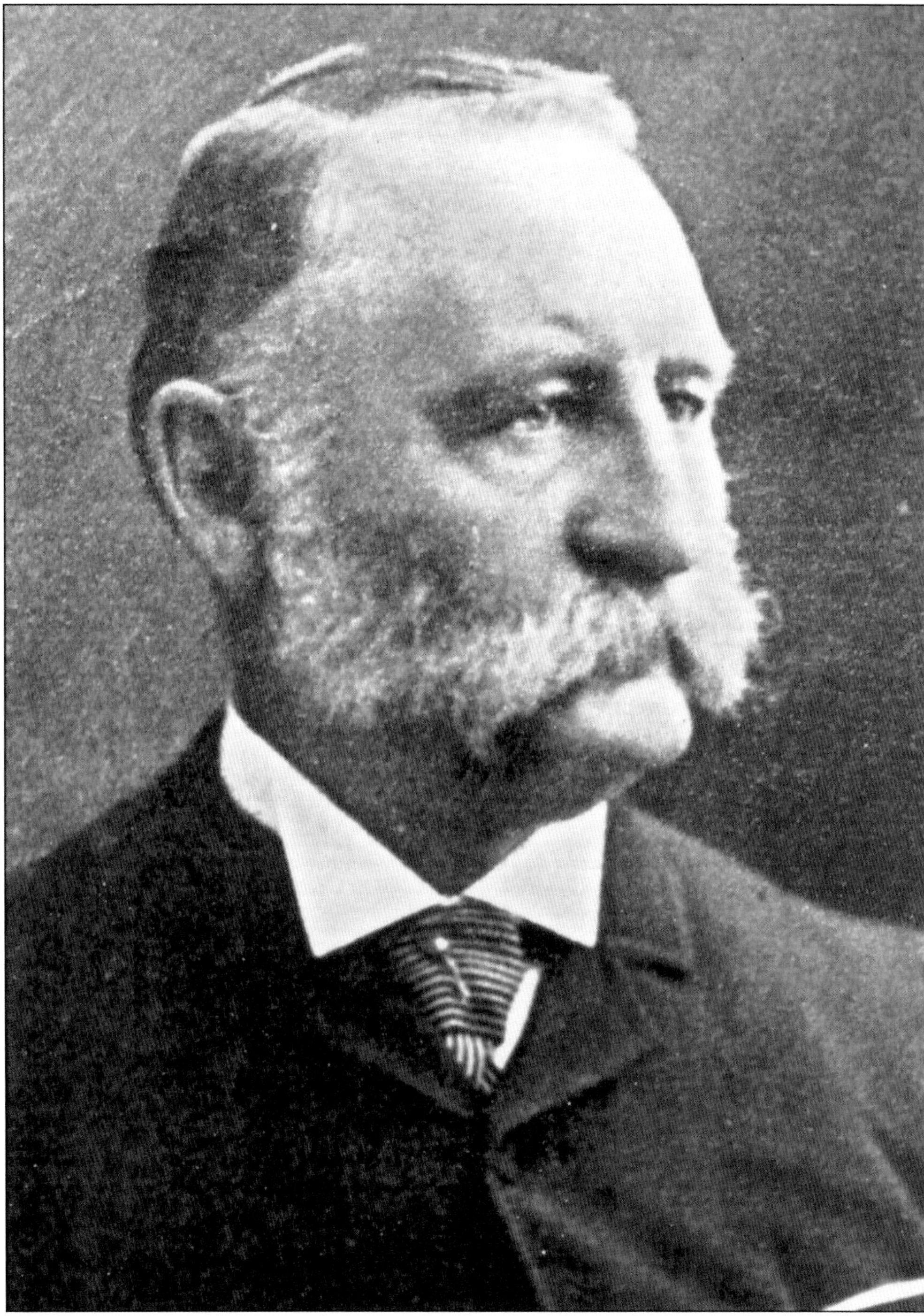

Julius Keeler came to the Owens Valley in the winter of 1879 and worked with the Owens Lake Mining and Milling Company. His namesake, Keeler, on the north shore of the Owens Dry Lake, was a terminal for the ships that transported ore from the smelter at Swansea across the lake to Cartago, where it was shipped on to Southern California by wagon. (Courtesy County of Inyo, Eastern California Museum.)

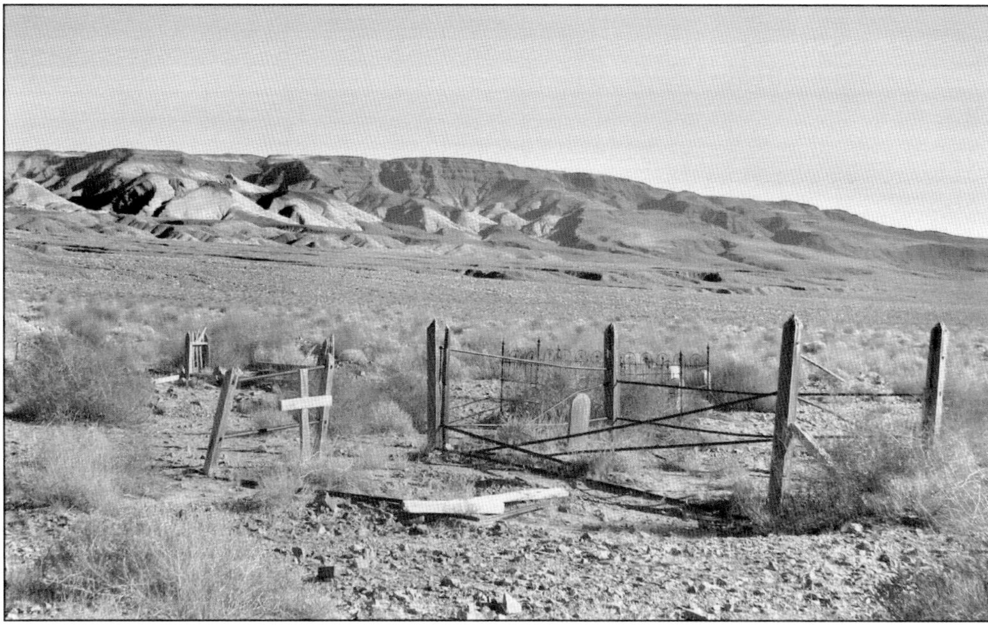

Only a handful of graves remain in this cemetery, just to the side of Highway 190. Mostly wooden crosses, only four of the headstones are readable. Known for its ties to mining and the Owens Valley's narrow-gauge railroad, Keeler was also immortalized in the 1899 novel *McTeague: A Story of San Francisco* by Frank Norris. (Courtesy of David Ortega.)

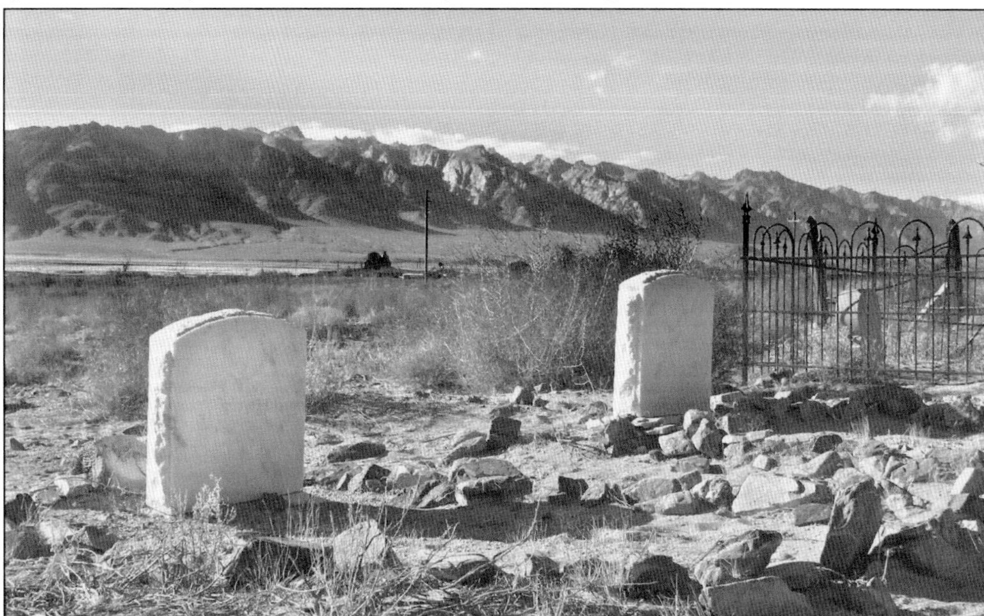

John and Luna Bean came to Inyo County from New Creek, West Virginia, where John served as the mayor. Luna died in 1909, and John, his five children, and his mother continued living together in Keeler. John was a Mason, and Luna had been a member of the Order of the Eastern Star, a Masonic auxiliary group for women and men. The Beans are buried in the Keeler cemetery. (Courtesy of David Ortega.)

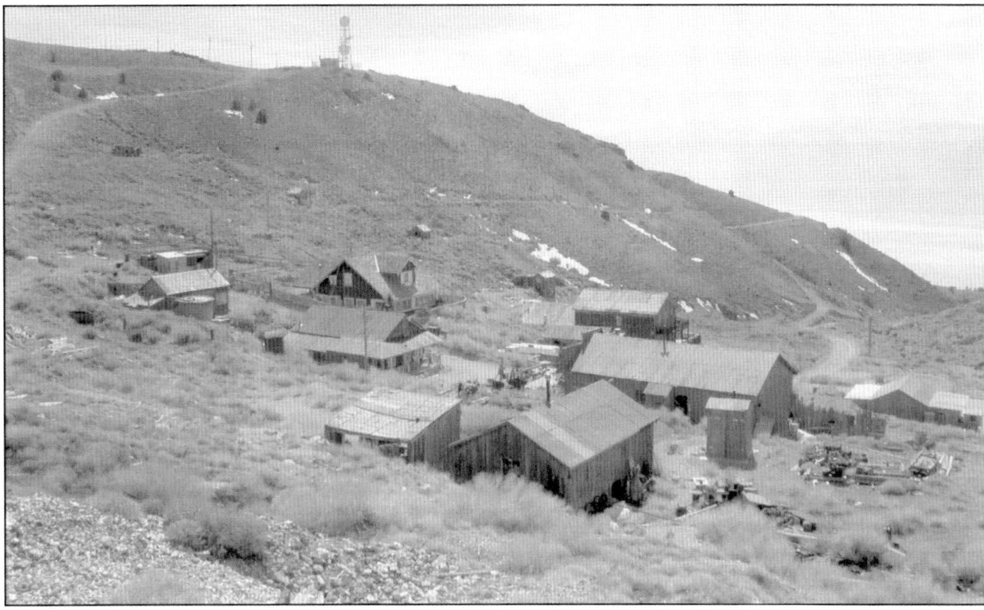

Cerro Gordo, Spanish for "Fat Hill," became the richest silver mining district in California history. It was discovered by Mexican prospectors in 1865. The American Hotel, shown here, was built in 1871 by John Simpson. Cerro Gordo is now privately owned; its owners have completed restorative work on this and other structures in the town. (Courtesy of Cat House.)

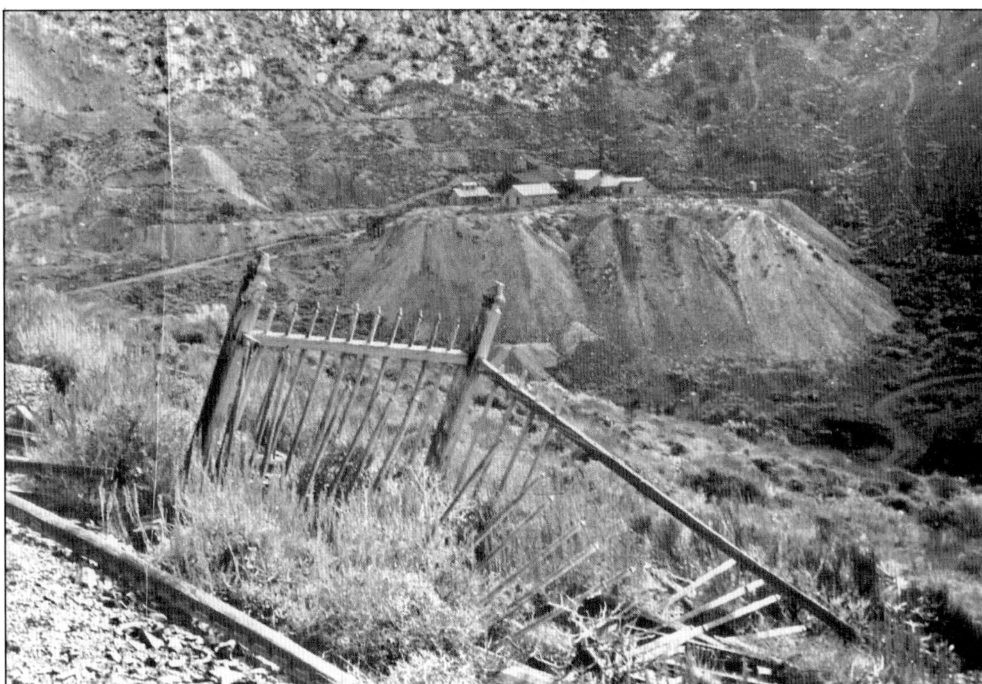

Like most early mining towns, Cerro Gordo was a place where lawlessness reigned supreme. Inyo County judge John Hannah noted that crime was pervasive in Cerro Gordo, and newspaperman P. A. Chalfant likened Cerro Gordo to a shooting gallery. (Courtesy of County of Inyo, Eastern California Museum; from *This Mountain—Cerro Gordo*.)

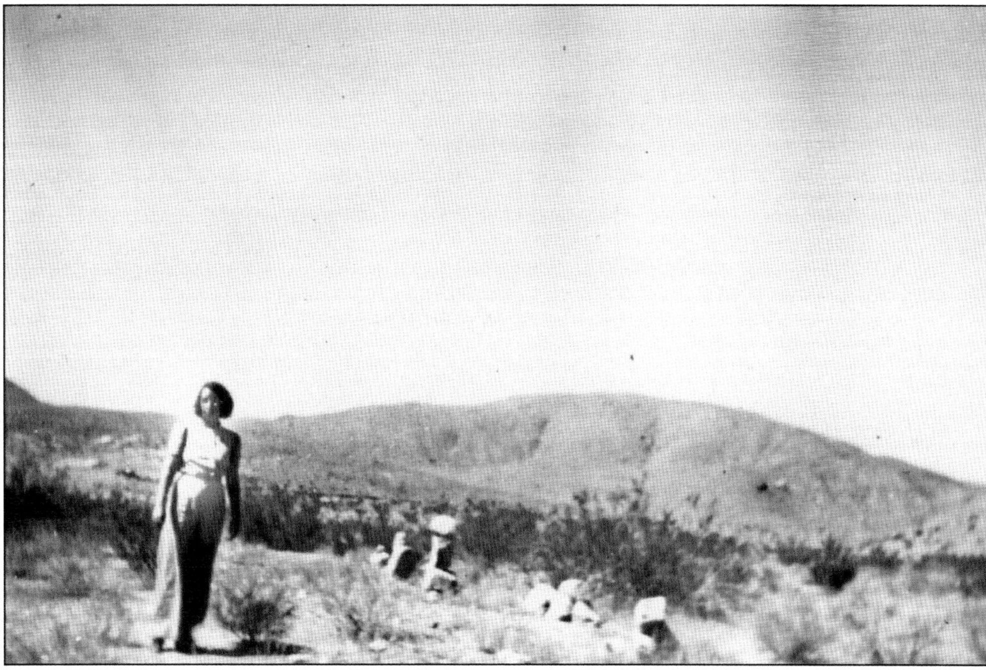

In 1860, miner W. H. Farley, working in the Silver Peak area of southern Inyo, mentioned the existence of hot springs to the south. Twenty-one years later, a government survey noted thousands of hot springs in the area. In 1909, a health resort was started there, with claims that the water would cure ailments from venereal disease to constipation. The resort was gone by 1947 and replaced by a naval facility. (Courtesy of County of Inyo, Eastern California Museum.)

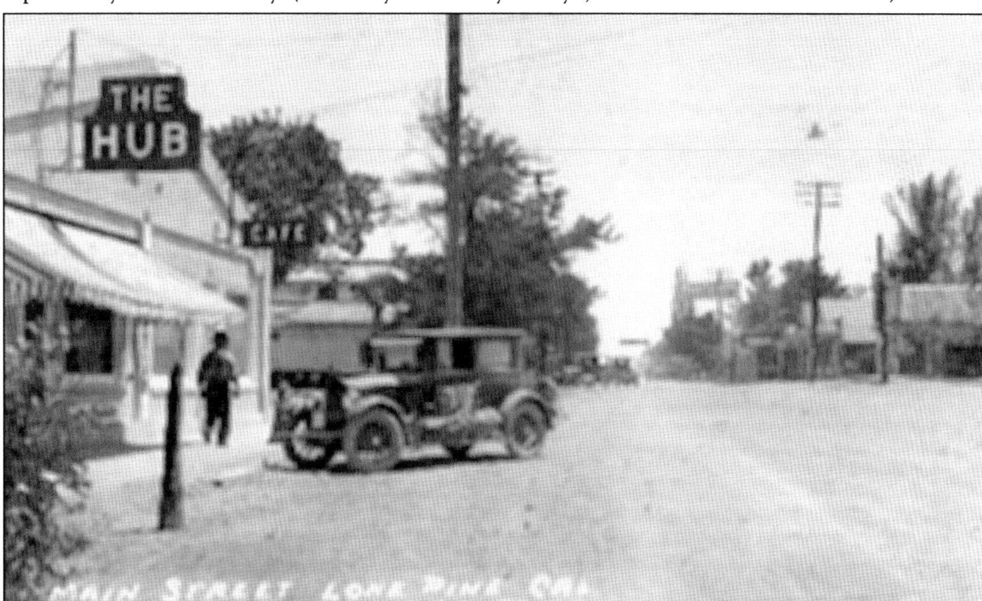

Prior to the white settlers arriving here, the Shoshone and Paiute Indians called this area home. The town of Lone Pine was founded in the 1860s as a supply hub for local mining and ranching operations and was named for a solitary pine tree found at the mouth of Lone Pine Canyon. Lone Pine is seen here in the 1940s. (Courtesy of June Bagwell.)

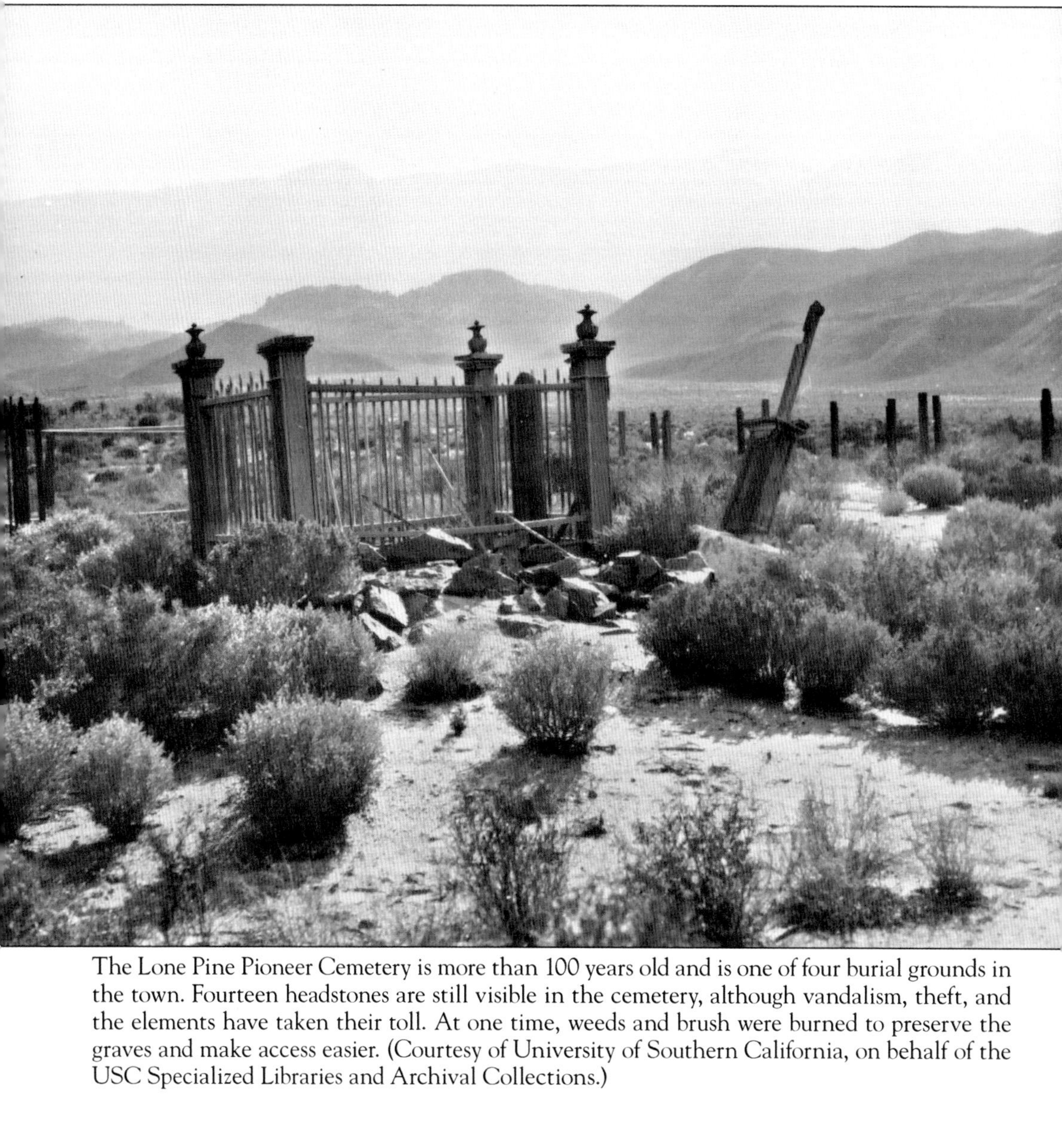

The Lone Pine Pioneer Cemetery is more than 100 years old and is one of four burial grounds in the town. Fourteen headstones are still visible in the cemetery, although vandalism, theft, and the elements have taken their toll. At one time, weeds and brush were burned to preserve the graves and make access easier. (Courtesy of University of Southern California, on behalf of the USC Specialized Libraries and Archival Collections.)

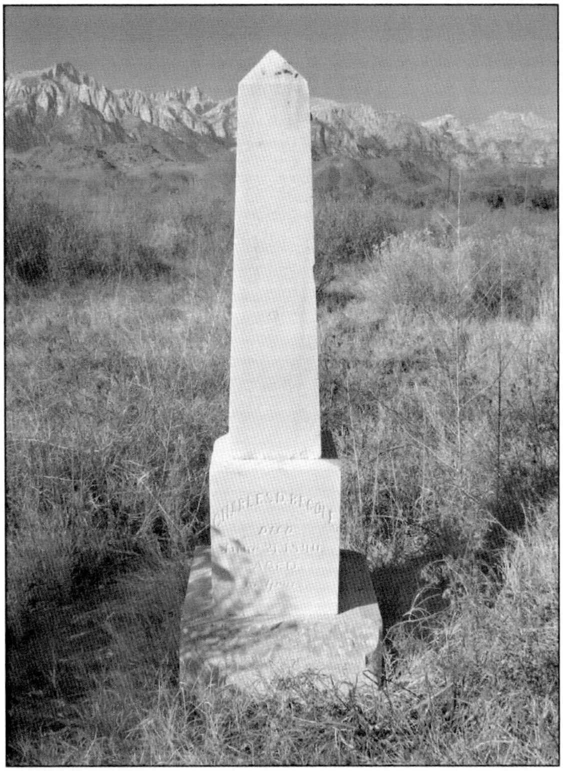

The Lone Pine Pioneer Cemetery is the resting place for many of the town's first settlers, among them Charles Becole and Albert Johnson. Along with John Lucas, they were the first three men to climb Mount Whitney on August 18, 1873. Originally locals wanted to rename the mountain Fisherman's Peak because these three men were fisherman. (Courtesy of David Ortega.)

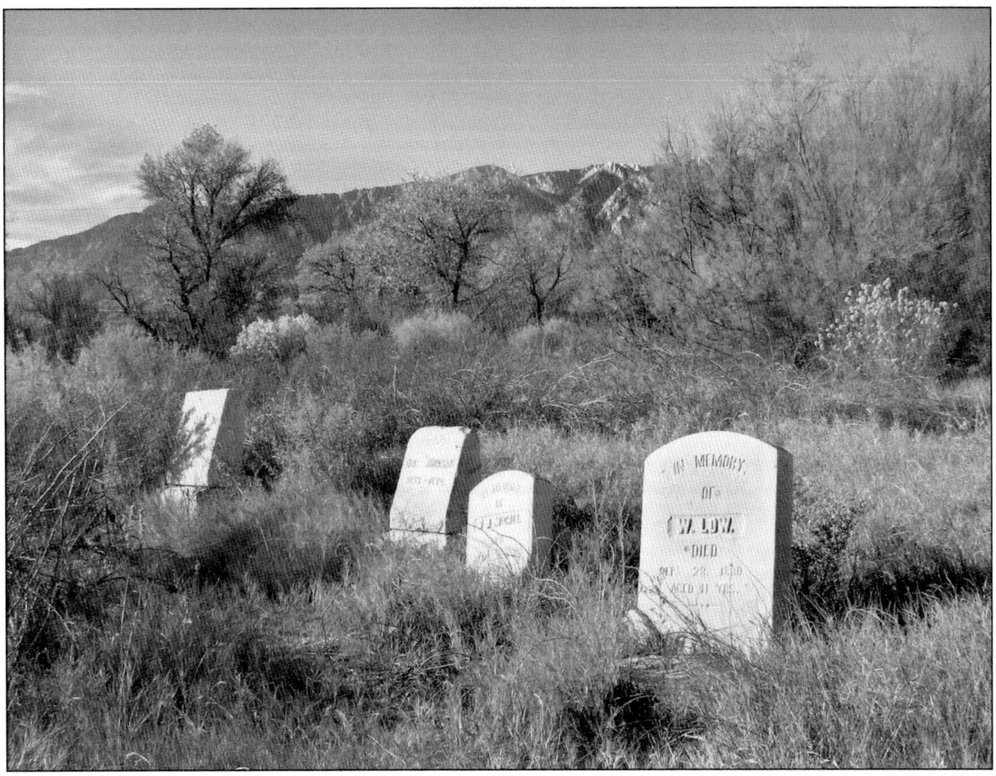

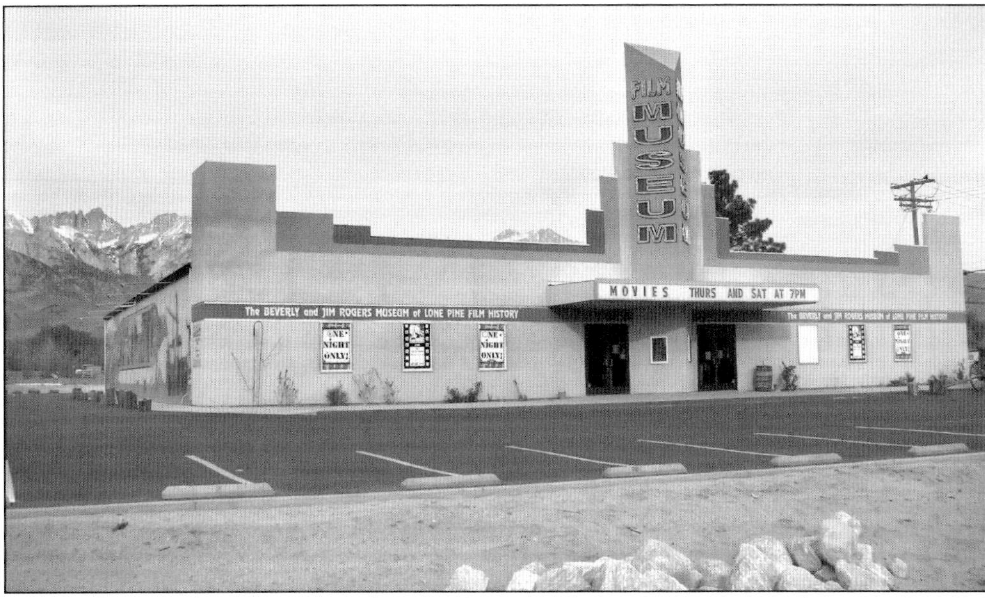

A recently opened museum on Highway 395 in Lone Pine commemorates the more than 300 movies and television series, and dozens of commercials, filmed in the region beginning in 1920. Displays include film posters and props from Westerns shot in the Alabama Hills. In October, an annual film festival remembers this moviemaking heritage. (Courtesy of David Ortega.)

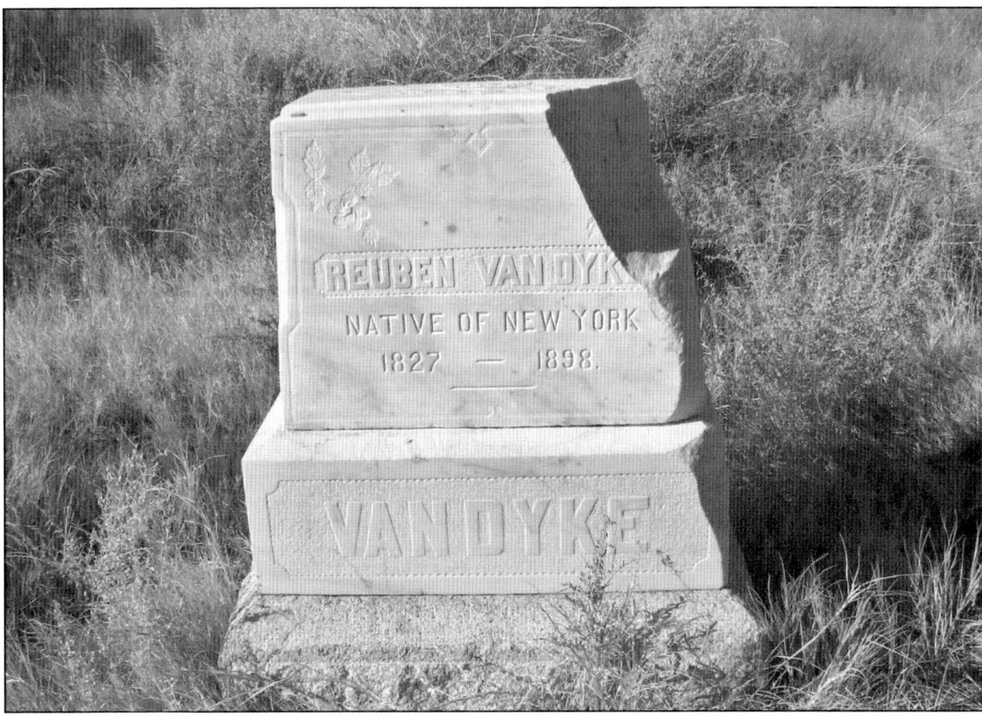

Reuben Van Dyke and his wife, Mary, lived in Lone Pine. Reuben is listed in the 1880 U.S. Census as being a farmer. His tombstone is one of several that have been vandalized over the years in the Lone Pine Pioneer Cemetery. Although many of the areas' pioneers are most likely buried here, only 14 marked graves remain. (Courtesy of David Ortega.)

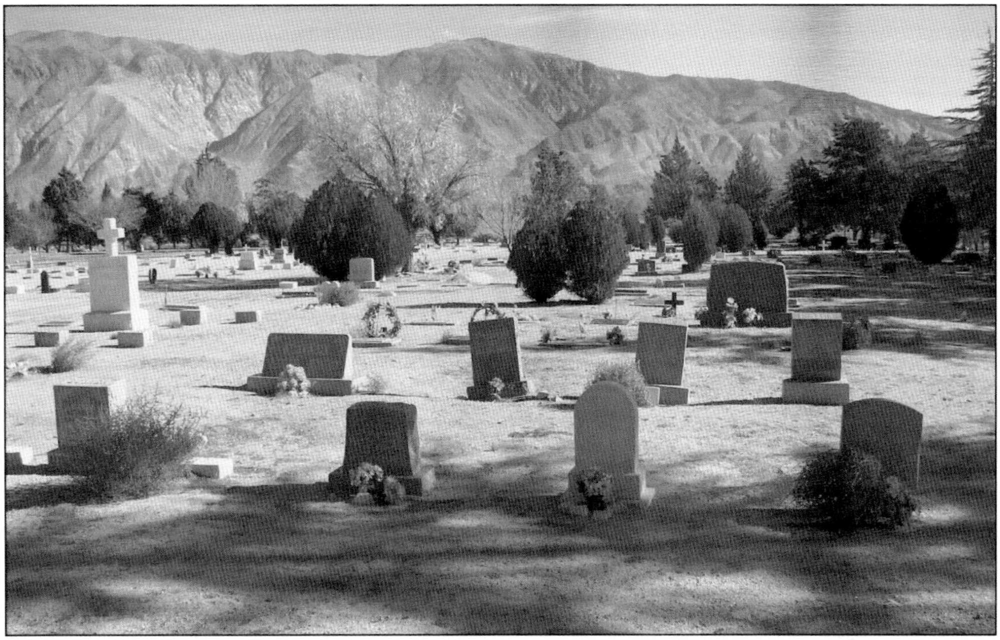

Mount Whitney Cemetery is located off Highway 395, across from the grave of the 1872 earthquake victims in Lone Pine. It is one of four cemeteries or burial grounds in a town with a population of only a little over 1,600. Mount Whitney is the main town cemetery and includes older and more recent burials. (Courtesy of David Ortega.)

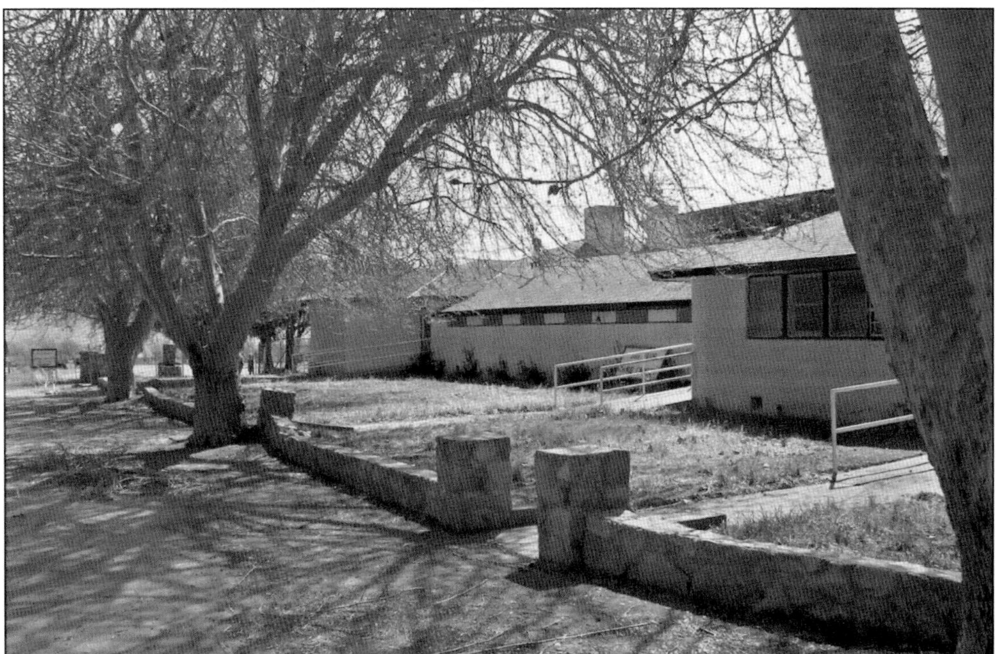

In the early 1900s, an Inyo County Poor Farm and Hospital were located about 2 miles north of Big Pine. This property is believed to have included a cemetery in a field near the buildings, but no records remain of any burials or of its exact location. Later the poor farm was a sanitarium and was sold to a private company. The buildings are now vacant. (Courtesy of David Ortega.)

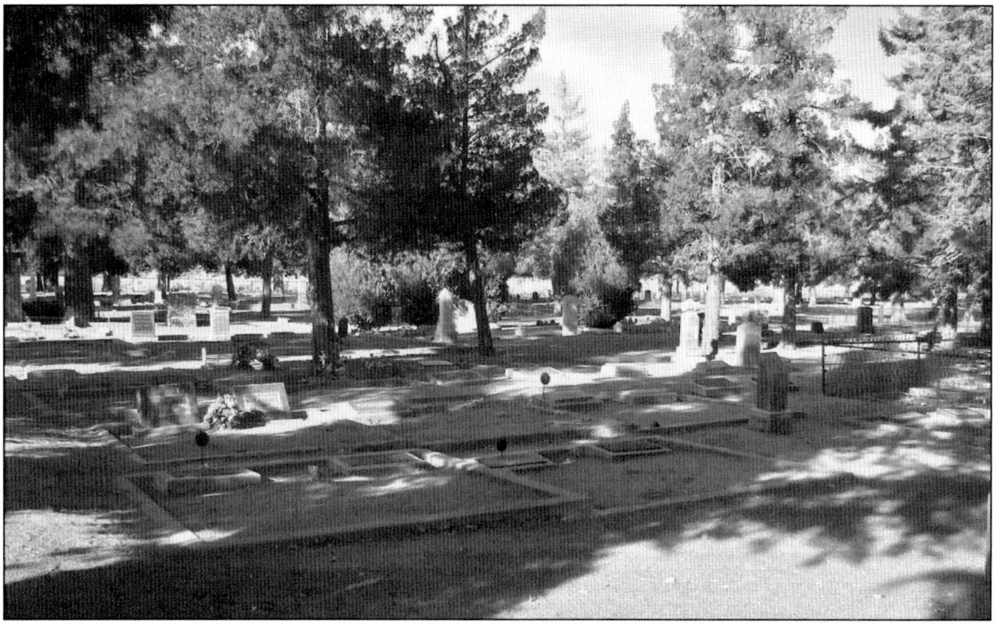

The Big Pine Cemetery on Crocker Street was deeded to the town for the sum of a $5 gold piece by James Crocker, a stockman, and his son Edwin Crocker on May 2, 1892. The earliest known burials are from 1884. It is believed that some unmarked pauper graves are located to the west of the cemetery grounds. (Courtesy of David Ortega.)

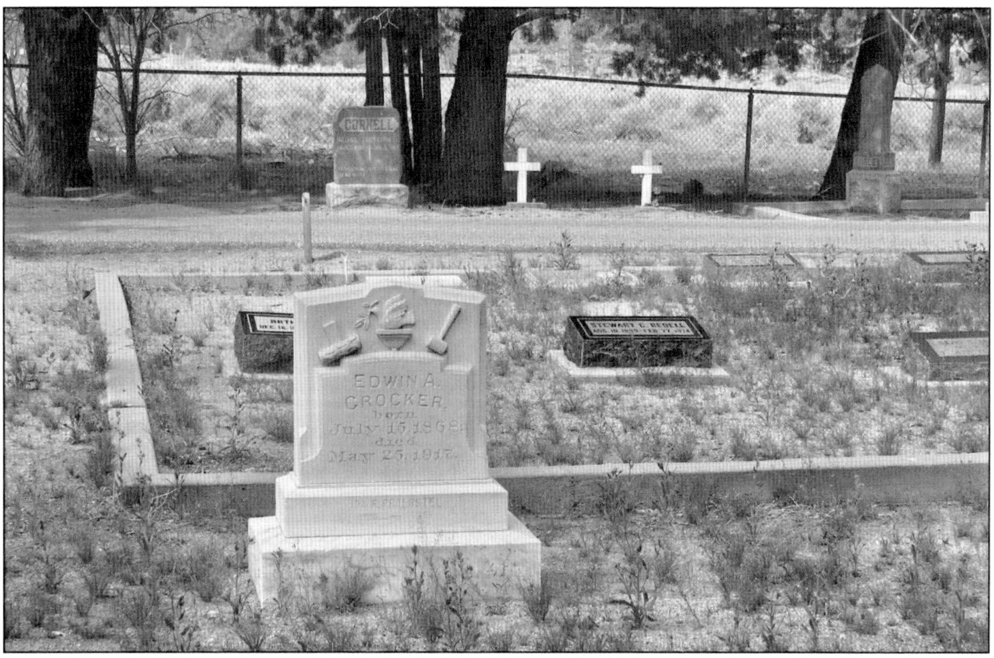

Edwin Crocker was the son of James and Mary Smith Crocker. He and his family came from Kern County to Big Pine in 1887. He, like his father, was a stock raiser by profession. His wife's name, Ida F. Hall Crocker Proebstel, is listed in small letters at the bottom of the headstone. The carved imagery indicates he was a member of the fraternal organization Woodmen of the World. (Courtesy of David Ortega.)

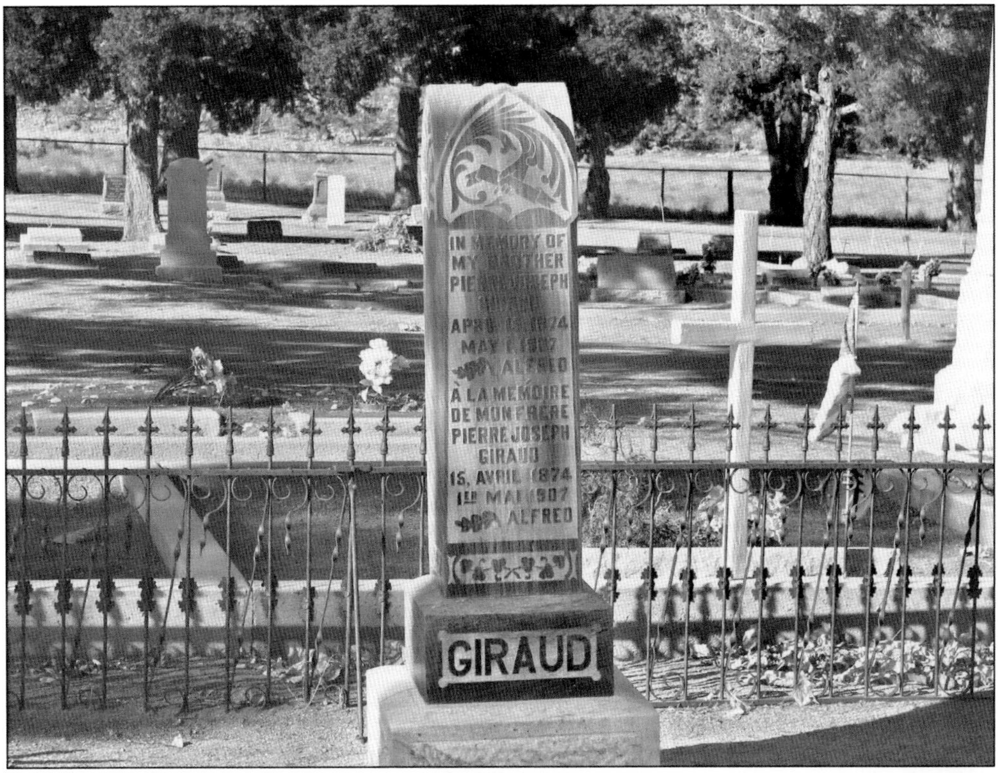

Pierre and his brother Alfred were French immigrants who came to the Owens Valley about 1901. They worked as sheepherders in Inyo County, learning from older French sheepherders. Alfred wrote a small book about his experiences entitled *My First Winter in California*, in which he describes his activities as a sheepherder and his trials on the long drives across the Sierra and through the Owens Valley. (Courtesy of David Ortega.)

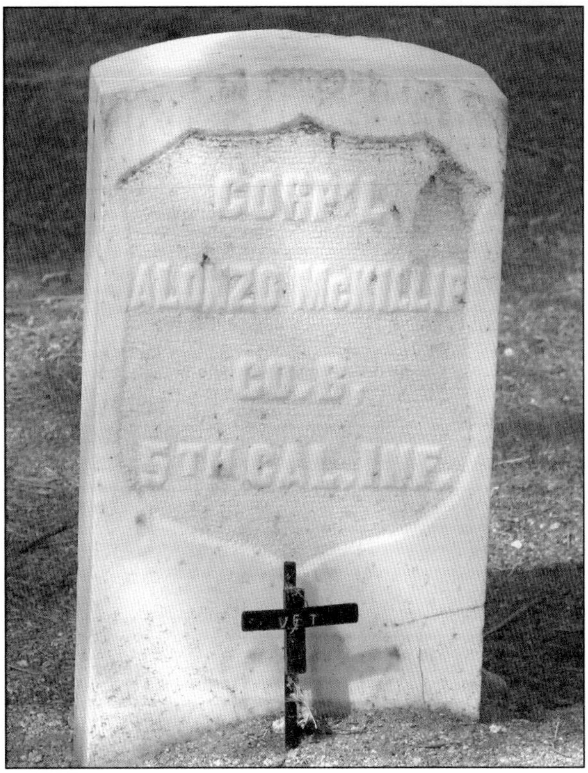

Alonzo McKellips was a Civil War veteran who came to California in the mid-19th century. He was the stationmaster at Orne Station, located 14 miles outside of Olancha on Highway 190. Two of his children are still buried there along the highway. His son Alonzo Inyo McKellips is said to have been the first white child born in Big Pine. (Courtesy of David Ortega.)

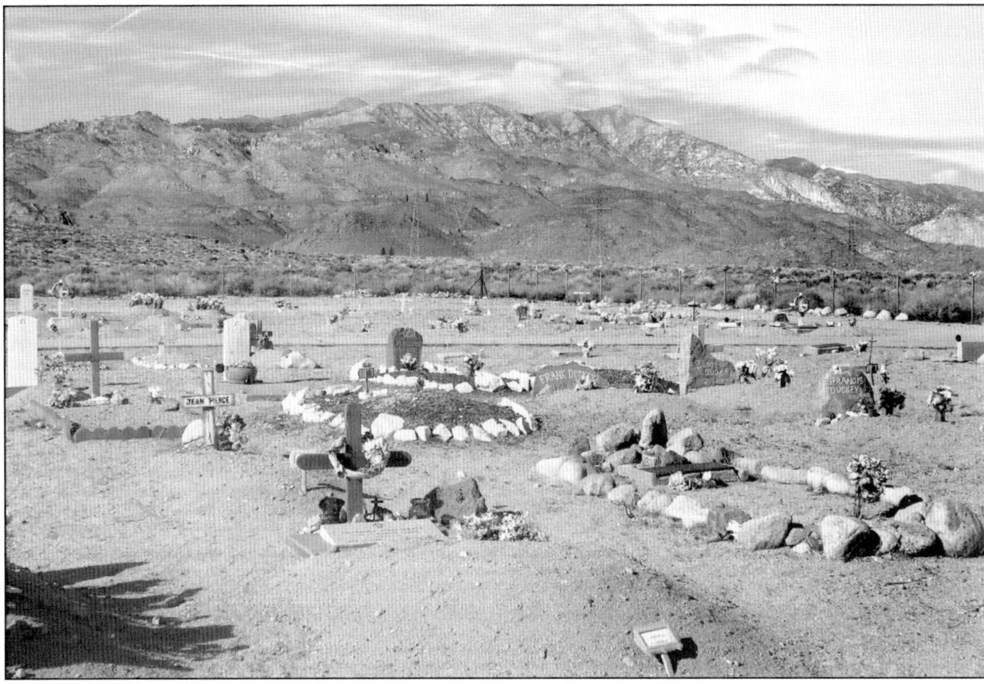

The Woodmen Cemetery was originally a cemetery of the fraternal group Woodmen of the World. It was deeded to the Big Pine Cemetery District in November 1940. While it includes some Big Pine pioneers, it is now used mainly by the local Paiute tribe. (Courtesy of David Ortega.)

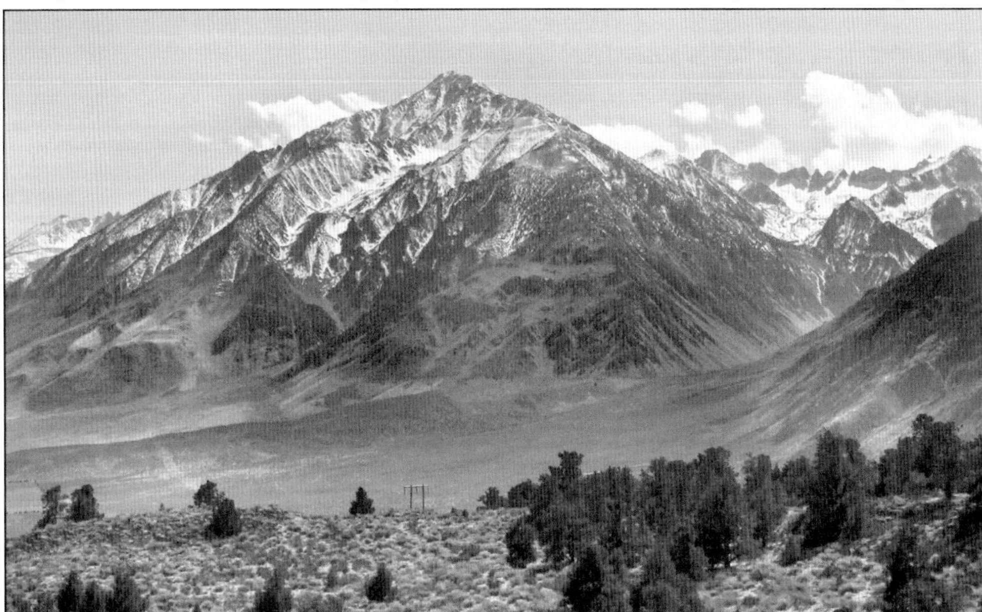

Mount Tom, at an elevation of 13,652, is located on the Eastern Sierra mountain range, west of Bishop in Round Valley. The beauty and serenity found here as well as through the entire mountain range has led some people to choose this as their final resting place. One such person is Robert William Wood, one of America's best known landscape painters and one-time resident of Bishop. He died in the spring of 1979. (Courtesy of David Ortega.)

Two

Manzanar

The area known as Manzanar lies just south of the town of Independence. Now a National Historic Site, Manzanar is today synonymous with the World War II–era internment camp for persons of Japanese ancestry. But Manzanar's history extends back hundreds of years to the Owens Valley Paiute communities who made use of the area's abundant water, native plants, and wildlife. In 1863, rancher John Shepherd homesteaded 160 acres in the area. The Shepherd ranch grew to over 2,000 acres.

Southern California developers George and Charles Chaffey bought Shepherd's land and nearby ranches in 1905. The Chaffeys' Owens Valley Improvement Company subdivided the land, offered irrigated farm parcels for sale, and planted 22,000 apple trees. A school, store, and town hall were built as well. The new project was called "Manzanar," Spanish for apple orchard. Los Angeles later bought all of Manzanar and other Owens Valley farmland to secure needed water rights. The city managed the orchards, with some farmers staying on as renters, but by 1935, with irrigation shut down, the town was abandoned.

On December 7, 1941, Japan attacked Pearl Harbor in Hawaii, and the following February, Pres. Franklin Roosevelt issued Executive Order 9066, which resulted in the forced removal of over 112,000 people of Japanese heritage living in the Pacific Coast states. Manzanar was selected as the site of the first of 10 "relocation centers" where they would be indefinitely confined. Evacuees, two-thirds of them American citizens, began arriving at Manzanar on March 21, 1942. By September, the population was more than 10,000, and Manzanar was the largest city in the Eastern Sierra.

Like any large city, provisions were made for the sick, injured, and dead. Internee doctors treated the ill in a modern, 250-bed hospital that also included a morgue. From March 1942 to November 1945, when the camp closed, approximately 150 people died. Funerals were conducted by Buddhists and Christians in churches converted from barracks. Many of the dead were cremated, to be buried eventually in the cemetery of the city they called home or to be interred in the Manzanar cemetery.

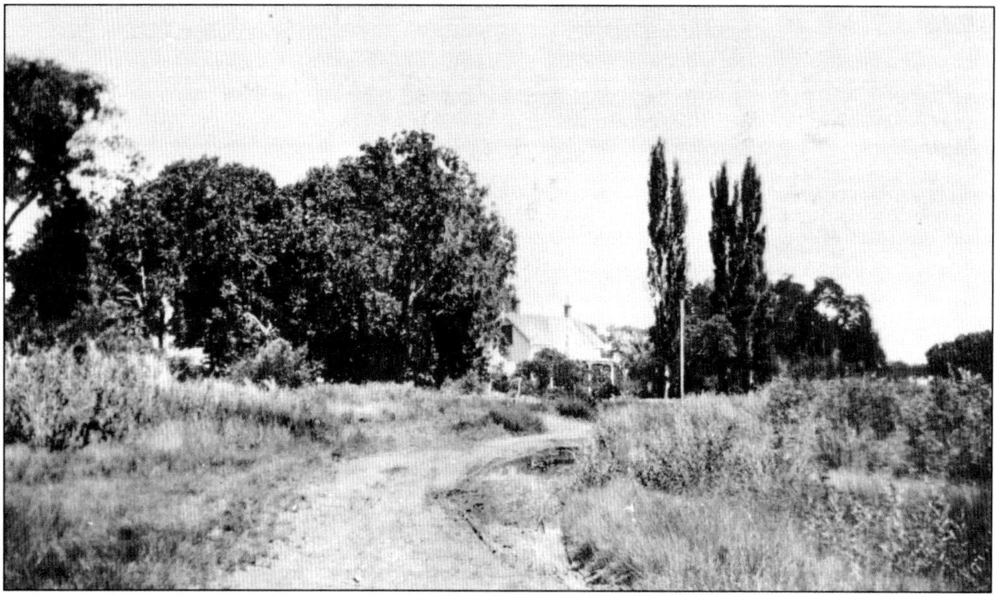

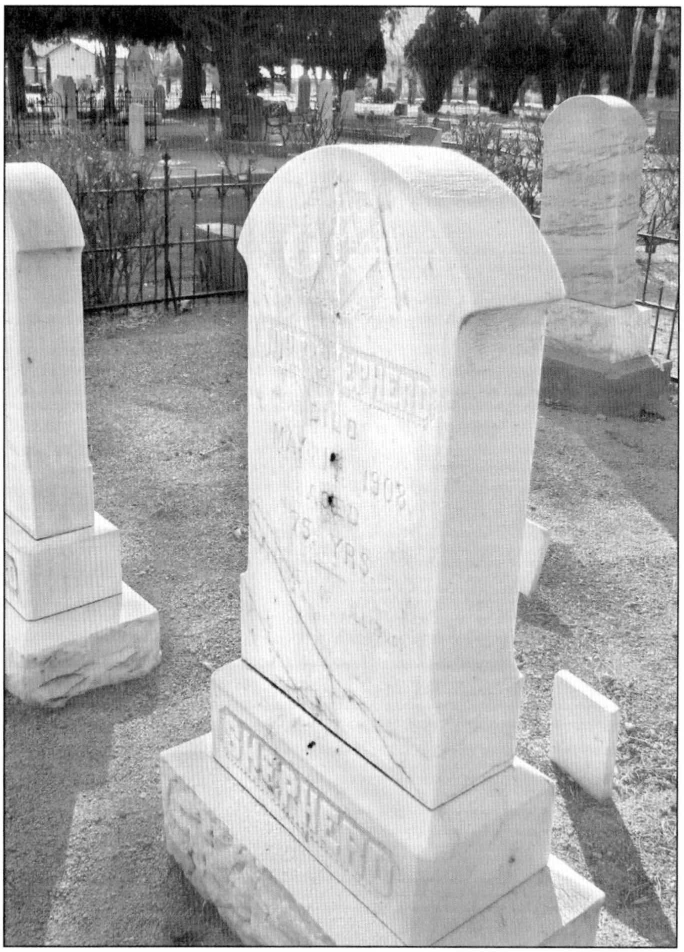

The Shepherd Ranch, in the area of George's Creek that would later become Manzanar, was one of the earliest Euro-American homesteads in the southern Owens Valley. Shepherd arrived in the Owens Valley in 1861 and rose to prominence in his community. He was elected constable in 1866, a district judge in 1871, and Masonic Lodge officer and an Inyo County supervisor in 1874. Shepherd later sold his ranch to developer Charles Chaffey, and in 1910, it became Manzanar, a subdivided orchard colony. The Shepherd family moved to San Francisco, where they met tragedy in the great 1906 San Francisco earthquake. Shepherd died in 1908 and is buried in Independence. (Above, courtesy of County of Inyo, Eastern California Museum; at left, courtesy of the author.)

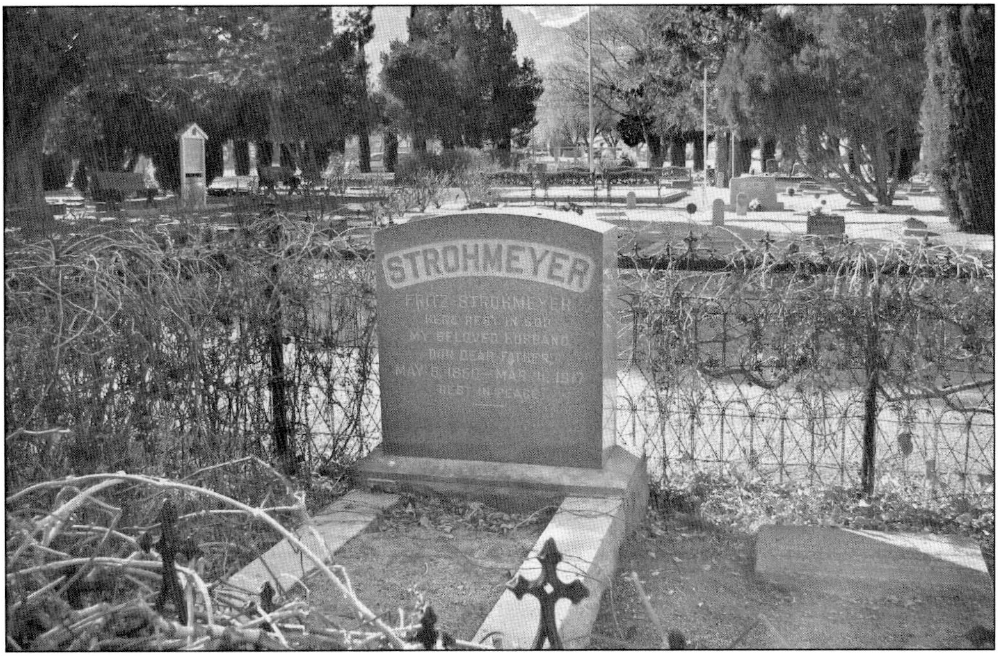

Fritz Strohmeyer came to the George's Creek area, south of Manzanar, around 1877, after emigrating from Germany. As described in his obituary, Fritz was "an honest, upright man and leaves many friends." Strohmeyer was buried in the Masonic Cemetery in Independence, which is now known as the Independence Town Cemetery. (Courtesy of the author.)

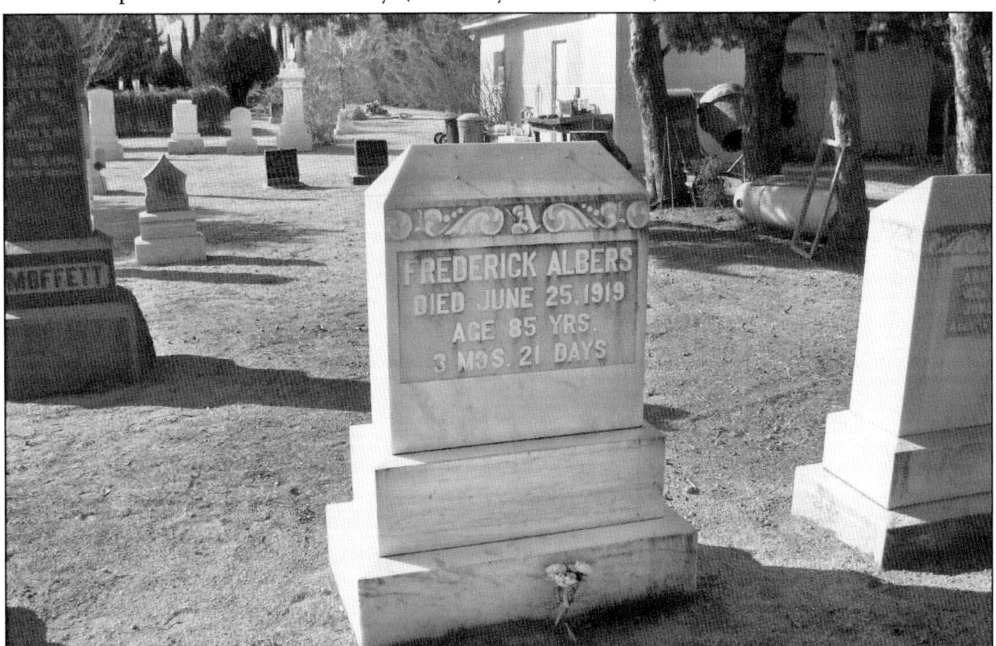

The Albers, Frederick and Anna, were German immigrants. With their seven children, they had a cattle ranch and orchard next to the John Shepherd ranch in the area known as George's Creek. At one time, their neighbors included Fritz Strohmeyer and William L. Hunter. The Alberses are buried in the Independence Cemetery. (Courtesy of the author.)

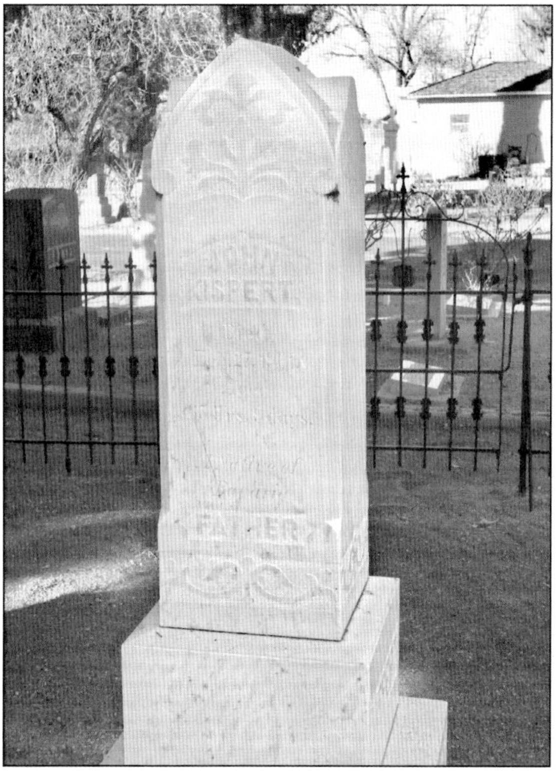

John Kispert was one of the first ranchers to homestead in the George's Creek area, along with John Shepherd. He came to the valley in 1859 as a trapper and returned in 1861, homesteaded 400 acres on George's Creek, and grew barley for the mines nearby. His original rock-and-adobe house was destroyed in the 1872 earthquake, and he rebuilt a wood-frame Victorian home on the same site. (Courtesy of the author.)

The family of Julius Roeper was also early homesteaders in the George's Creek area, and like others, they were emigrants from Germany. They eventually sold the land there and moved to the Fort Independence area and later into Independence proper, where Julius was a butcher and ran the town post office. (Courtesy of the author.)

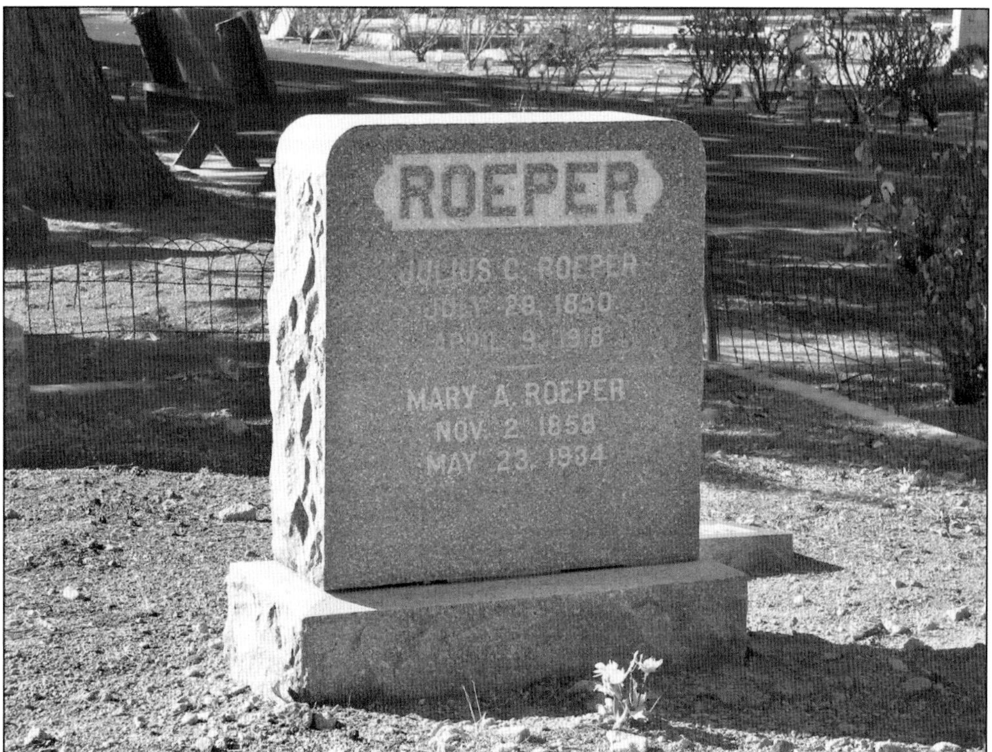

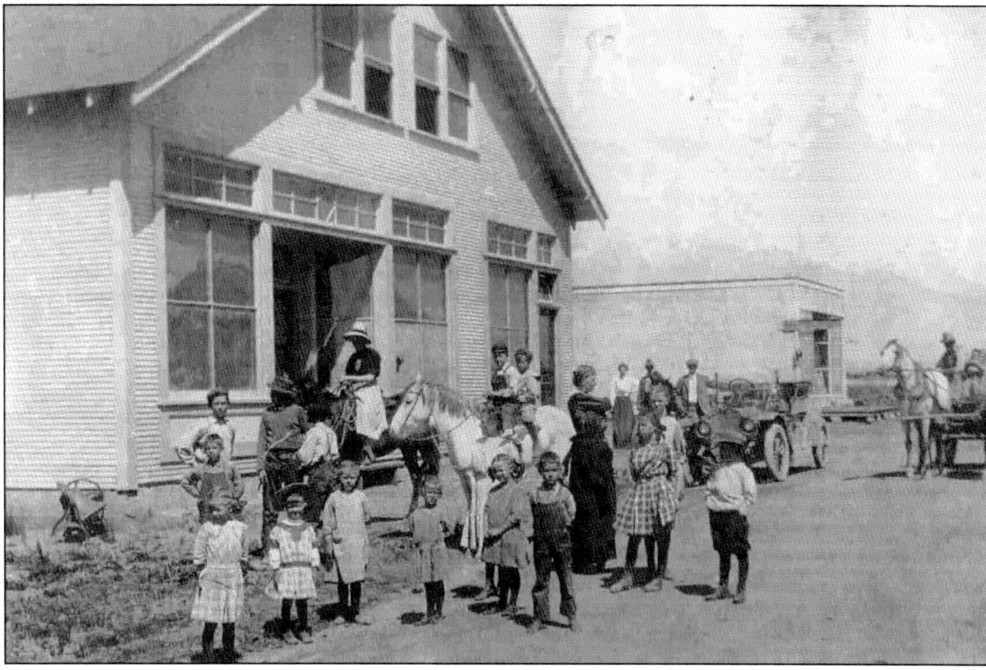

Manzanar Town Hall, shown *c.* 1912, was built by developer George Chaffey's Owens Valley Improvement Company, which subdivided the former John Shepherd land and sold irrigated parcels for fruit growing starting in 1910. By 1926, the hall was also a packinghouse for the tons of apples, pears, and peaches shipped out from Manzanar. The general store is also visible in the background. (Courtesy of the County of Inyo, Eastern California Museum.)

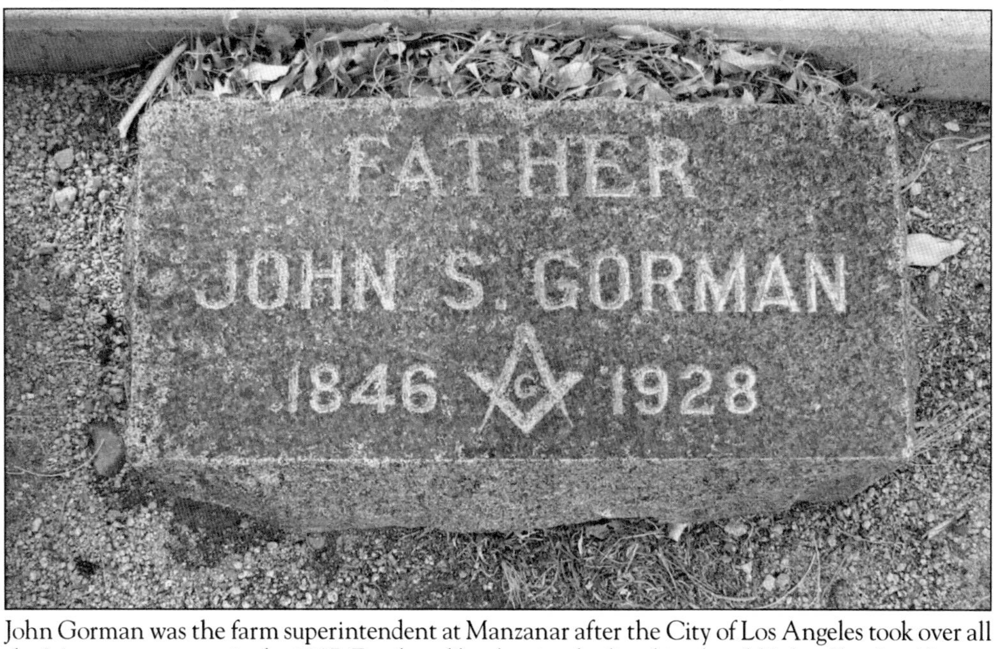

John Gorman was the farm superintendent at Manzanar after the City of Los Angeles took over all the Manzanar properties by 1927. Employed by the city, he lived in the old John Shepherd home, since 1905 the headquarters for Manzanar's orchard operations. He is buried in the Independence cemetery. (Courtesy of the author.)

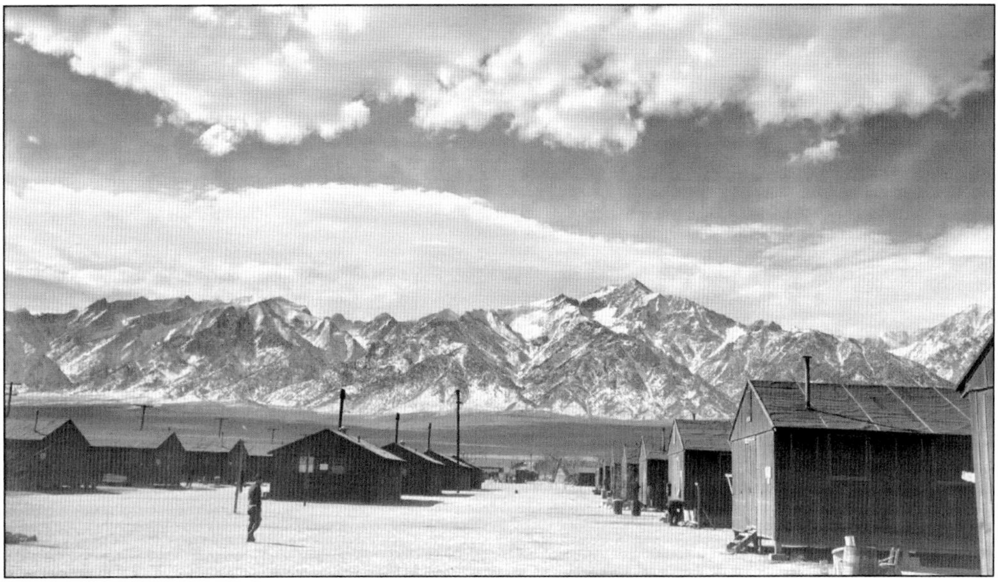

Manzanar's newest residents found themselves living with wind, dust, and extreme fluctuations in temperatures. Manzanar quickly became a self-contained city where children went to school, people had jobs, and letters were sent out via a post office. An internee-produced newspaper kept residents informed. Gardens and abandoned orchards thrived under the care of camp gardeners. Internee photographer Toyo Miyatake documented camp life, along with renowned photographers Ansel Adams and Dorothea Lange. (Courtesy of Library of Congress, Prints and Photographs Division, Ansel Adams, photographer, LC-DIG-ppprs-00284.)

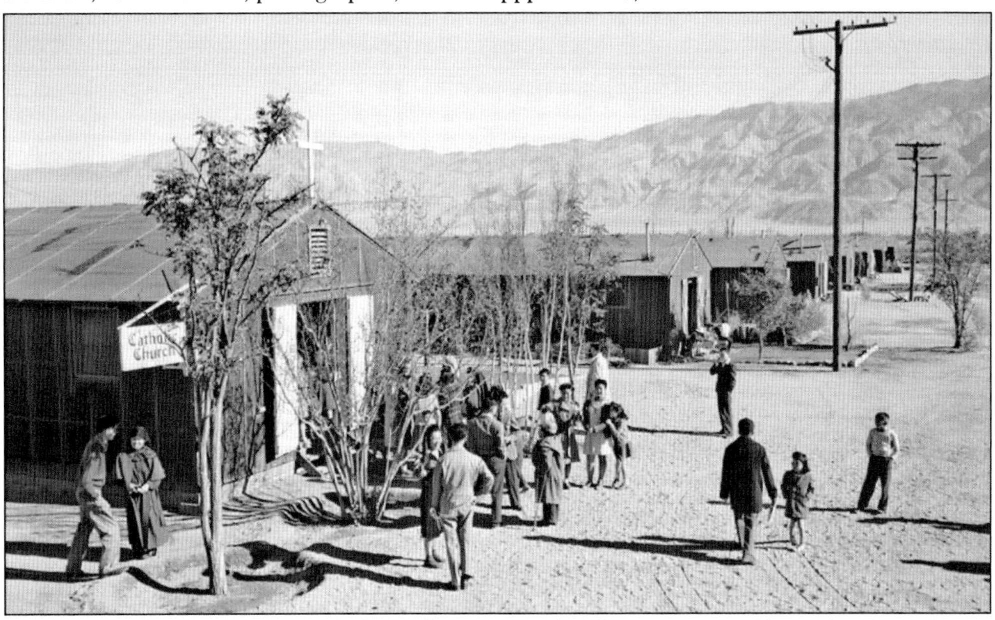

Manzanar included Buddhist, Catholic, and Protestant churches in converted barracks. According to a March 20, 1943, article in the *Manzanar Free Press*, the camp's newspaper, the purpose and function of the Manzanar Catholic Church was "to enable people to obtain eternal happiness." Funerals were held at these churches for those who died at Manzanar. (Courtesy of Library of Congress, Prints and Photographs Division, Ansel Adams, photographer, LC-DIG-ppprs-00196.)

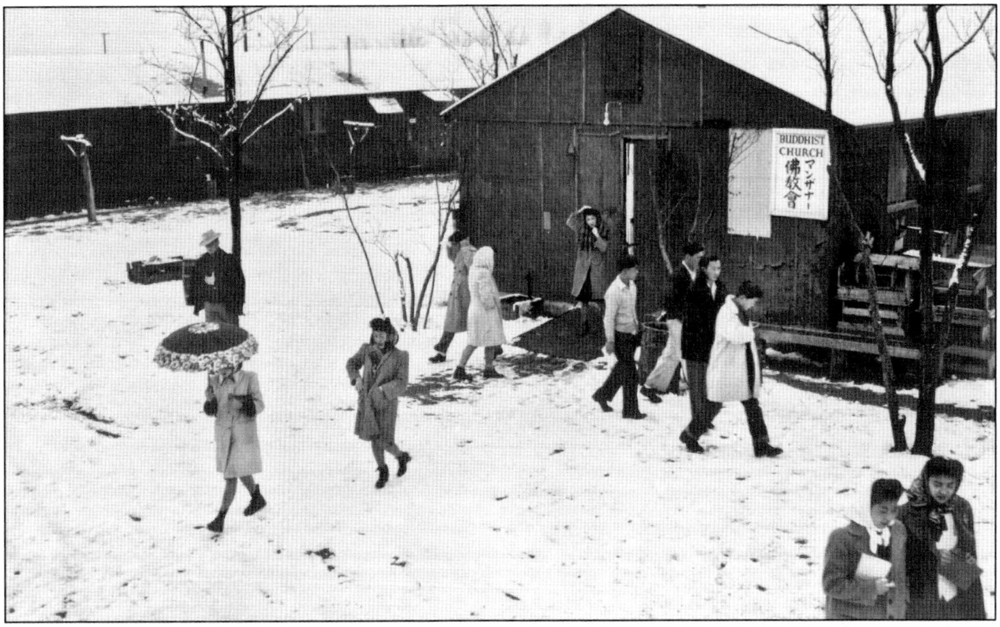

Shown here in a 1943 print by Ansel Adams, the Manzanar Buddhist Church was located in a barrack in Block 13. Worship services, holiday celebrations, and funerals took place here. Many of those who died at Manzanar were cremated. Their ashes were often kept in the Buddhist church until other arrangements were made. (Courtesy of Library of Congress, Prints and Photographs Division, Ansel Adams, photographer, LC-DIG-ppprs-00359.)

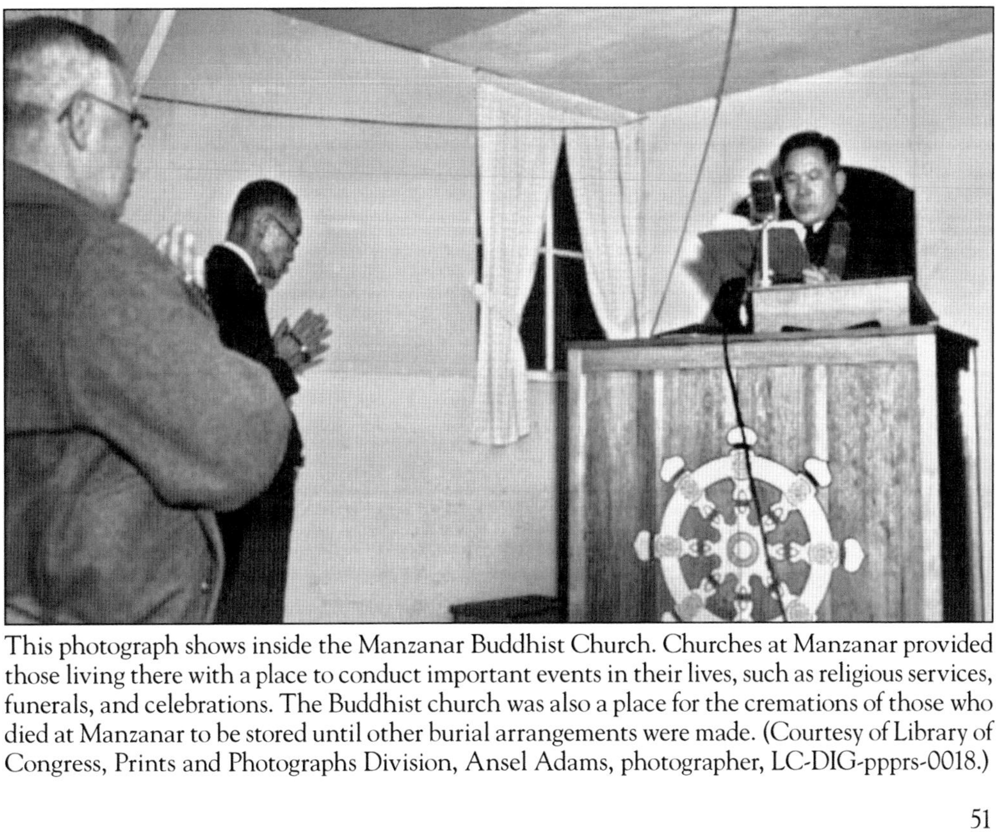

This photograph shows inside the Manzanar Buddhist Church. Churches at Manzanar provided those living there with a place to conduct important events in their lives, such as religious services, funerals, and celebrations. The Buddhist church was also a place for the cremations of those who died at Manzanar to be stored until other burial arrangements were made. (Courtesy of Library of Congress, Prints and Photographs Division, Ansel Adams, photographer, LC-DIG-ppprs-0018.)

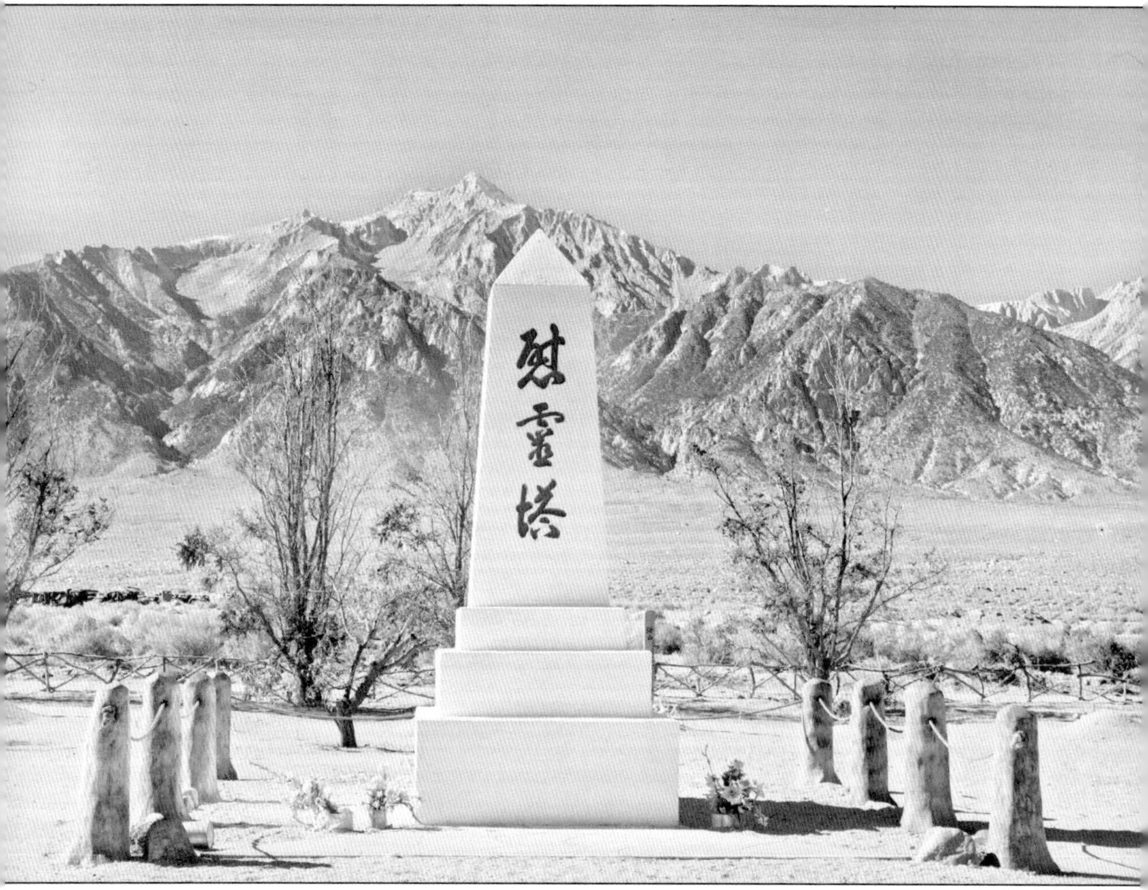

Located west of the camp and outside the living area fence, the now-restored cemetery is dominated by a large stone monument whose Japanese characters translate to "soul consoling tower." The tower project was supervised by internee Ryozo Kado, a former stonemason for the Los Angeles Catholic Diocese. Each family in Manzanar contributed 15¢ to purchase cement for the memorial. The monument was dedicated in August 1943. (Courtesy of Library of Congress, Prints and Photographs Division, Ansel Adams, photographer, LC-DIG-ppprs-00210.)

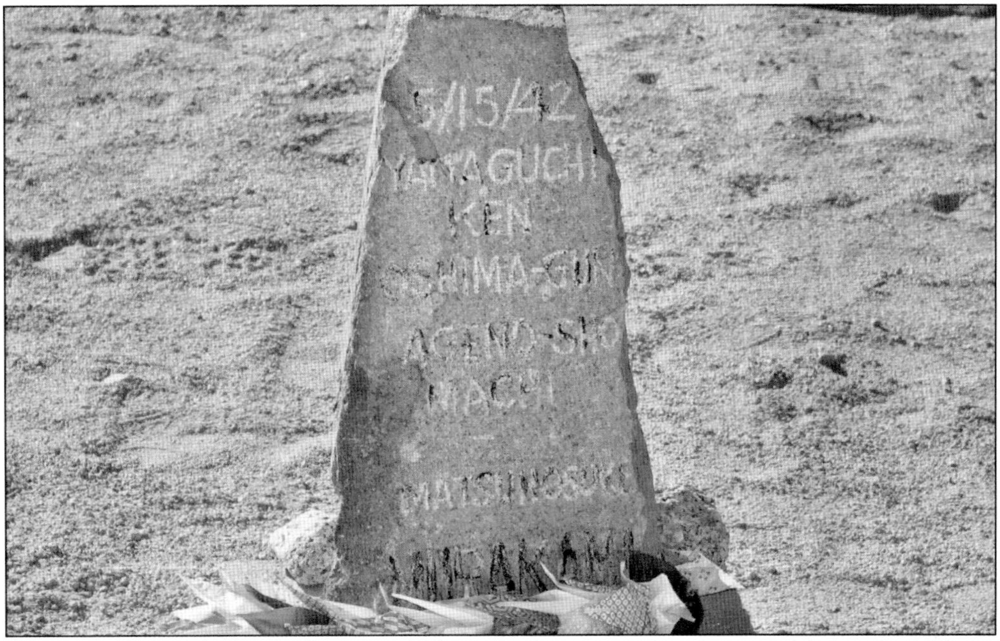

Matsunosuke Murakami was the first to be buried at Manzanar. A widower and former farm laborer without relatives, he died on May 16, 1942, at age 63 from myocardial failure and pneumonia. Between 1942 and 1945, one hundred fifty people died at Manzanar, two from gunshot wounds suffered during the December 1942 riot. Only 15 people were buried in the cemetery; six graves remain today. Most who died were cremated or buried elsewhere at their families' request. (Courtesy of David Ortega.)

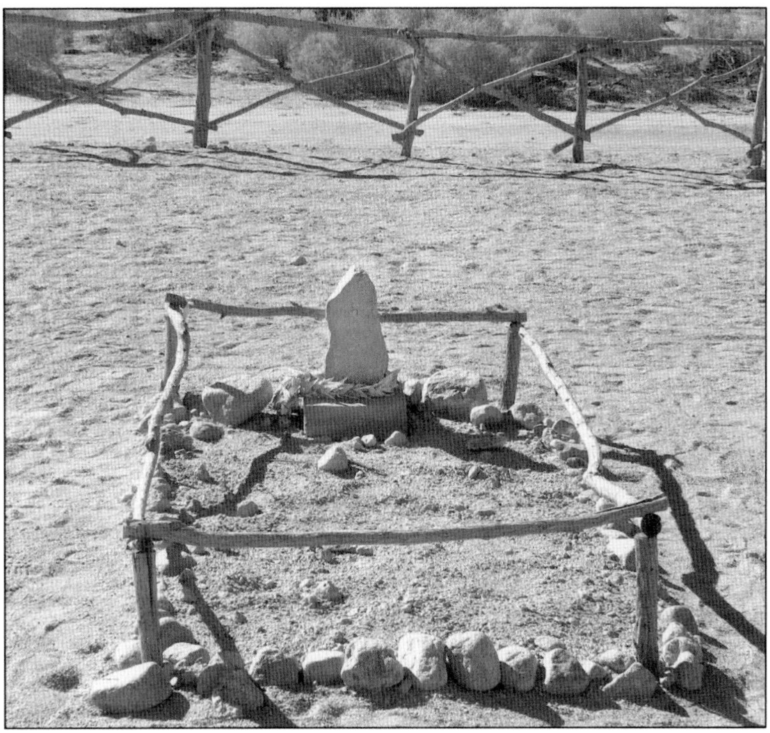
This is the marker for Sachiko Sawamura, a six-month-old girl who died on November 26, 1942, from tuberculosis-related meningitis. Like many of those who were temporarily buried at Manzanar, her body was later exhumed and reburied, possibly where her parents lived after the war. (Courtesy of David Ortega.)

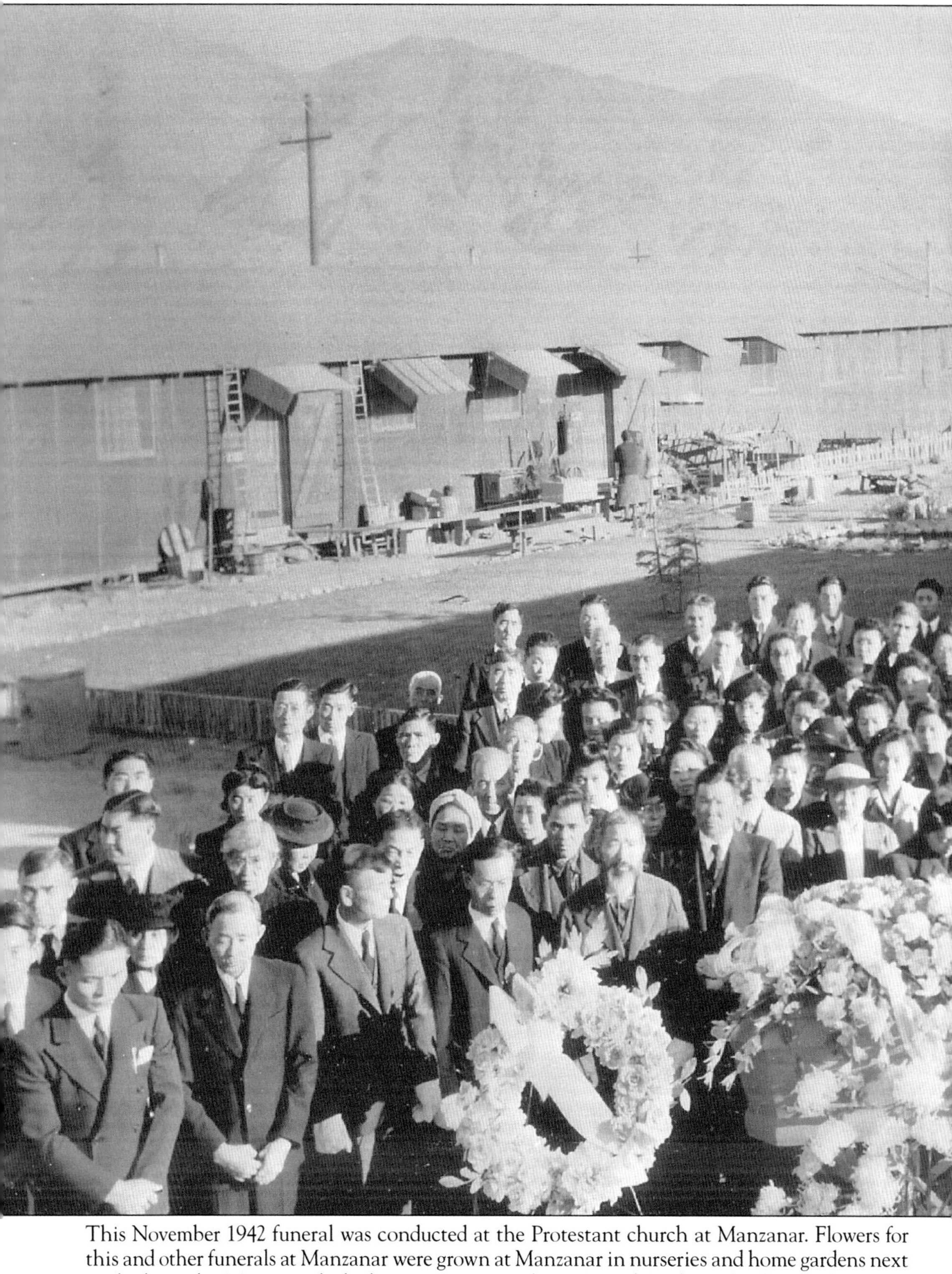

This November 1942 funeral was conducted at the Protestant church at Manzanar. Flowers for this and other funerals at Manzanar were grown at Manzanar in nurseries and home gardens next to the barracks. Manzanar lacked maintenance workers to conduct the task of grave digging. It

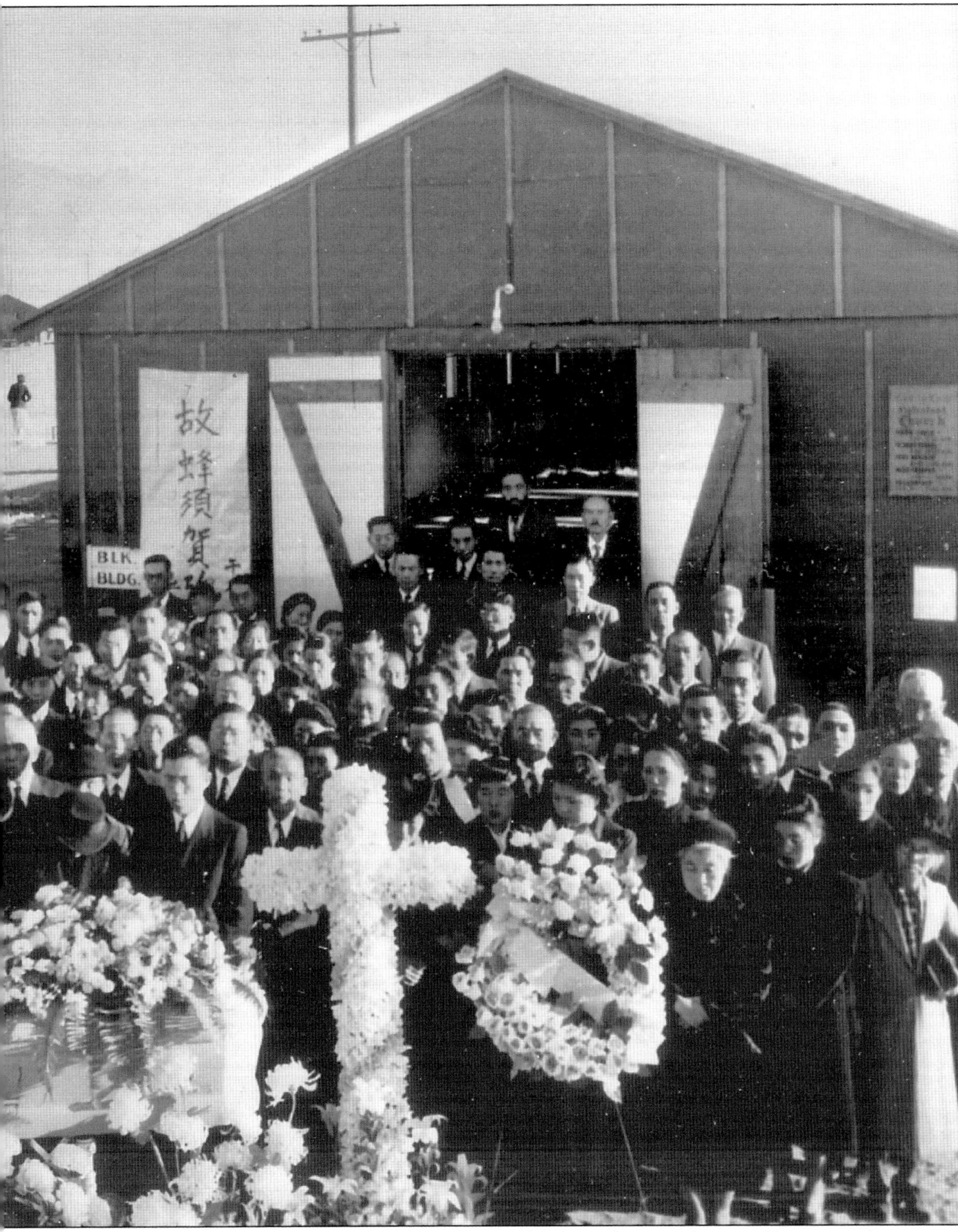

was decided that friends and neighbors of the deceased help with grave digging. (Courtesy of County of Inyo, Eastern California Museum.)

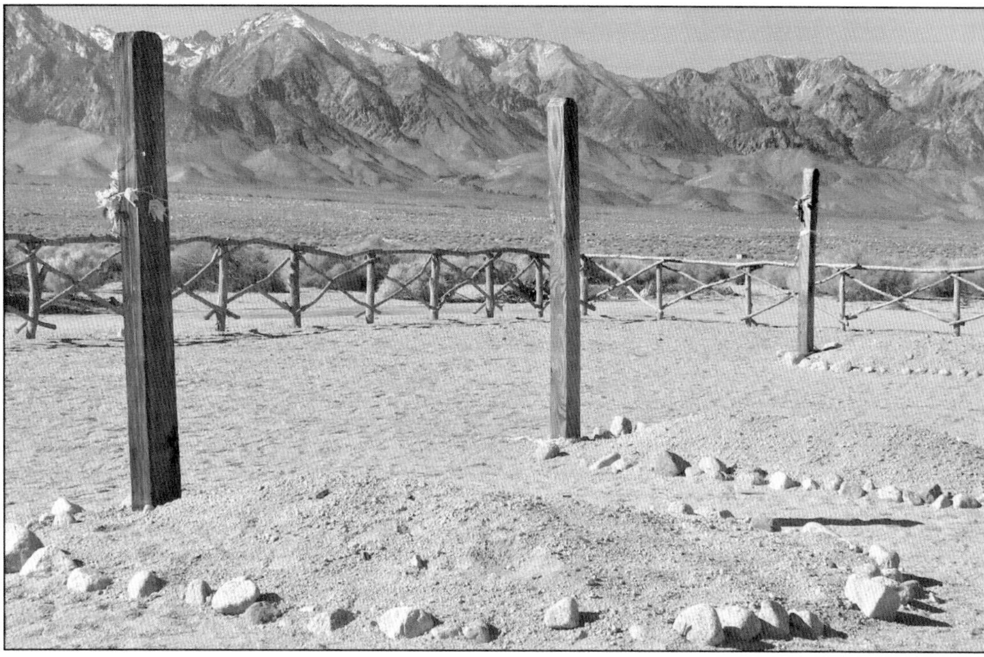

These simple wooden posts mark the graves of Minoru Kihara, Susan Midori Furuya, and Shinnojio Fukumoto. Kihara, 63 years old, died on November 27, 1942. He lived at Manzanar for just eight months prior to his death. Susan Midori Furuya, a premature baby, died on August 14, 1943. Shinnojio Fukumoto was a 62-year-old cook at Manzanar who died on December 19, 1944. (Courtesy of David Ortega.)

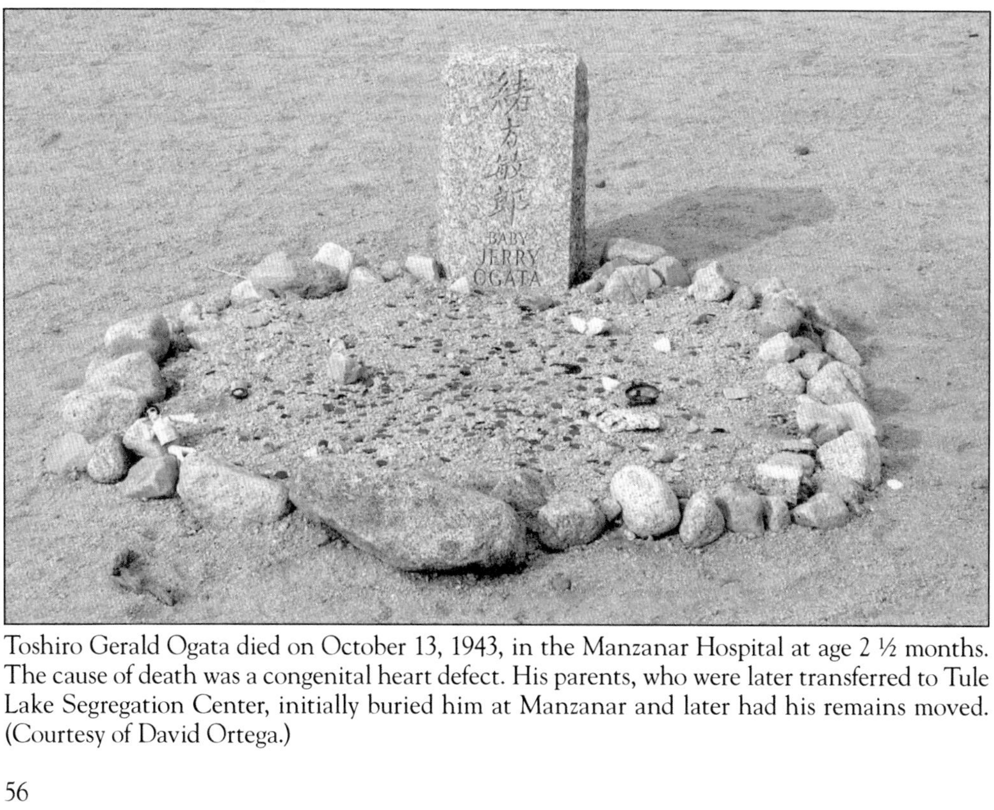

Toshiro Gerald Ogata died on October 13, 1943, in the Manzanar Hospital at age 2 ½ months. The cause of death was a congenital heart defect. His parents, who were later transferred to Tule Lake Segregation Center, initially buried him at Manzanar and later had his remains moved. (Courtesy of David Ortega.)

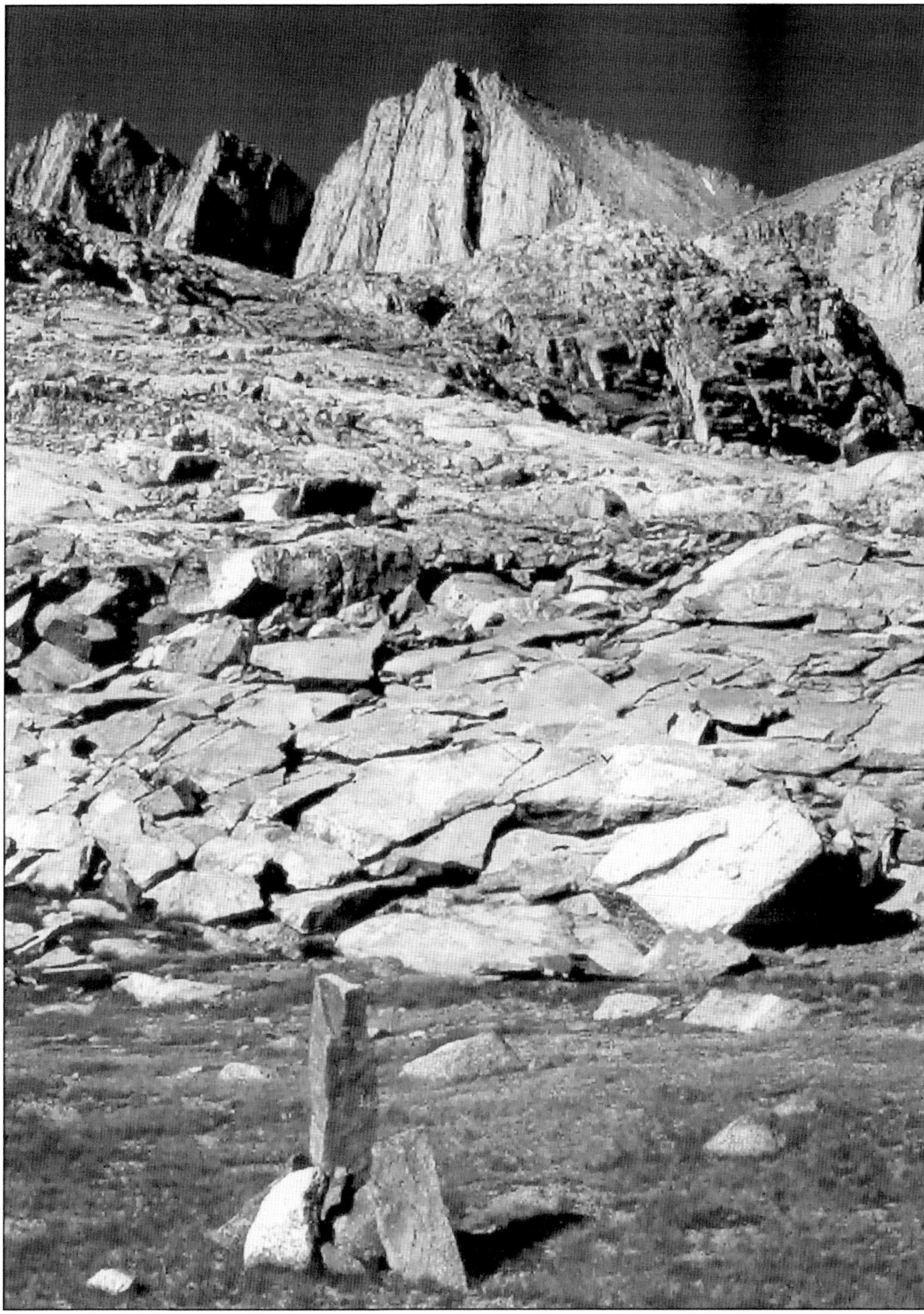

On August 2, 1945, Giichi Matsumura hiked with fellow internees into the Williamson Lake area to fish and oil paint. At some point, he became separated from the group and either became ill from the altitude or suffered a heart attack. His body was found September 2, 1945, by hikers from Independence. Because of the difficult terrain, it was decided that he would be buried where he was found. (Courtesy of Edwin P. Pister.)

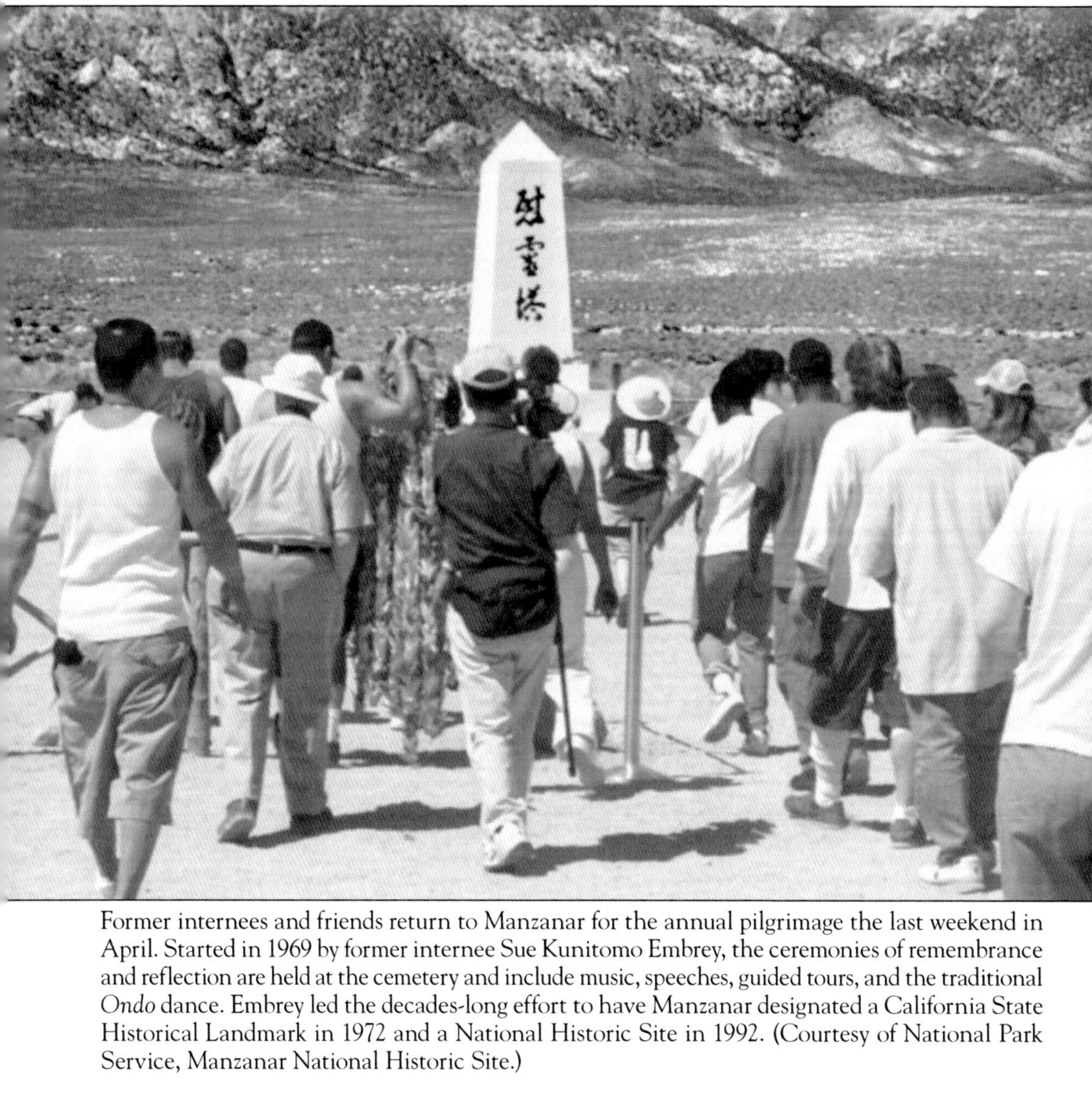

Former internees and friends return to Manzanar for the annual pilgrimage the last weekend in April. Started in 1969 by former internee Sue Kunitomo Embrey, the ceremonies of remembrance and reflection are held at the cemetery and include music, speeches, guided tours, and the traditional *Ondo* dance. Embrey led the decades-long effort to have Manzanar designated a California State Historical Landmark in 1972 and a National Historic Site in 1992. (Courtesy of National Park Service, Manzanar National Historic Site.)

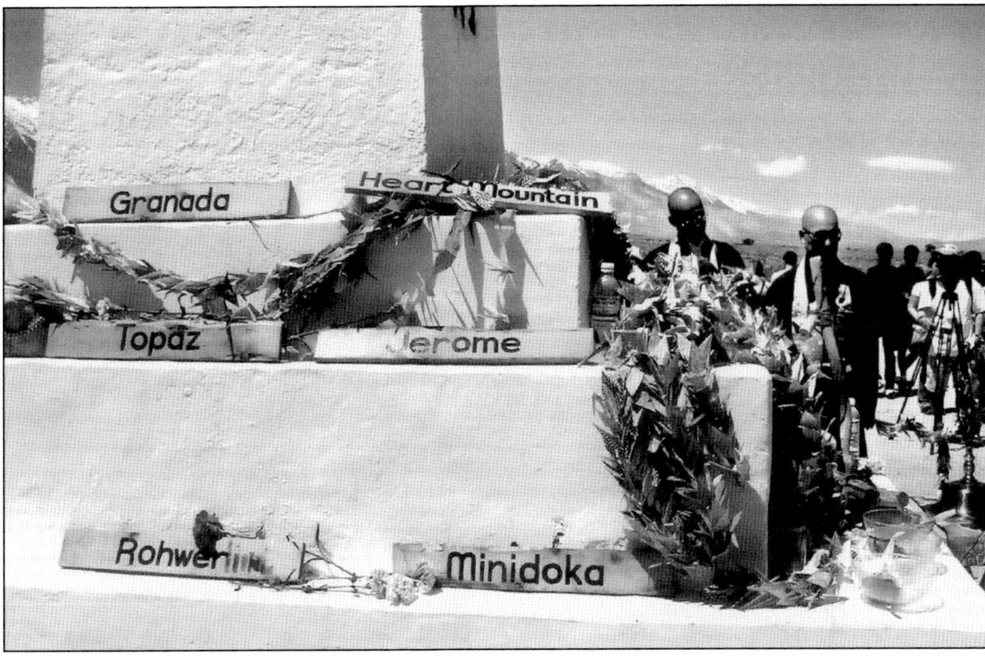

The wooden plaques resting on the Manzanar cemetery tower are engraved with the names of other internment camps. Ten U.S. internment camps held people of Japanese ancestry during World War II; they were Poston and Gila River in Arizona, Manzanar and Tule Lake in California, Minidoka in Idaho, Topaz in Utah, Heart Mountain in Wyoming, Granada in Colorado, and Jerome and Rohwer in Arkansas. (Courtesy of National Park Service, Manzanar National Historic Site.)

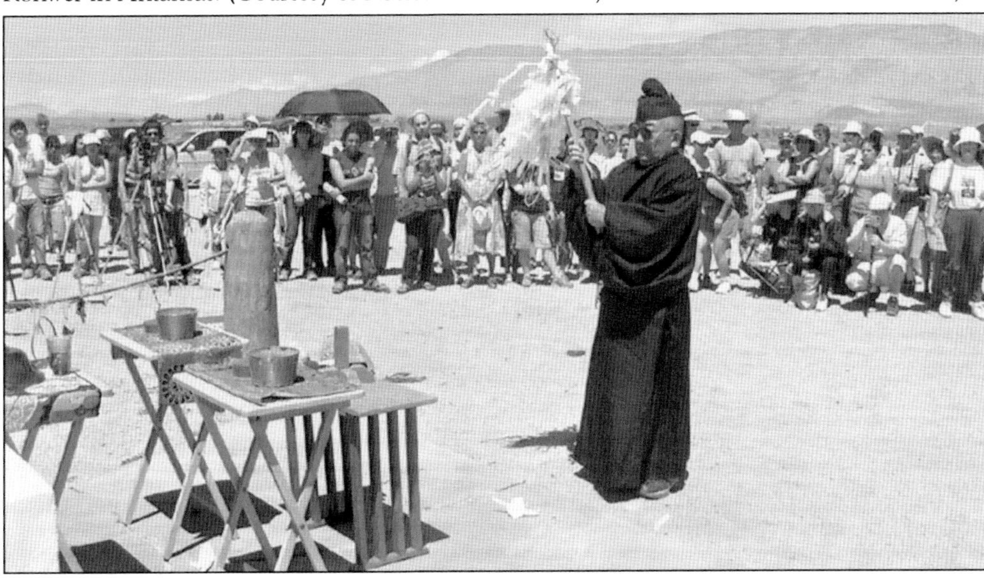

Prior to the formal pilgrimage begun in 1969, two Issei clergymen—the late Rev. Sentoku Maeda, a Buddhist, and Rev. Shoichi Wakahiro, a Christian—returned to Manzanar annually for 25 years after it closed in 1945. Today the annual Manzanar pilgrimage includes a traditional Buddhist service of remembrance. Pilgrimage attendees participate in Buddhist and Christian religious services held at the cemetery monument. (Courtesy of National Park Service, Manzanar National Historic Site.)

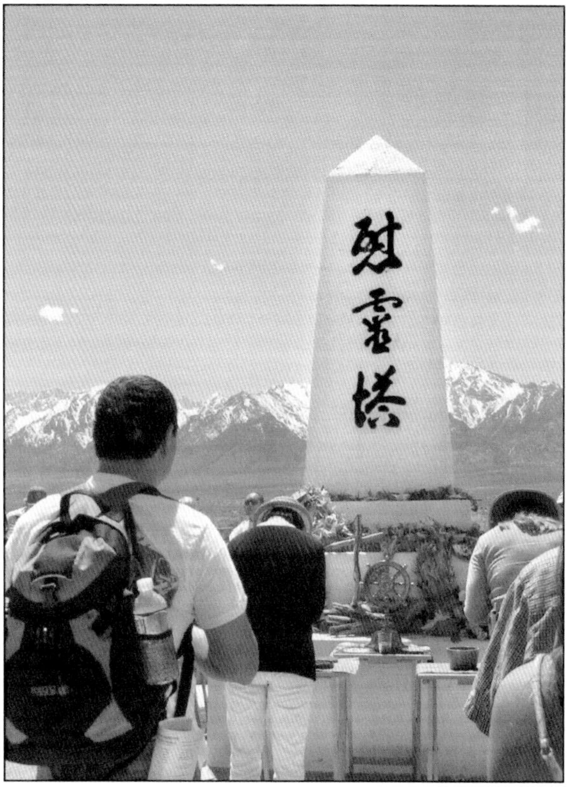

The Manzanar pilgrimage is attended by people who come from all over to remember and honor those who were interned. One of the events, Manzanar After Dark, held since 1997, provides a time for the generations to come together and learn through sharing, group discussions, oral histories, and cultural performances. Approximately 400 people attend the annual pilgrimage. (Courtesy of National Park Service, Manzanar National Historic Site.)

Internees were not allowed to bring their pets into camp, but stray dogs and cats from the local communities often found their way to Manzanar. North of the human cemetery is a small pet cemetery where three visible graves, outlined by rocks, hold the remains of two dogs and five cats who found a home at Manzanar. (Courtesy of David Ortega.)

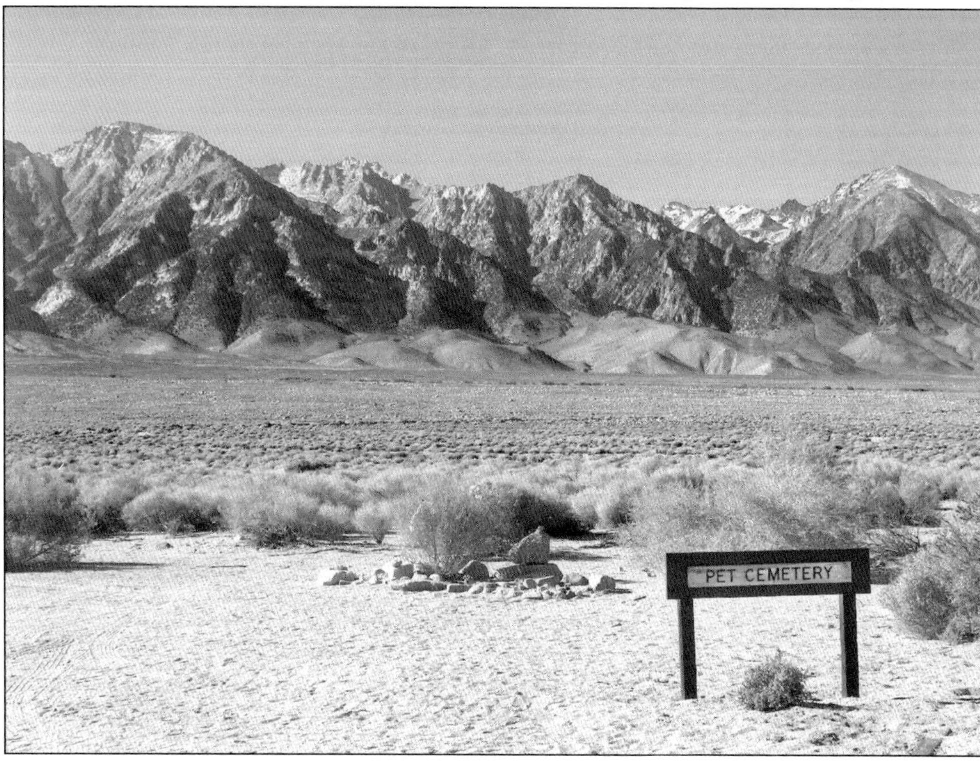

Three

Mono County

Mono County was formed in 1861 and stretches from the town of Benton, north of Bishop, to the Nevada state border. By 1877, the influx of new residents into Mono County was reflected in the voting register that showed men of various professions, as well as women, settling in the area. Today the county has just over 12,000 residents.

The county's only incorporated city, Mammoth Lakes, is best known for its ski resort, beautiful mountain lakes, and Ice Age mascot. Mono Lake to the north is familiar to many for the bumper stickers, popular 30 years ago, that proclaimed "Save Mono Lake." It is California's largest lake and is a salt lake akin to the Great Salt Lake in Utah. Like something from another world, it is nestled in a treeless environment, with its strange tufa formations reaching out of azure water.

Ghost towns like Lundy and Dogtown were home to Mono County's mining boom. But no ghost town is as well-known or well preserved as Bodie. A state park since 1862, Bodie is today in a state of "arrested decay." In 1859, W. Bodey discovered a vein of gold that would turn the area into a booming city. Twenty years later, the town had a population of 8,000. Unlike other area mining boomtowns, Bodie experienced a longer period of wealth, which resulted in a population limited not just to miners, but which included women and families. Stores, saloons, and a red-light district flourished. During one six-week period in 1889, the Bodie mines shipped over $1 million in gold bouillon.

Mono County's is a rich history, and names associated with its localities hint at its colorful past. Deadman Creek, near Mammoth Lakes, was originally named for Robert Hume, a prospector whose burned and headless body was found nearby in a shallow grave in 1861. Suspicion soon pointed to his partner, a man named Farnsworth, who later disappeared. A few years later, the remains of two more prospectors were found near here. And in December 1879, William Haines, a mailman, was found, along with his mailbags, after being reported missing.

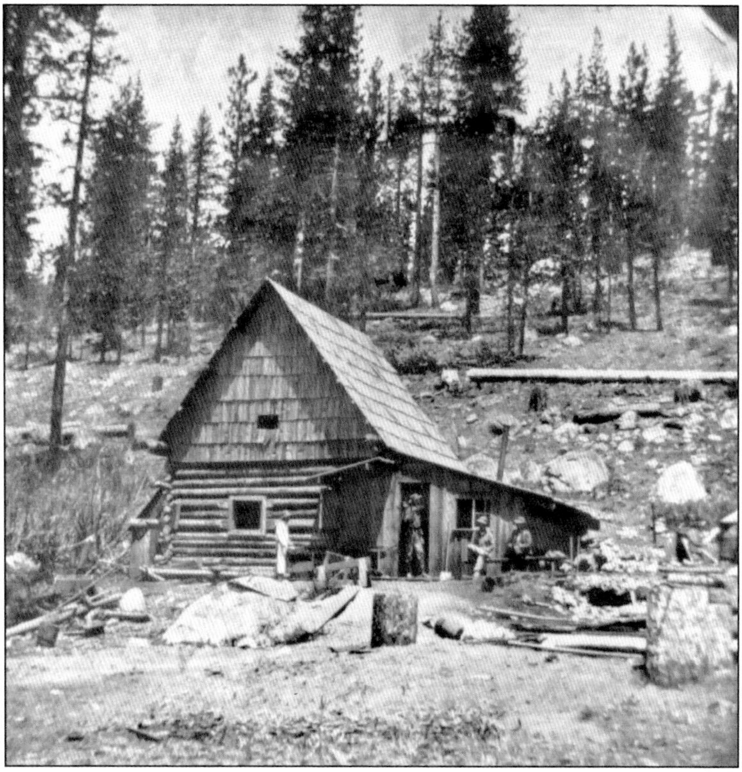

Men flocked to the West with dreams of striking it rich in gold or silver, and many left wives and children behind in hopes that one day they could make a new life for their families in California. Living alone for years in primitive cabins or even tents, only a few miners found the wealth they had dreamed of; most went back to families brokenhearted and financially ruined. (Courtesy of the Library of Congress, Prints and Photographs Division, LC-USZ62-13121.)

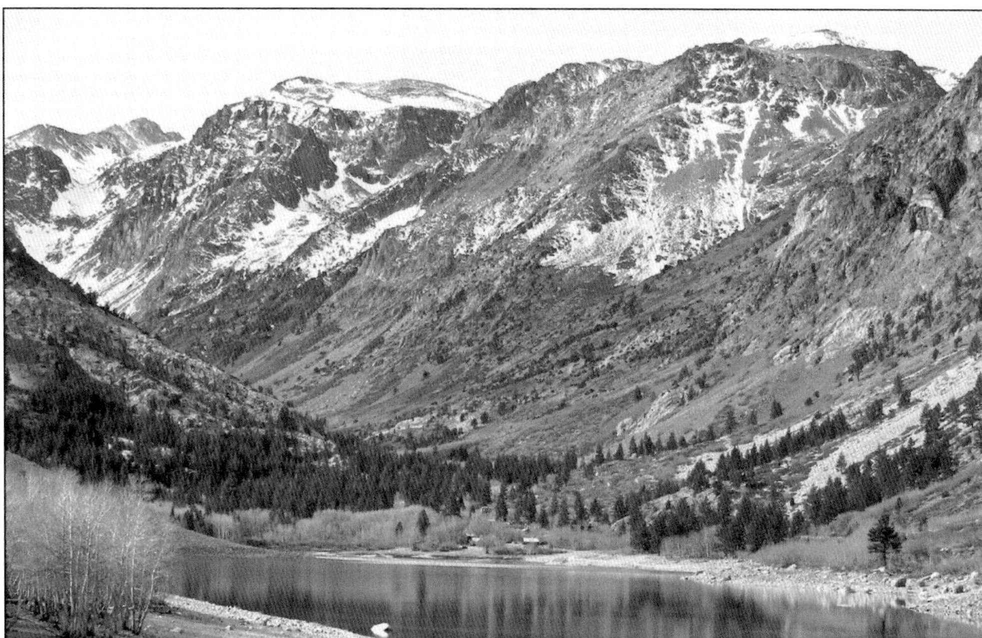

Lundy, located in a steep canyon at about 7,000 feet just north of Lee Vining, was once a mining town brimming with hope. The May Lundy mine was organized in 1879 and disbanded in 1884. Lundy was the site of many avalanches and the deaths that accompanied them. (Courtesy of David Ortega.)

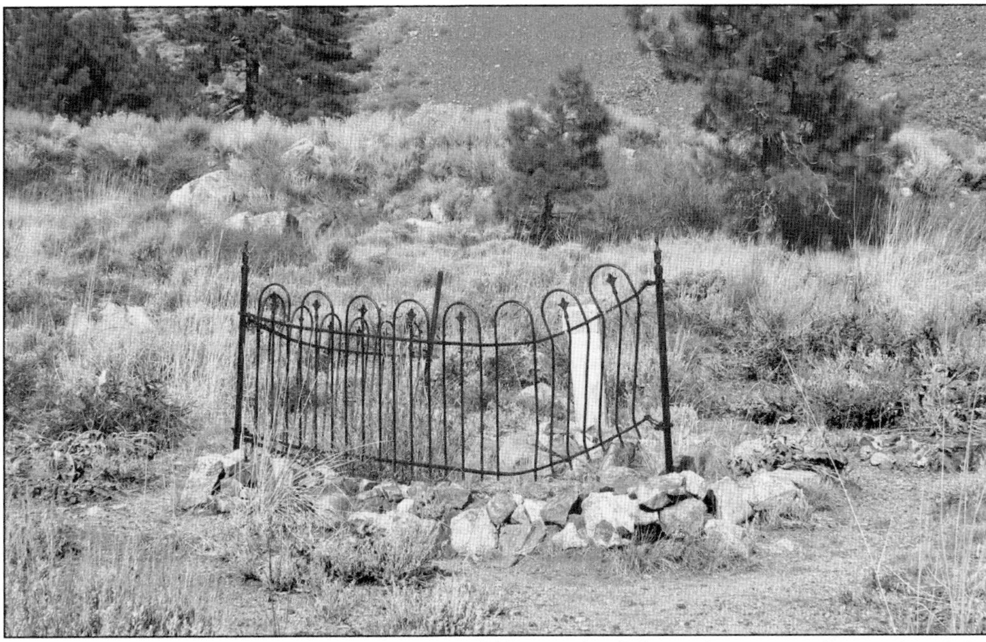

One story involving the Lundy cemetery, as told by Emil Billeb, is of a Mono Lake rancher, John Dondero, who came into Lundy to sell produce. He would stake his horse in the Lundy cemetery and allow it to eat the grass there. Some locals thought they would play a trick on John and waited one night with white sheets in the darkened cemetery. As he approached, the men jumped out, yelling and carrying on like they were ghosts. Not missing a beat, Dondero went after the "ghosts," yelling, "Get back in your holes!" Today Lundy's cemetery is almost completely gone save one fence and a memorial marker recently erected to those early settlers. (Courtesy of David Ortega.)

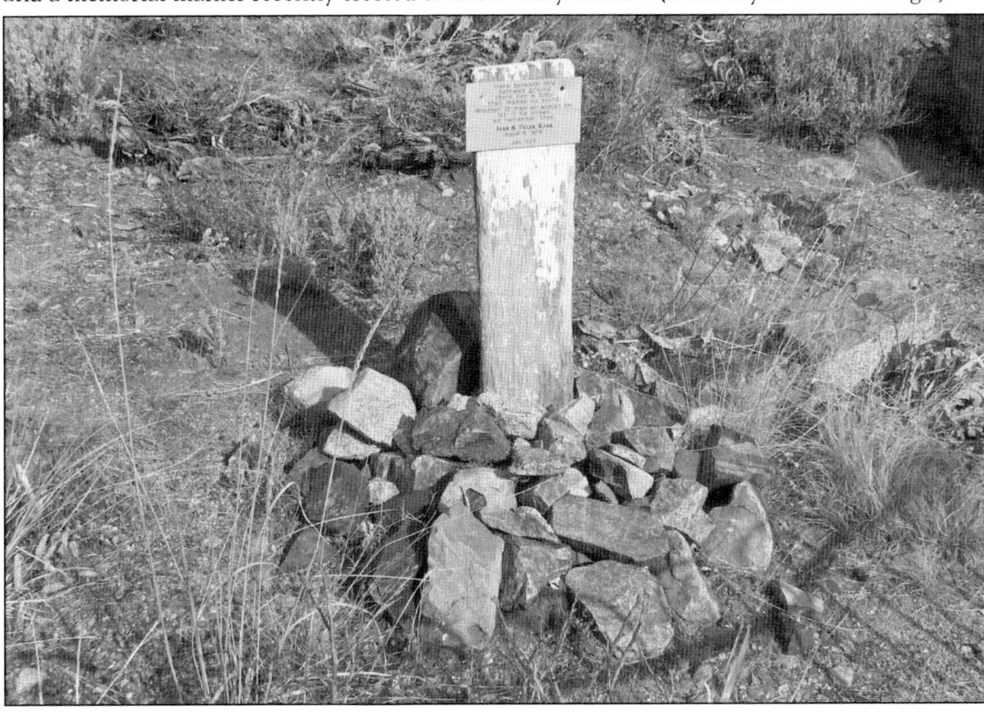

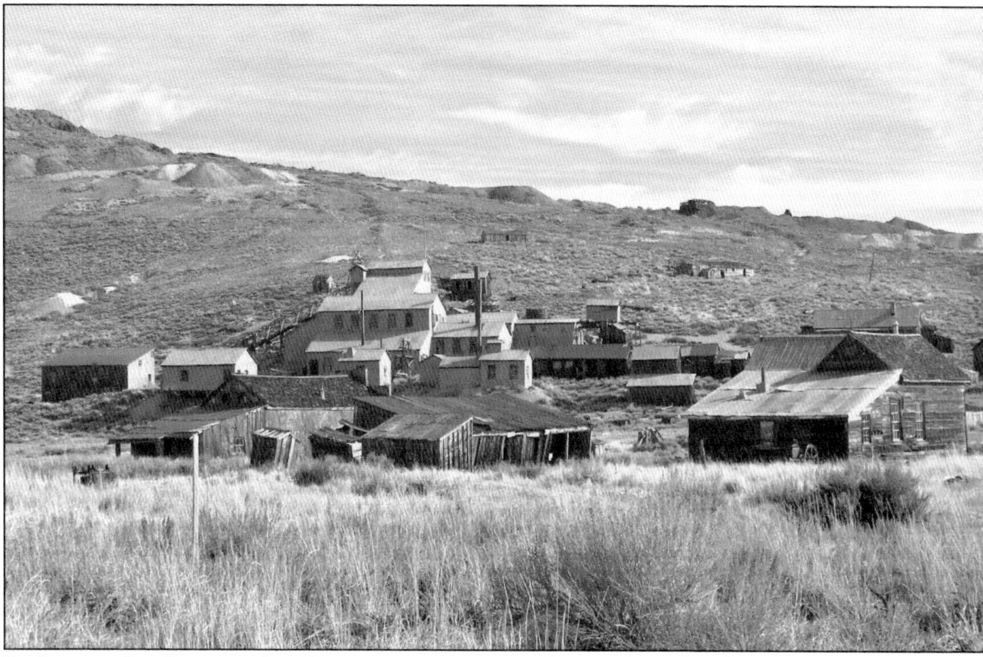

Bodie in its heyday was a bustling mining town complete with a school, mills, stores, and its own red-light district. Miners and their families lived there, along with those who operated hotels, stores, and restaurants. In 1879, the local paper boasted that the population had grown to 8,000 people. But the gold and the dreams that come with mining dried up, and by 1887, only 1,500 people were living in town. (Courtesy of David Ortega.)

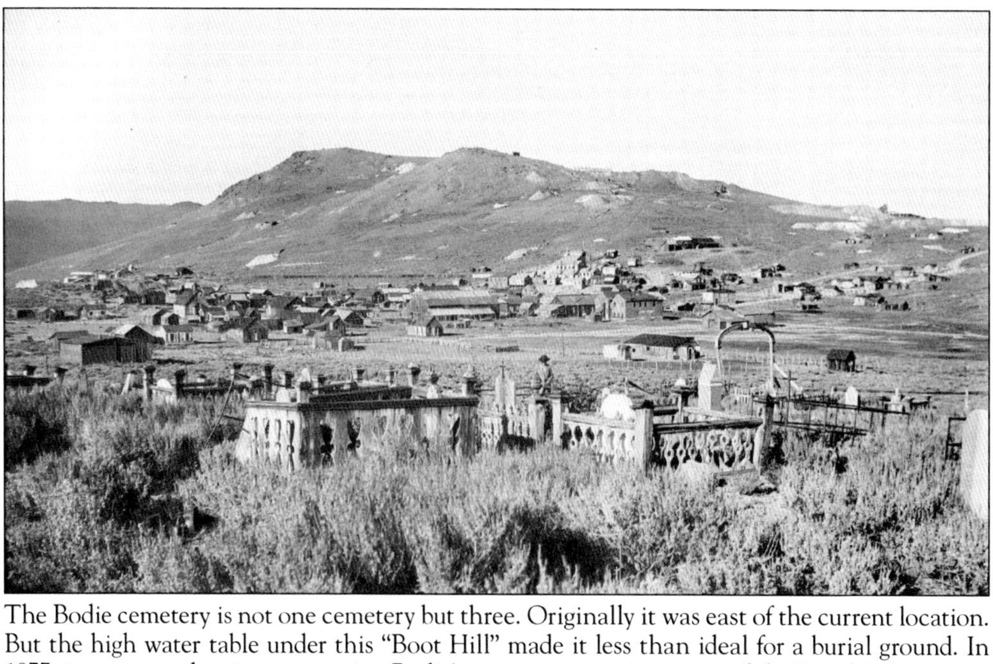

The Bodie cemetery is not one cemetery but three. Originally it was east of the current location. But the high water table under this "Boot Hill" made it less than ideal for a burial ground. In 1877, it was moved to its present site. Bodie's cemetery contains parts of the People's Cemetery, the Masonic Cemetery, and the Miners Union cemetery. (Courtesy of University of Southern California, on behalf of the USC Specialized Libraries and Archival Collections.)

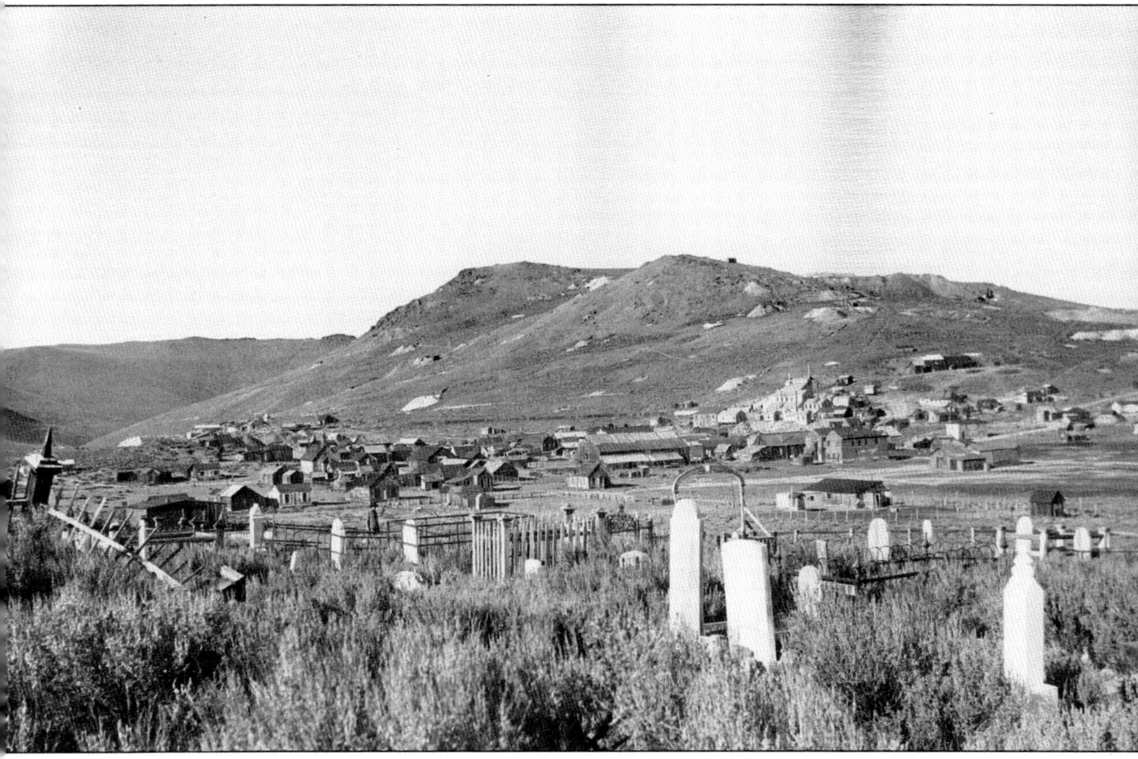

Some burials were also placed outside of the parameters of the three cemeteries when locals felt that certain types of people were unworthy to be buried with the "regular" citizens. Prostitutes often had this status and were frequently denied burial inside the cemetery gates. Like many old-time cemeteries, those at Bodie include other burials not recorded and graves for which there are no headstones. (Courtesy of University of Southern California, on behalf of the USC Specialized Libraries and Archival Collections.)

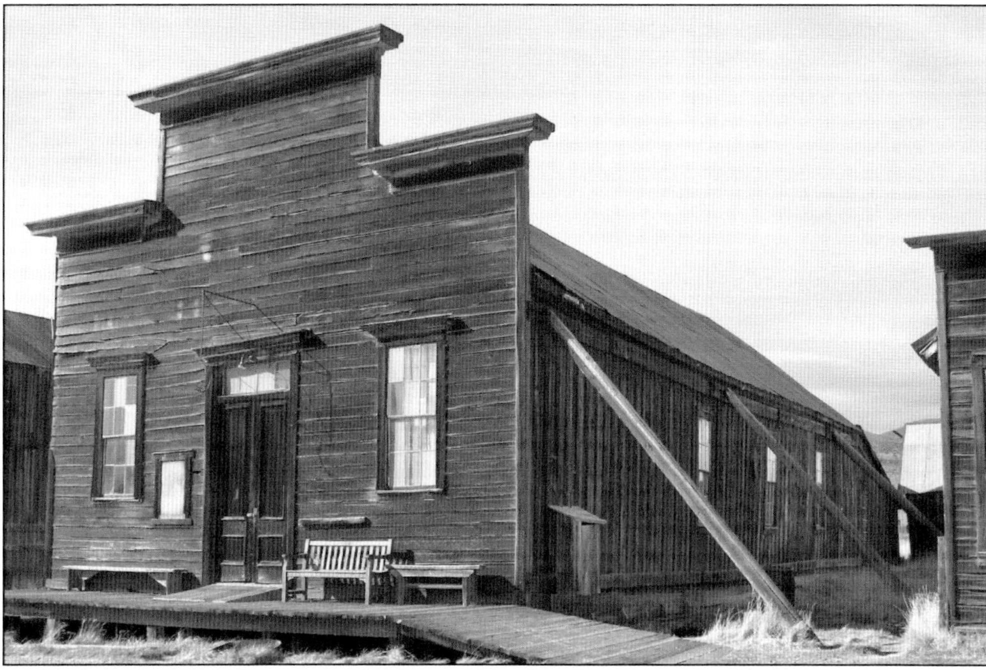

Bodie's burials included numerous deaths attributed to the rough way of life immortalized in the countless retellings of the town's history, including the moniker, "The Bad Man of Bodie," which could have referred to several area residents. But delays in medical attention also resulted in the early demise of many citizens. (Courtesy of David Ortega.)

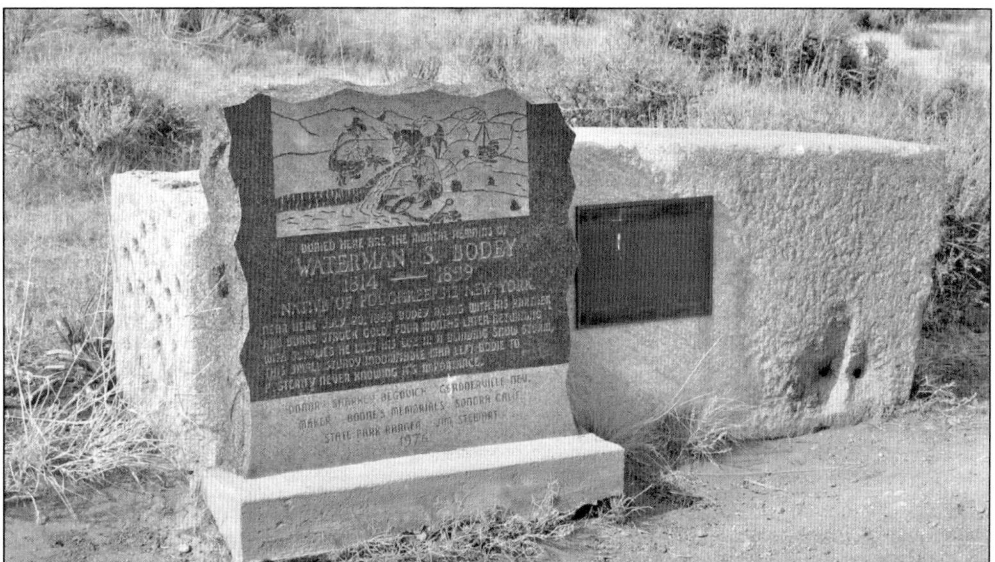

Waterman Bodey, also known as Wakeman or William Bodey, is the town's namesake. In 1859, while recovering a wounded rabbit at the foot of the Bodie bluff, he discovered a vein of gold, but he died the same year at the age of 45 trying to find shelter from a snowstorm. He didn't live long enough to enjoy the success of his namesake. This is a more modern monument placed by the group E Clampus Vitus. (Courtesy of David Ortega.)

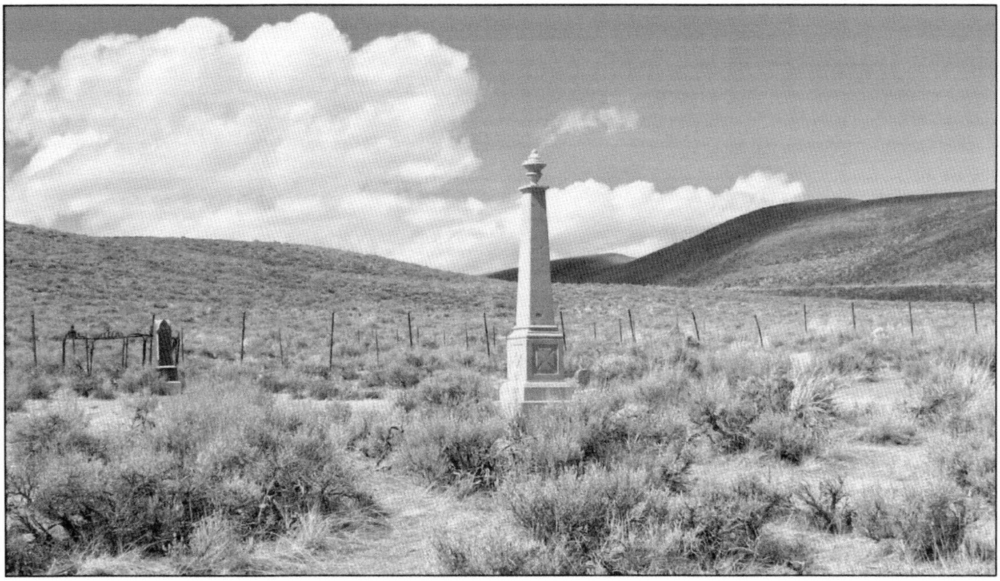

Another monument originally meant to honor the Bodie founder instead honors assassinated U.S. president James A Garfield. Bodey's remains were rediscovered in 1879, and a monument was commissioned for him. Unhappy about not being paid for his work, the stonecutter stopped work on the monument. When Garfield was assassinated on July 2, 1881, it was decided to finish the monument and dedicate it instead in his honor. (Courtesy of David Ortega.)

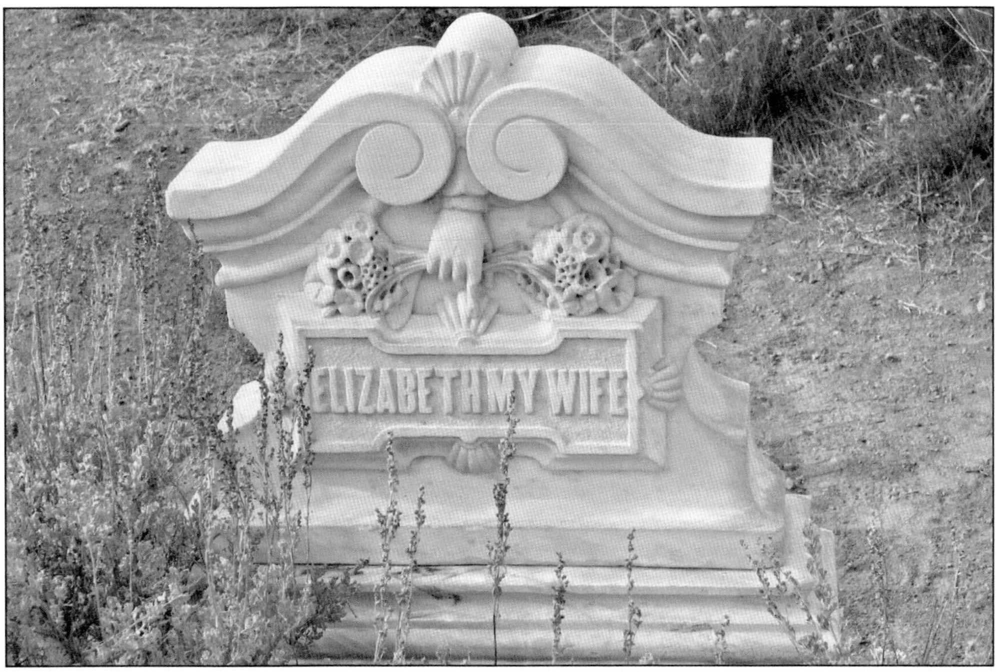

Women's lives in the 19th century were difficult at best. Childbirth was a potentially fatal part of life. Children typically came every two years, and a mother often saw at least one of her children die before they reached adulthood. The chores taken for granted today took all day in the 1800s and meant that, from morning to night, women were struggling to keep their families clothed and fed. (Courtesy of David Ortega.)

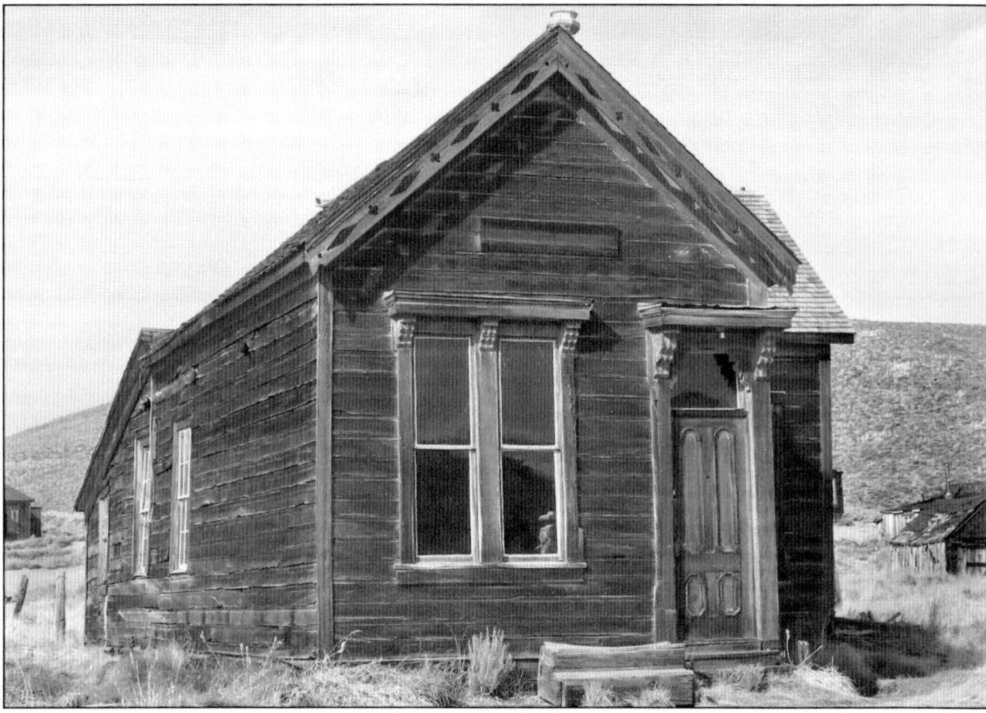

This was the home of Eli and Lottie Johl. Lottie, a Bodie prostitute, met local butcher Eli Johl and became his wife. Although she was loved by her husband, some townspeople, including the wife of her husband's business partner, could not accept her. One day, Lottie became ill and was given a prescription from a physician. The pharmacist accidentally gave Lottie poison instead of the prescribed medicine, and her life ended tragically. (Courtesy of David Ortega.)

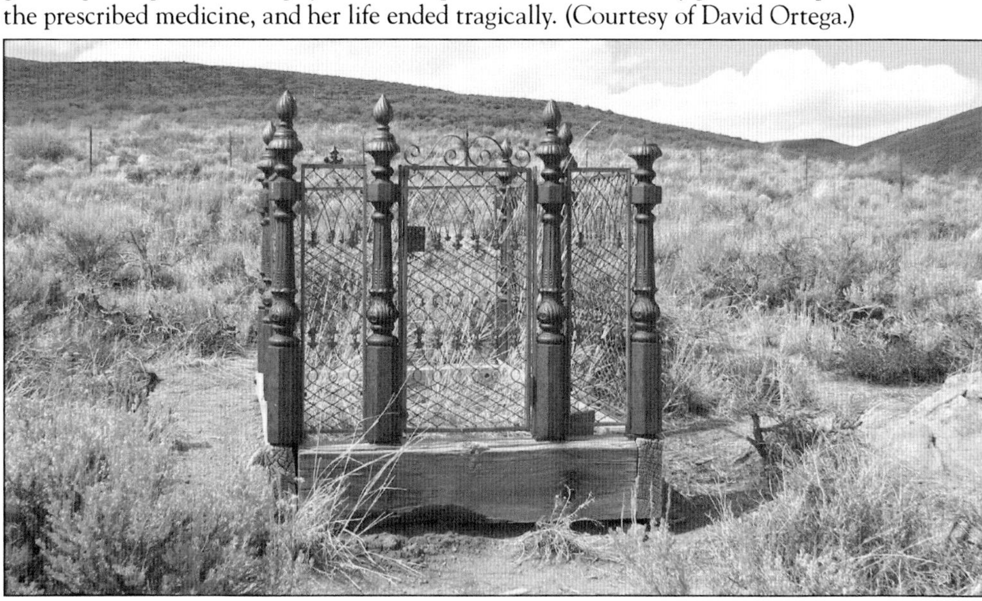

After arguments involving whether a reformed prostitute could be buried with the "normal" townsfolk, Lottie was buried on the edge of the cemetery. Eli erected the most elaborate fence around her grave and decorated it each Memorial Day. Eventually Eli left Bodie and never returned. Today only the fence remains. (Courtesy of David Ortega.)

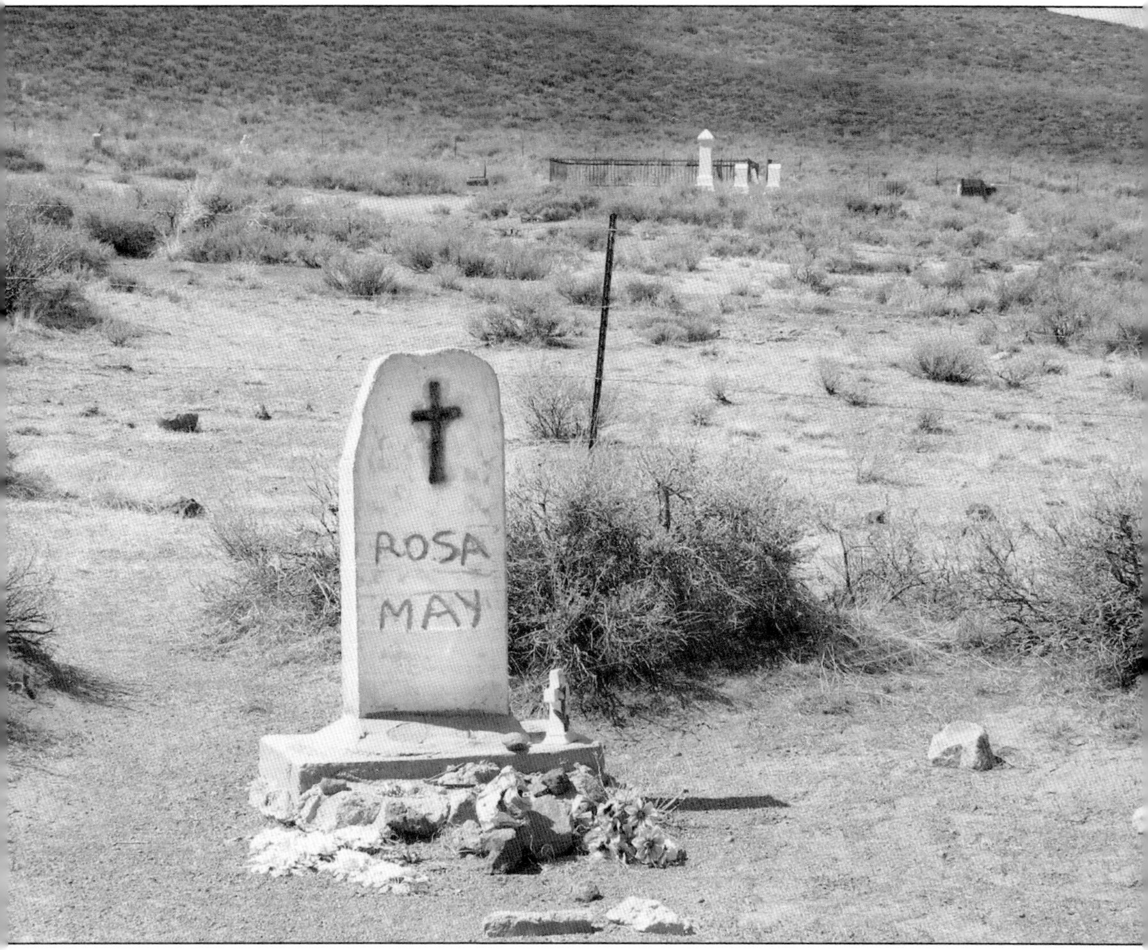

Rosa May was one of the many prostitutes who made a living in the brothels of Bodie. Like many western characters, Rosa and her life are shrouded in legend. Whatever is true about Rosa, like other prostitutes, she was not welcome inside the gates of the cemetery. Although her current headstone is outside the cemetery gates, it is unknown where her actual grave lies. (Courtesy of David Ortega.)

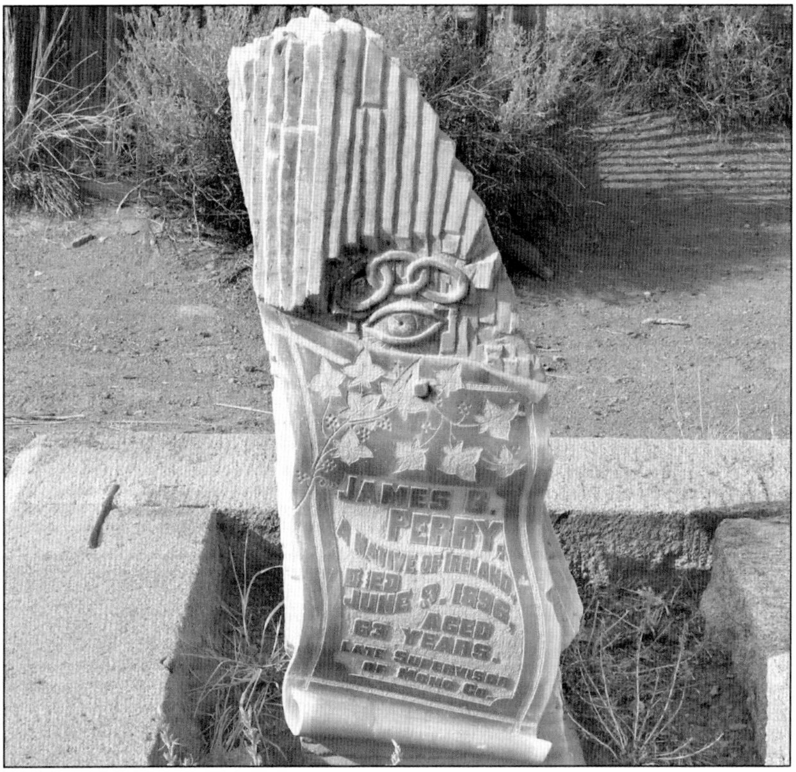

This interesting headstone is for James Perry, who served as a Mono County supervisor. The 1892 Bodie fire began in the restaurant that was operated by his wife. The three chains over the eye at the top of his tombstone represent the fraternal organization the Odd Fellows. (Courtesy of David Ortega.)

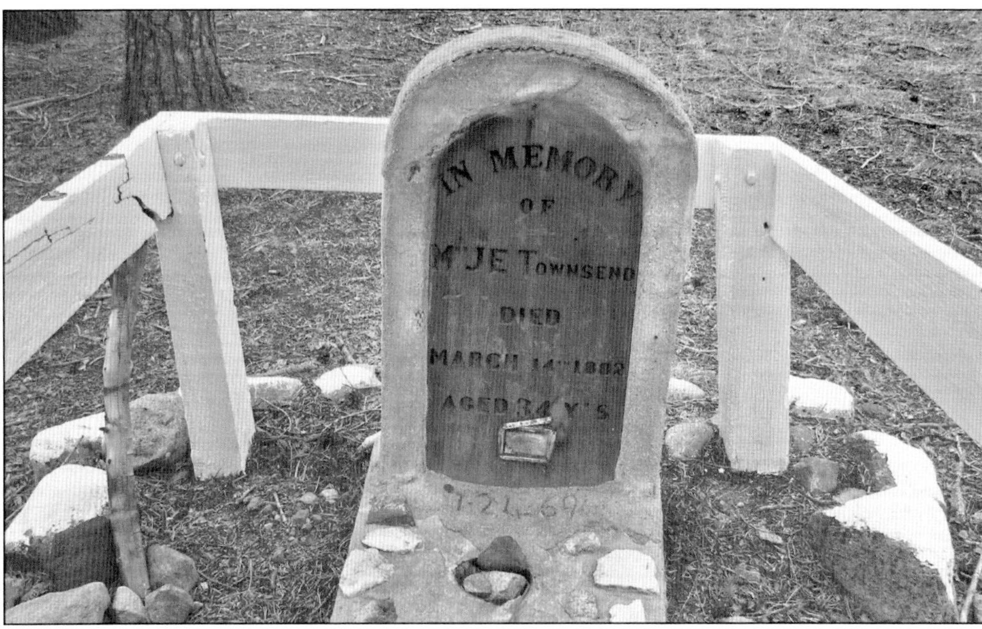

This solitary grave in Mammoth memorializes Mrs. J. E. Townsend. According to a story told to pioneer Owens Valley physician, Dr. Helen MacKnight Doyle, Townsend was accidentally shot by her husband when he was trying to discharge a jammed bullet. Townsend buried his wife with a white picket fence around her grave in memory of the home with a white picket fence she dreamed of. (Courtesy of David Ortega.)

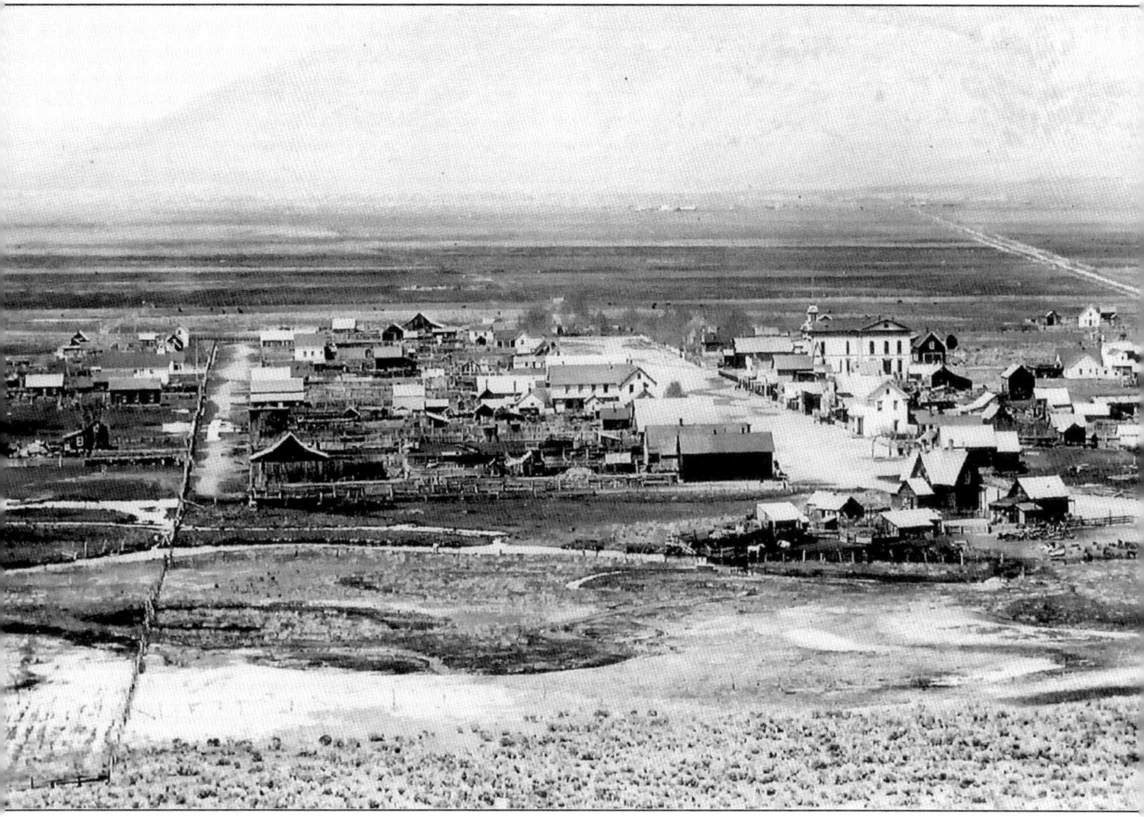

Prior to the white man coming to the Bridgeport Valley, Paiute Indians lived near the area hot springs and along the shores of Mono Lake. Later known for its agriculture, cattle ranching, and sawmills that supplied neighboring mining towns, Bridgeport was settled about 1859 by the Whitney brothers, William T. and G. A. It is now the county seat for Mono County. (Courtesy of the Mono County Historical Society.)

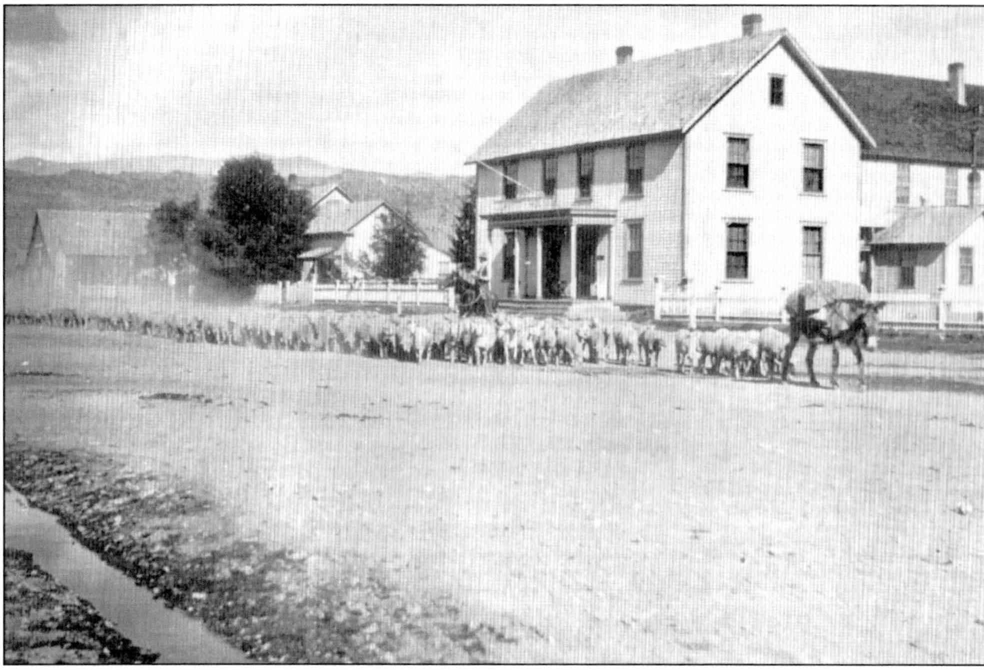

Formerly a Victorian home, the Bridgeport Inn on Highway 395 in the center of town was built in 1877 for Hiram Leavitt. Hiram and his family came to Indian Valley, now named after the Leavitts, in 1865. Leavitt owned a stage stop business and was at one time a judge for Mono County. Today the Bridgeport Inn operates as a hotel and restaurant. (Courtesy of the Mono County Historical Society.)

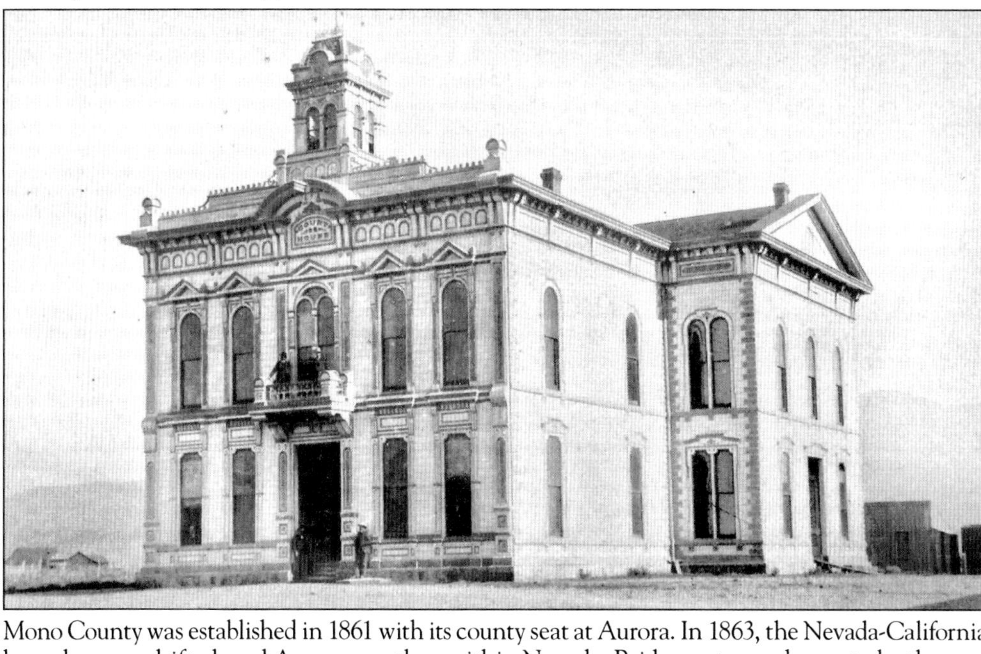

Mono County was established in 1861 with its county seat at Aurora. In 1863, the Nevada-California boundary was shifted, and Aurora was then within Nevada. Bridgeport was chosen to be the new county seat. This Mono County Courthouse was built in 1881. (Courtesy of the Mono County Historical Society.)

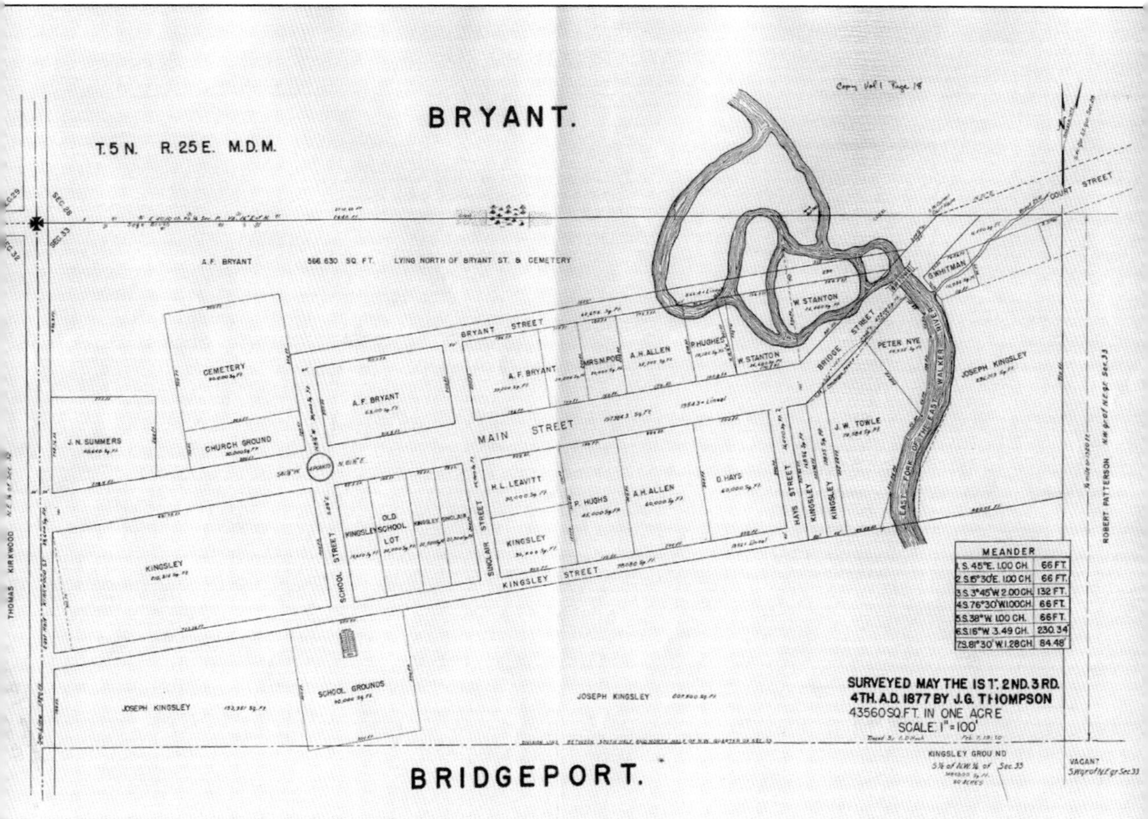

This map from 1877 shows the original city cemetery on Main Street. In front of the cemetery is a church, but by 1930, it was replaced by a gas station and two residences that extended onto the cemetery grounds. Names of burials are shown on a 1930 map, including six unknowns. (Courtesy of the Mono County Historical Society.)

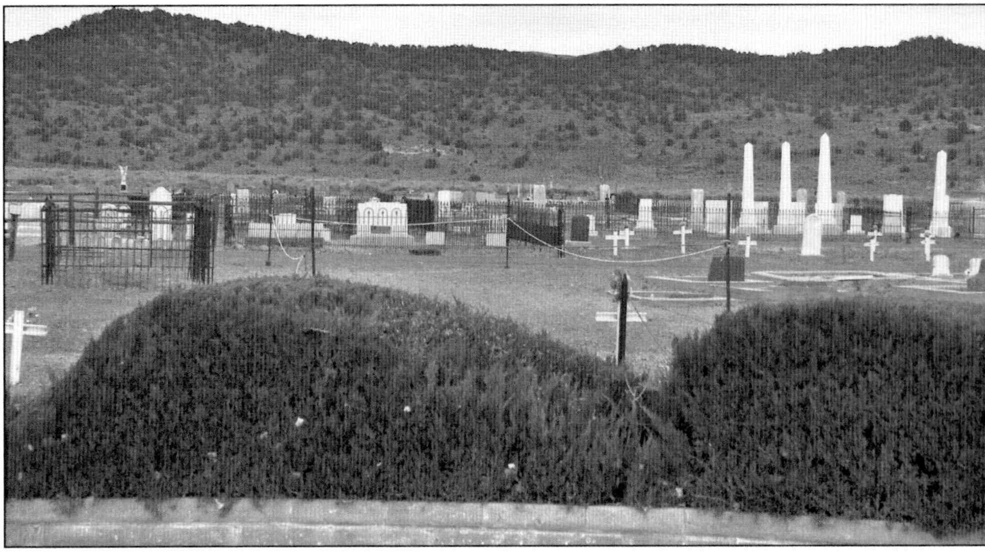

The Bridgeport Cemetery, originally located just west of the county courthouse where the current location of Bridgeport Park and Memorial Hall are, was moved in the 1930s to make room for a community center and a motor court. The current cemetery is on Bureau of Land Management land and was acquired by the county in 1940 with the stipulation that it be used as a cemetery. (Courtesy of David Ortega.)

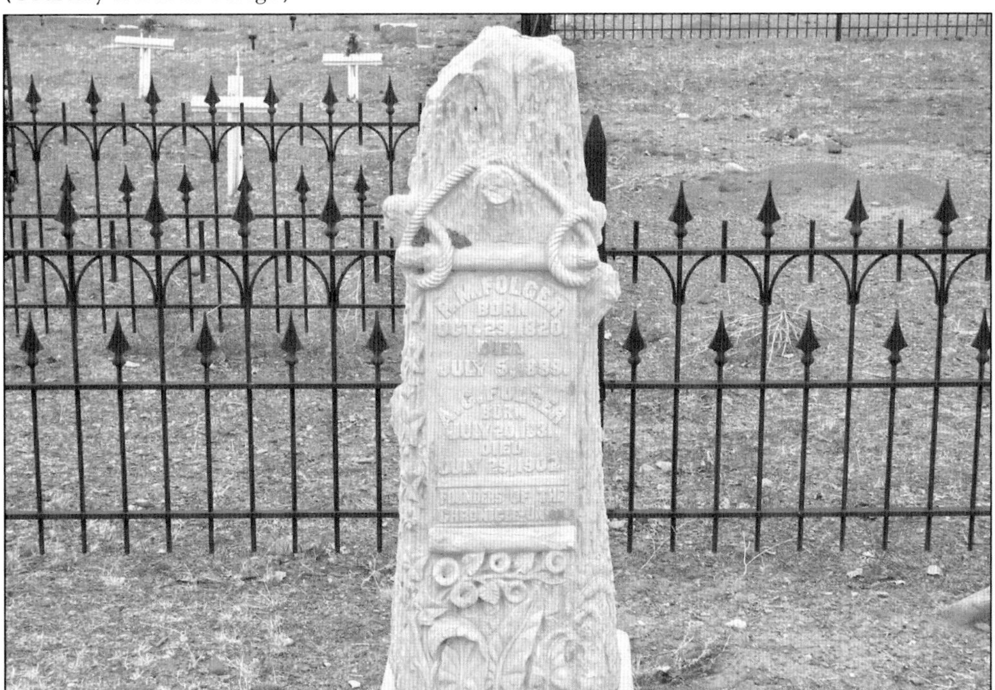

Alexander and Robert Folger, publishers of the *Alpine Chronicle* and the *Bridgeport Chronicle Union*, are buried in the Bridgeport Cemetery. The brothers, who were members of the Society of Friends, were well respected for their patriotism and defense of ethical journalism. When Robert died in 1902, he was the oldest working journalist on the West Coast. After Robert's death, Alexander continued to do the reporting, writing, and printing. (Courtesy of David Ortega.)

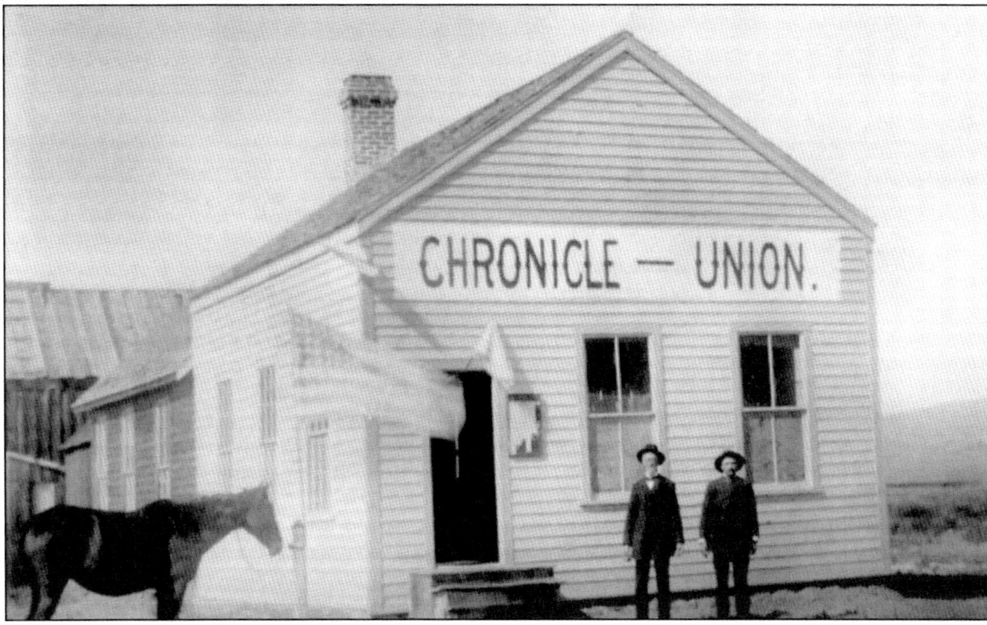

The Folgers' first office for the *Bridgeport Chronicle Union* was on Main Street in Bridgeport. They later had an office built on School Street, complete with a home and a warm padded stable for their beloved horse Jinny. When Jinny died, the Folgers hired local Native Americans to dig her a grave in their backyard. Jinny had her own tombstone that read, "Our beloved Jinny—The Faithful." (Courtesy of the Mono County Historical Society.)

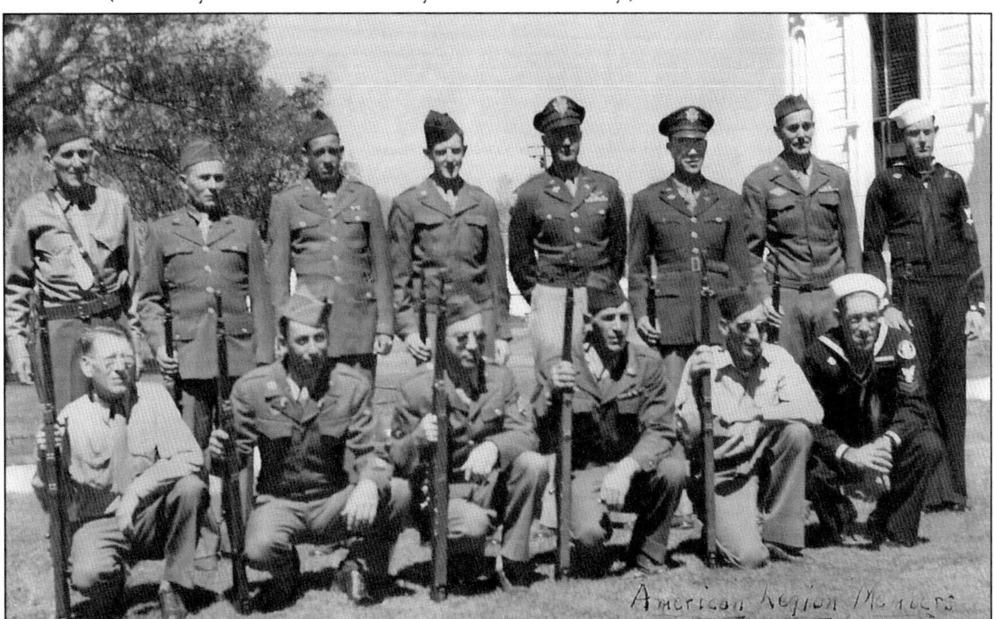

This picture is just one example of pictures taken of people attending funerals. Here members of the American Legion, Mark Twain Post, Bridgeport are dressed in uniform for a 1942 funeral. The American Legion, chartered in 1919, is a patriotic, wartime veteran's organization. (Courtesy of the Mono County Historical Society.)

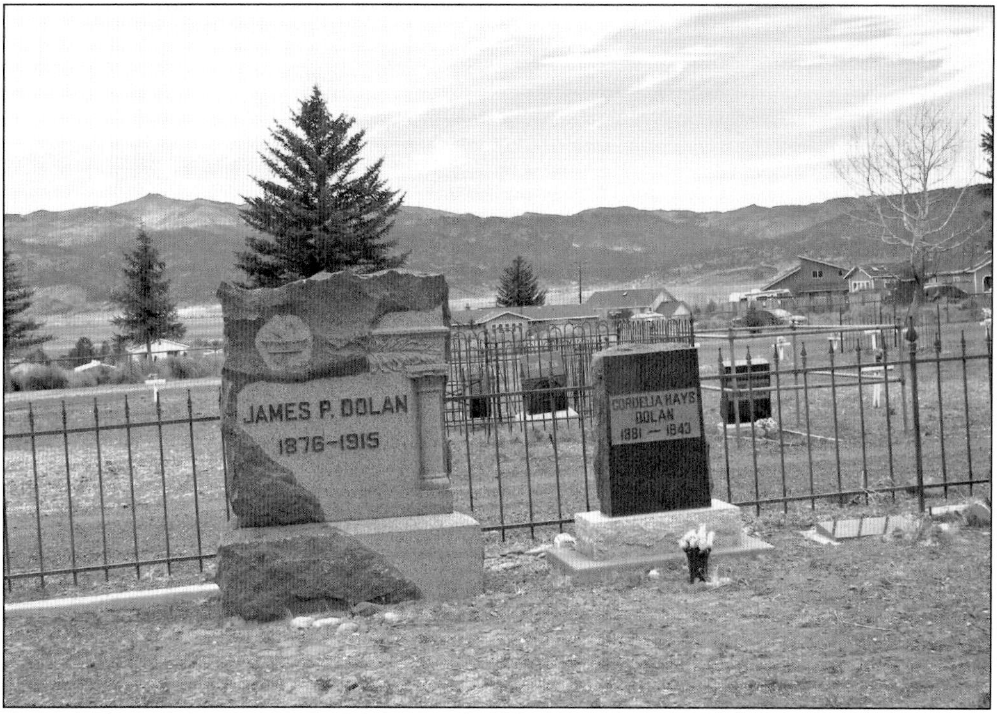

In November 1915, two Mexican laborers with stolen weapons raided local ranches in the Mono Basin. Local citizens informed Sheriff Jim Dolan, who then went looking for the men. After locating them, he approached them without drawing his weapon, believing that he could take them into custody without incident. Dolan was shot and killed. Later a posse exchanged gunfire with the two men and killed them. (Courtesy of David Ortega.)

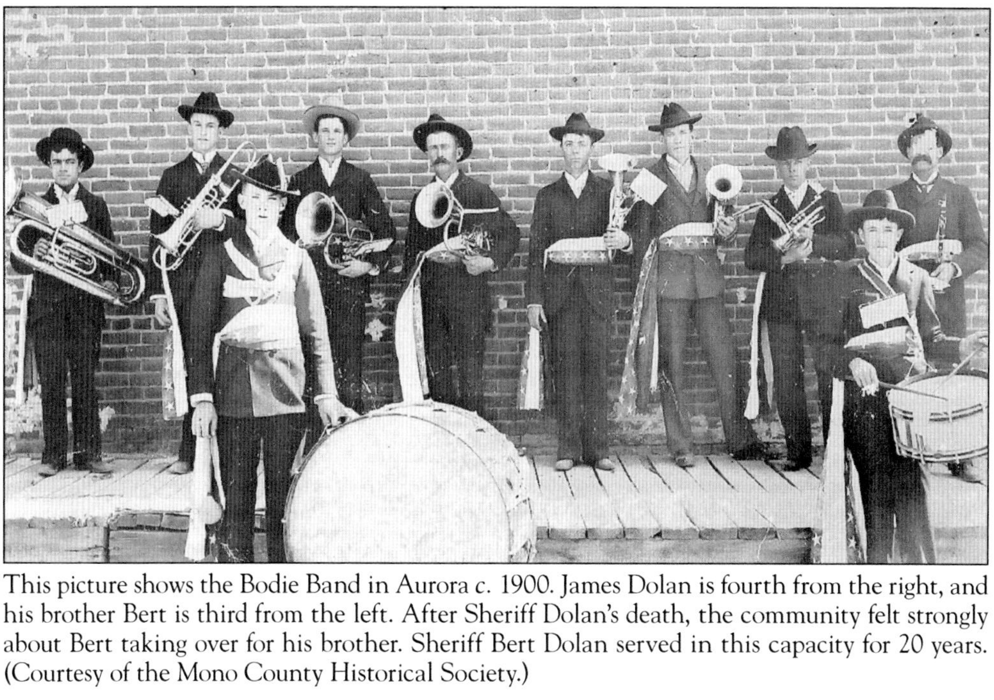

This picture shows the Bodie Band in Aurora c. 1900. James Dolan is fourth from the right, and his brother Bert is third from the left. After Sheriff Dolan's death, the community felt strongly about Bert taking over for his brother. Sheriff Bert Dolan served in this capacity for 20 years. (Courtesy of the Mono County Historical Society.)

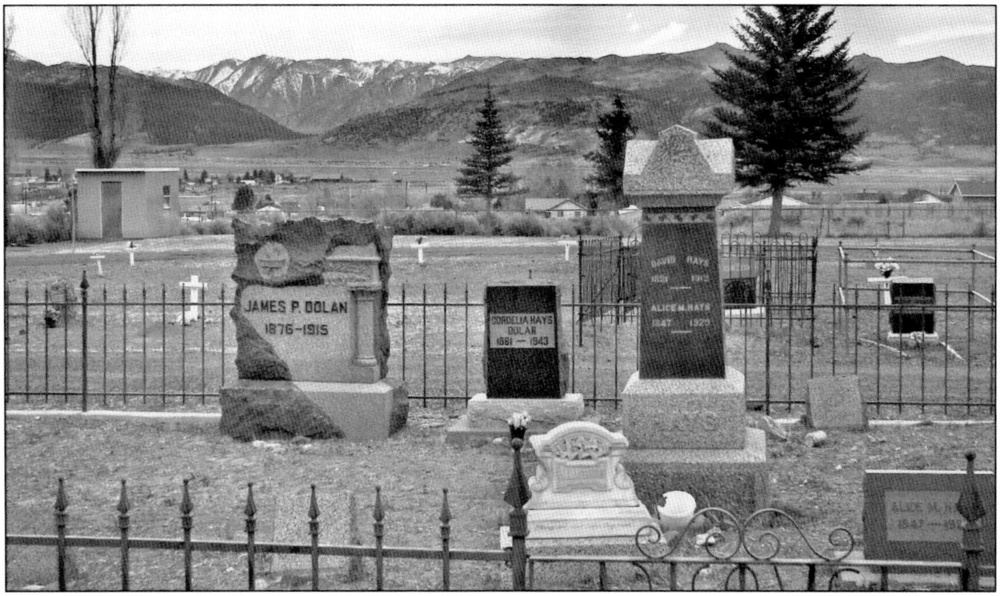

Alice M. Walker Hays was a teacher in Mono and Tuolumne Counties. Serving from 1876 to 1878, she was the first woman to be a superintendent of schools in the state of California. Her daughter Cordelia Hays Dolan was also a teacher and a superintendent for the Mono County Schools. Cordelia was the widow of Sheriff Jim Dolan. (Courtesy of David Ortega.)

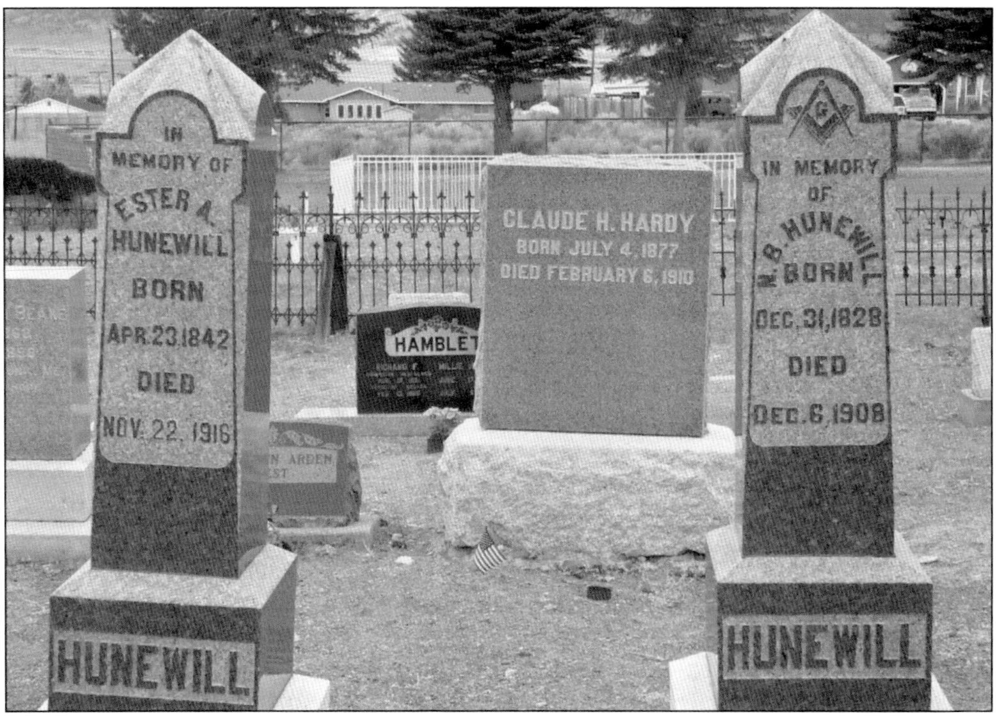

Bridgeport was initially known as Big Meadows. Napoleon Bonaparte Hunewill was among the early pioneers to the area in the 1850s. Hunewill, a Mason, farmer, and rancher, is buried next to his wife, Ester. The ranch he and his wife started in 1861 is now a guest ranch and vacation destination. (Courtesy of David Ortega.)

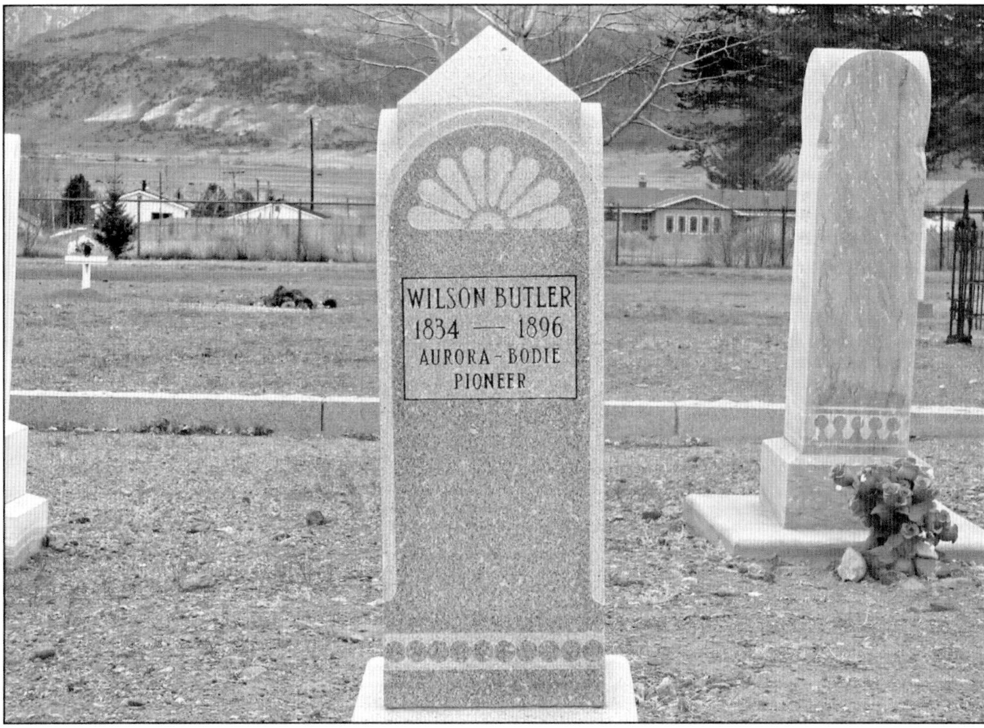

Wilson Butler, a pioneer of the Bodie area, was the son of Dan Butler. He arrived in Bodie in 1864 and was the town's first blacksmith. On one occasion, Butler's blacksmith shop was used as the site for a hanging for a man who killed another over a woman. Butler is buried in the Bridgeport Cemetery. (Courtesy of David Ortega.)

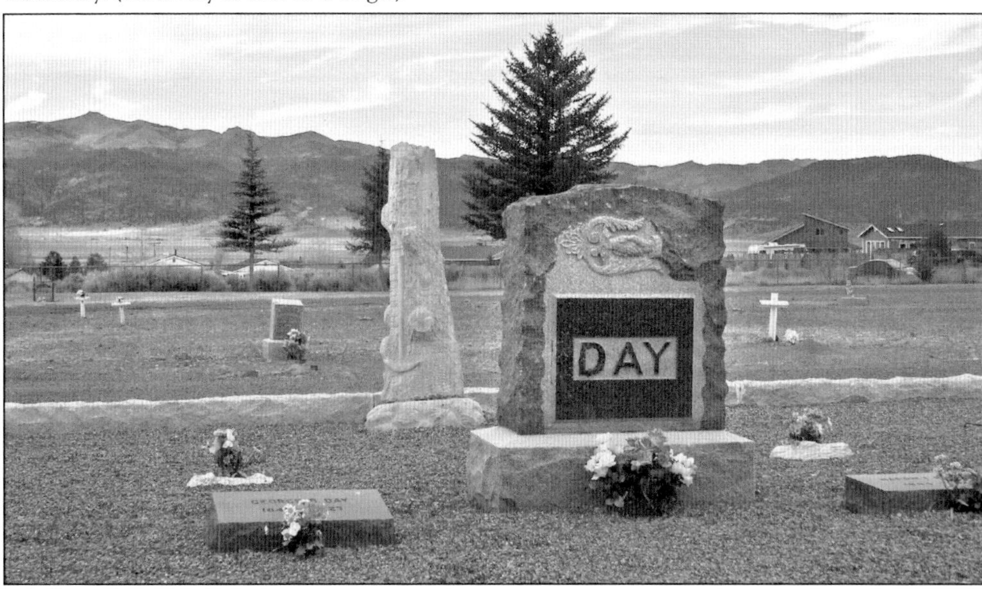

George Byron Day, who became later known as "By Day," was the first white man to spend a winter in Big Meadows and had settled in Bridgeport by the late 1850s. Day was a farmer, and his home has included over five generations of descendants. George Day is buried in the Bridgeport Cemetery. (Courtesy of David Ortega.)

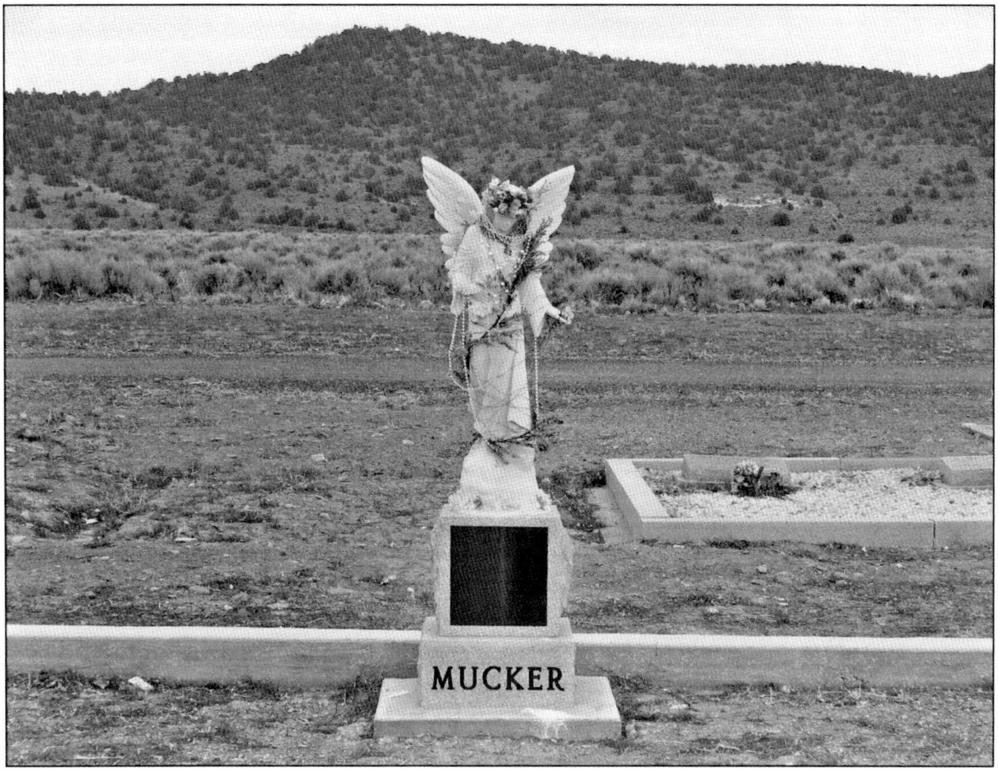

One of the unique qualities of many of the graveyards in the Eastern Sierra is the decorations, referred to as grave goods by cemetery caretakers. Because these cemeteries are rural, there are fewer rules about types of tombstones and what can be left at a grave as there are in larger urban cemeteries. (Courtesy of David Ortega.)

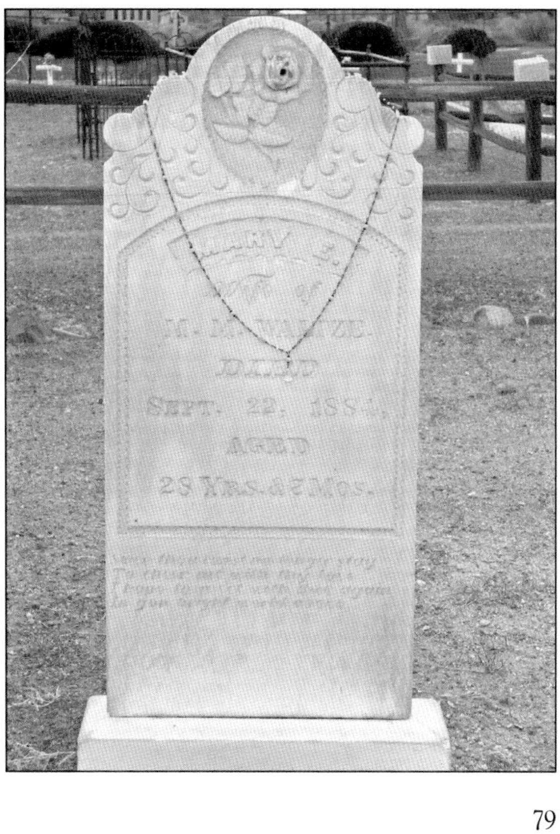

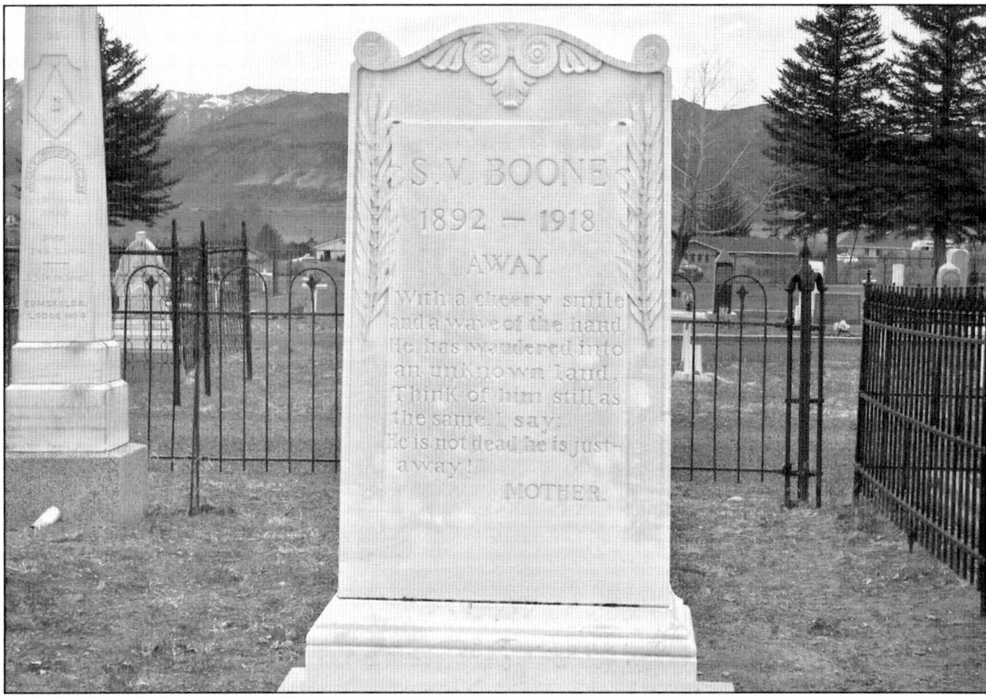

S. V. Boone's headstone includes his mother's belief that she would be separated from her son for a limited time. The verse entitled "Away" reads, "With a cheery smile and a wave of the hand, He has wandered into an unknown land, Think of him still as the same, I say: He is not dead he is just away!" (Courtesy of David Ortega.)

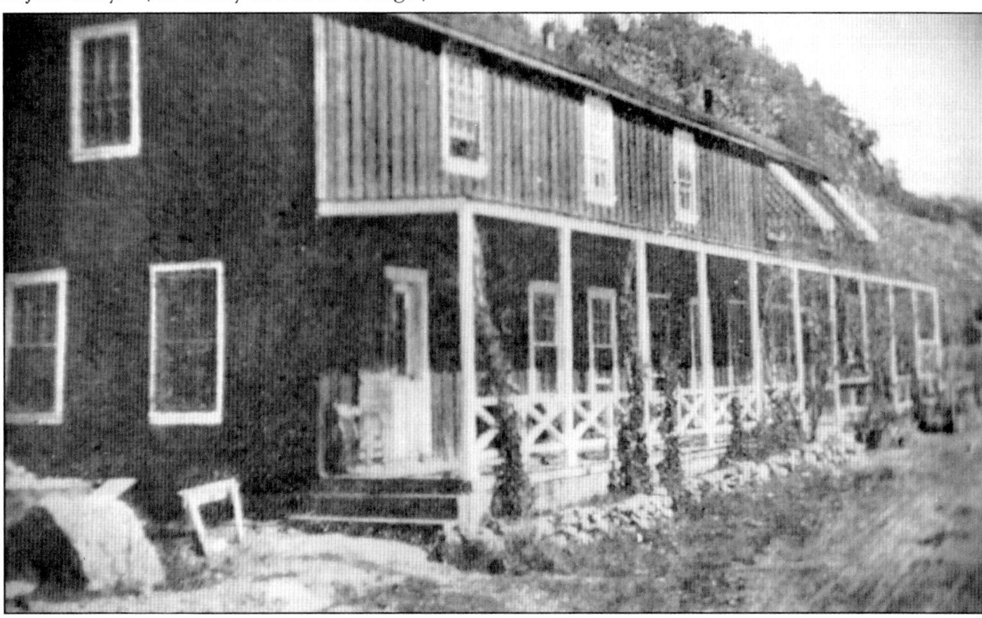

The poor farm, once located on Highway 395 and Green Creek Road, about 4 miles from Bridgeport, began as a hospital. Like many poor farms, a cemetery soon was part of the property. And like most poor farms, that cemetery is now just a piece of history with no visible remains of what once was. (Courtesy of the Mono County Historical Society.)

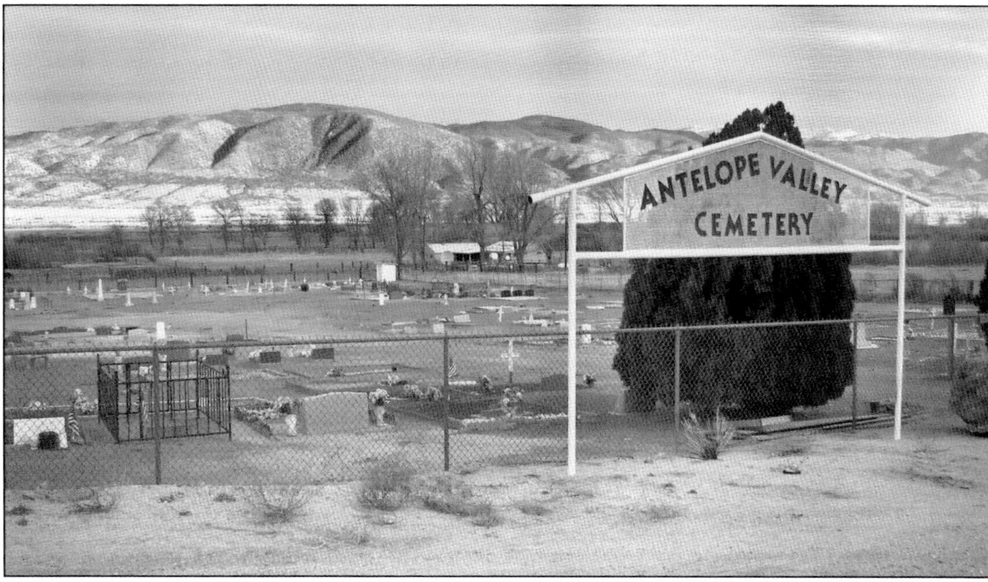

Antelope Valley Cemetery is located in Coleville, California. In the 1800s, the site was adjacent to a Methodist church, which later moved. At one time, the cemetery was run by the county, but today the cemetery is now taken care of by the Antelope Valley Cemetery Association. The cemetery holds pioneer burials, including many that are not marked. (Courtesy of David Ortega.)

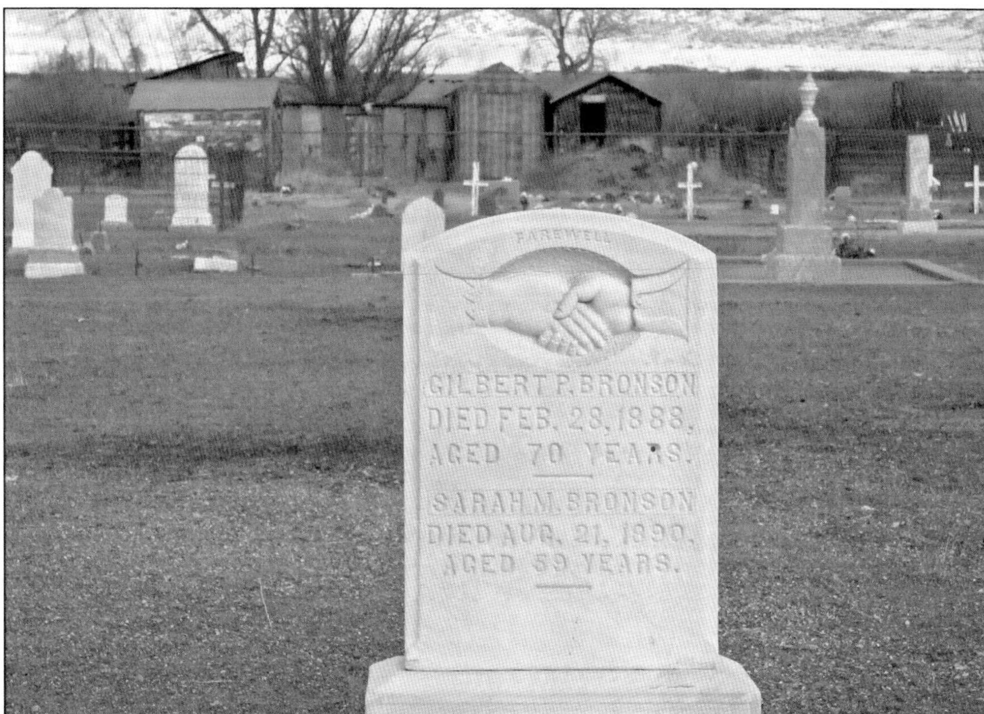

Husband and wife Gilbert and Sara Bronson's headstone at Antelope Valley Cemetery includes a carving with a female hand, depicted with a lace cuff, and a male hand, shown with a more masculine shirt cuff, clasped together. This is symbolic of unity and their relationship as husband and wife. Above the hands is the word "Farewell." (Courtesy of David Ortega.)

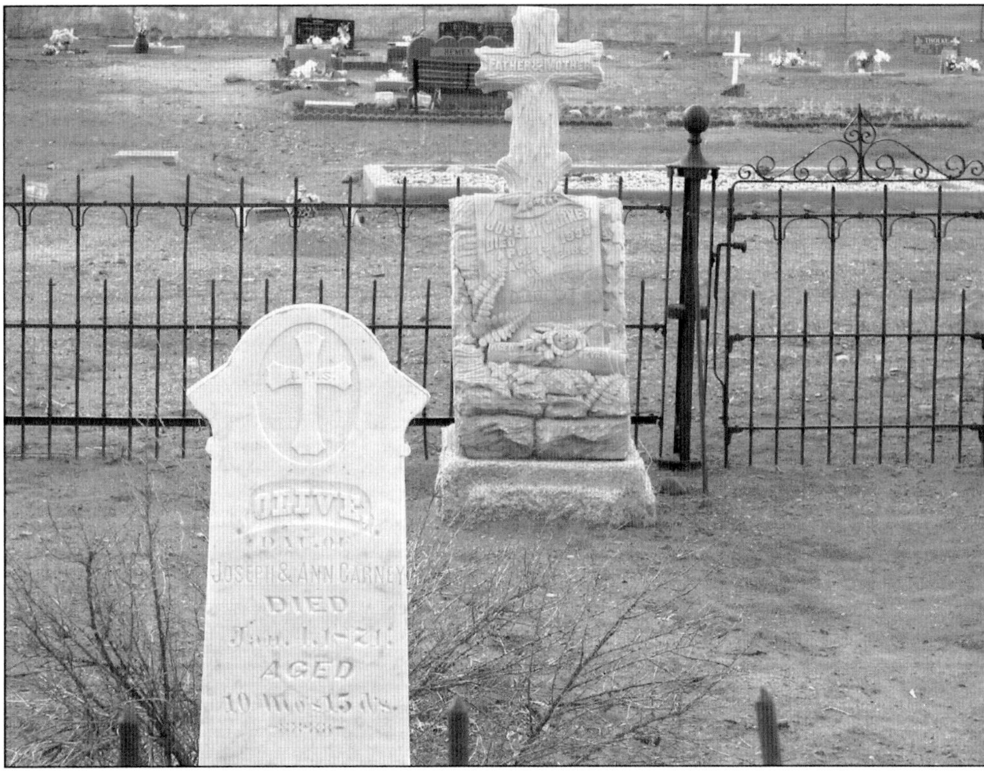

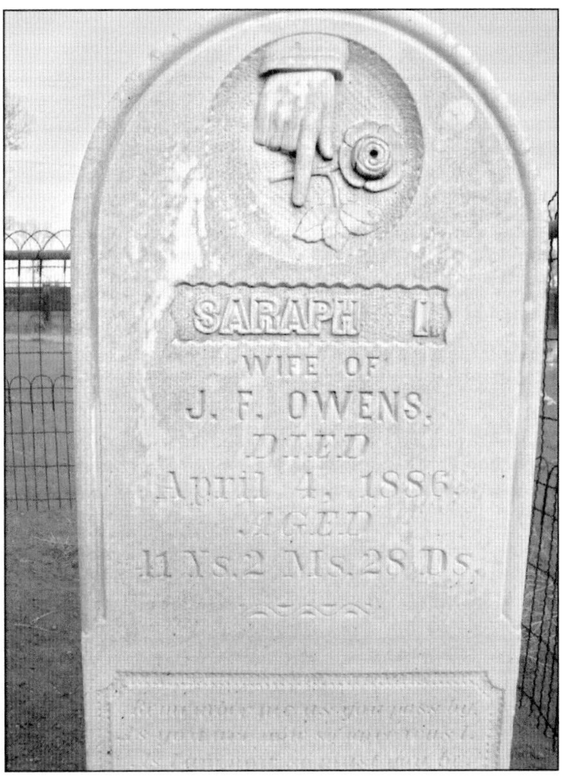

Olive Carney, a child of 10 months who died in 1871, has a headstone with a cross and the letters I. H. S. engraved in the cross, the first three letters in the Greek spelling of Jesus' name. Olive's parents, Joseph and Ann, are buried behind her under a tombstone that resembles a tree with sculpted ivy clinging to it. (Courtesy of David Ortega.)

Victorian headstones often had detail that is not seen on modern-day markers. Examples are symbolic etchings and poetry verse. The verse found on Sarah Owens grave at the Antelope Valley Cemetery reminds readers of where they will one day be, "Remember me as you pass by. As you are now so once was I. As I am now so must you be. Prepare yourself to follow me." (Courtesy of David Ortega.)

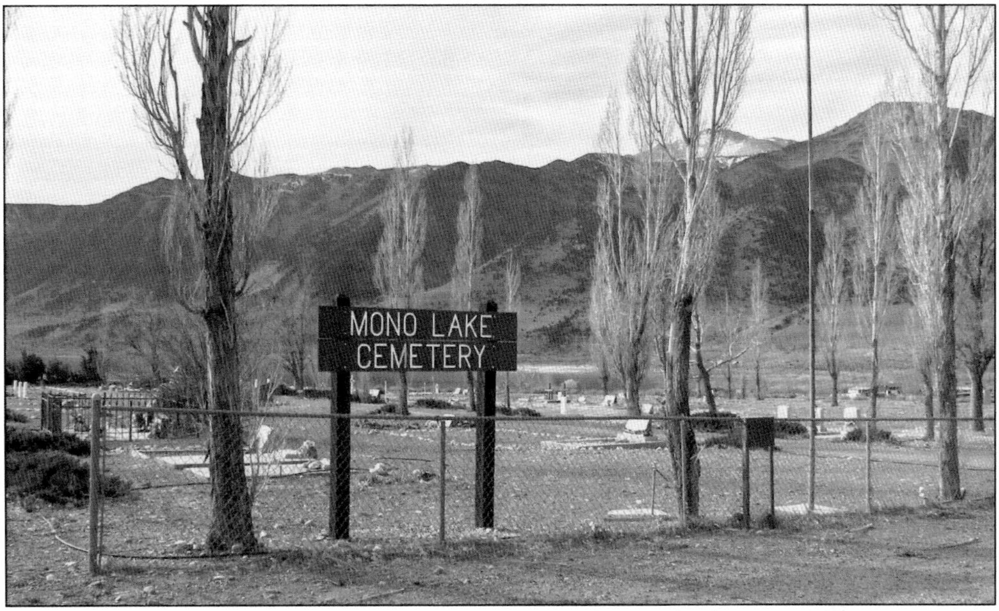

Mono Lake contains approximately 280 million tons of dissolved salt. One of the more unusual aspects of Mono Lake is the tufa towers, limestone deposits that date back 200–900 years. Mono Lake Cemetery overlooks Mono Lake on the northern side. (Courtesy of David Ortega.)

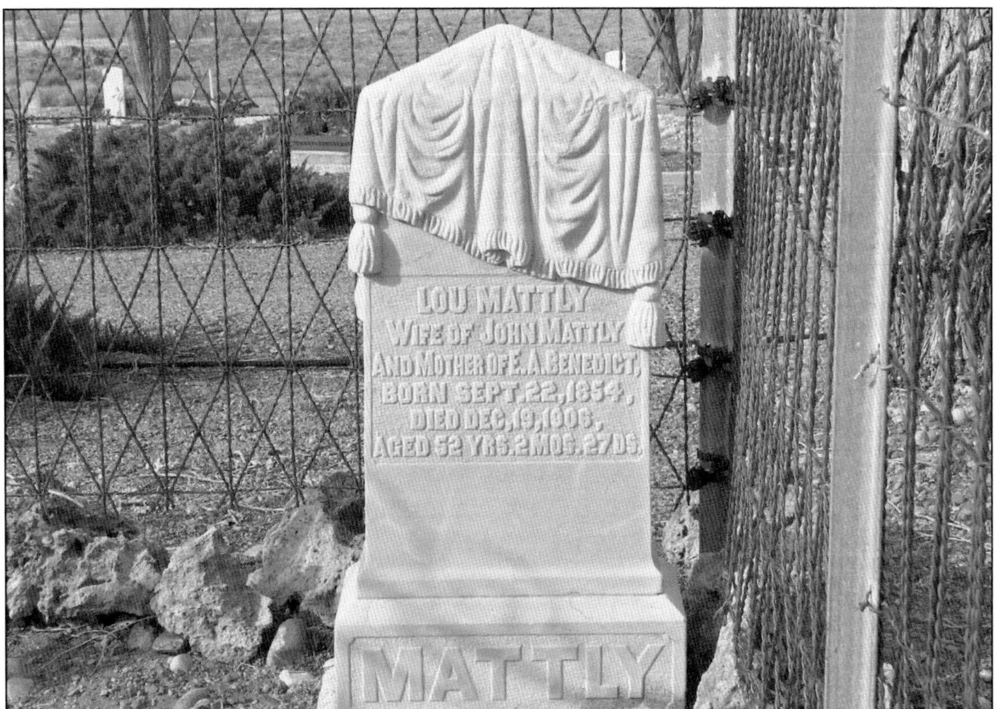

The Mattlys were an early pioneer family of the Mono Lake area. John Mattly's nephew Chris came to live with him and his wife, Lou, after he arrived in the United States from Switzerland. Chris sold salt from Mono Lake and later founded the town of Lee Vining, located across the highway from Mono Lake. (Courtesy of David Ortega.)

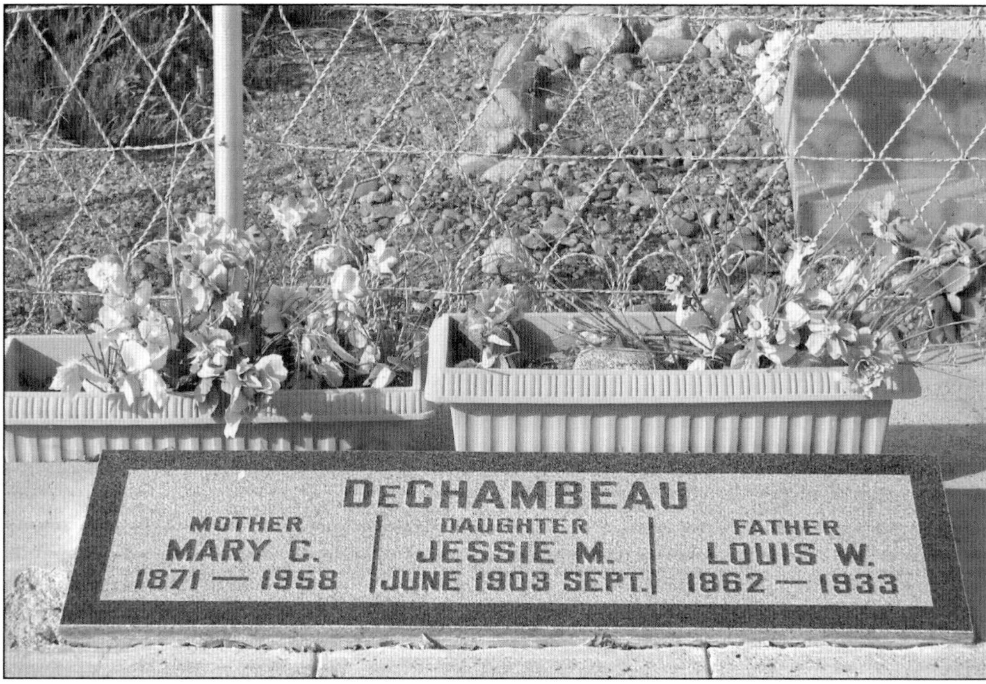

Louis DeChambeau, originally from Quebec, came to Bodie in 1880 with his family and worked as a miner. He later acquired a ranch in the Mono Basin that prospered until it was the third largest ranch; he and his family raised livestock, chickens, cattle, and sheep. He and his family are buried in the Mono Lake cemetery. (Courtesy of David Ortega.)

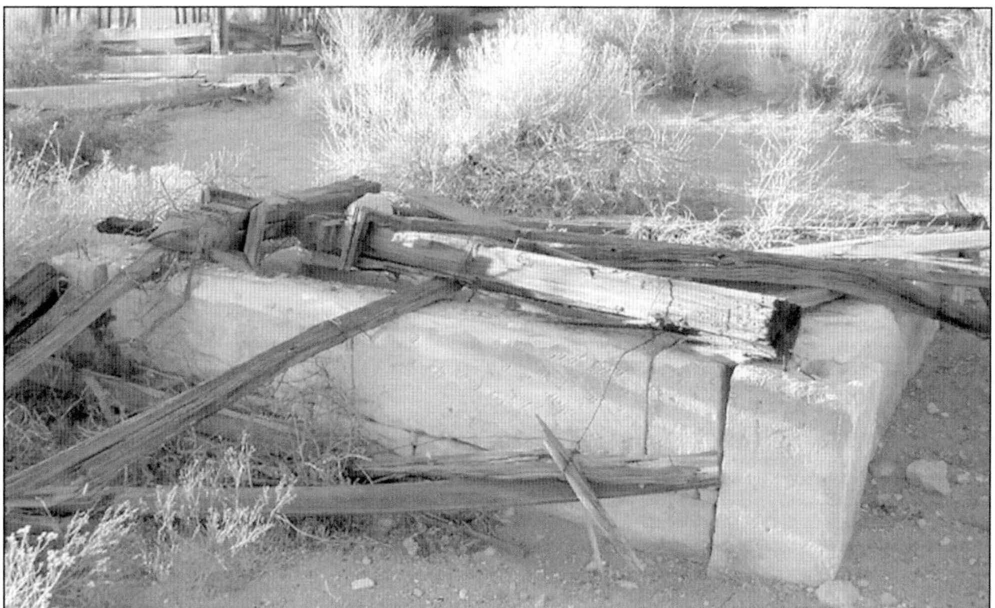

Benton, north of Bishop, California, was a mining town whose heyday was from 1862 to 1889. Unlike many of the mining camps in the Eastern Sierra, Benton survives today with a small population and a town that includes a bed-and-breakfast. The Benton cemetery, located on private land, includes pioneer headstones as well as recent burials. (Courtesy of Cat House.)

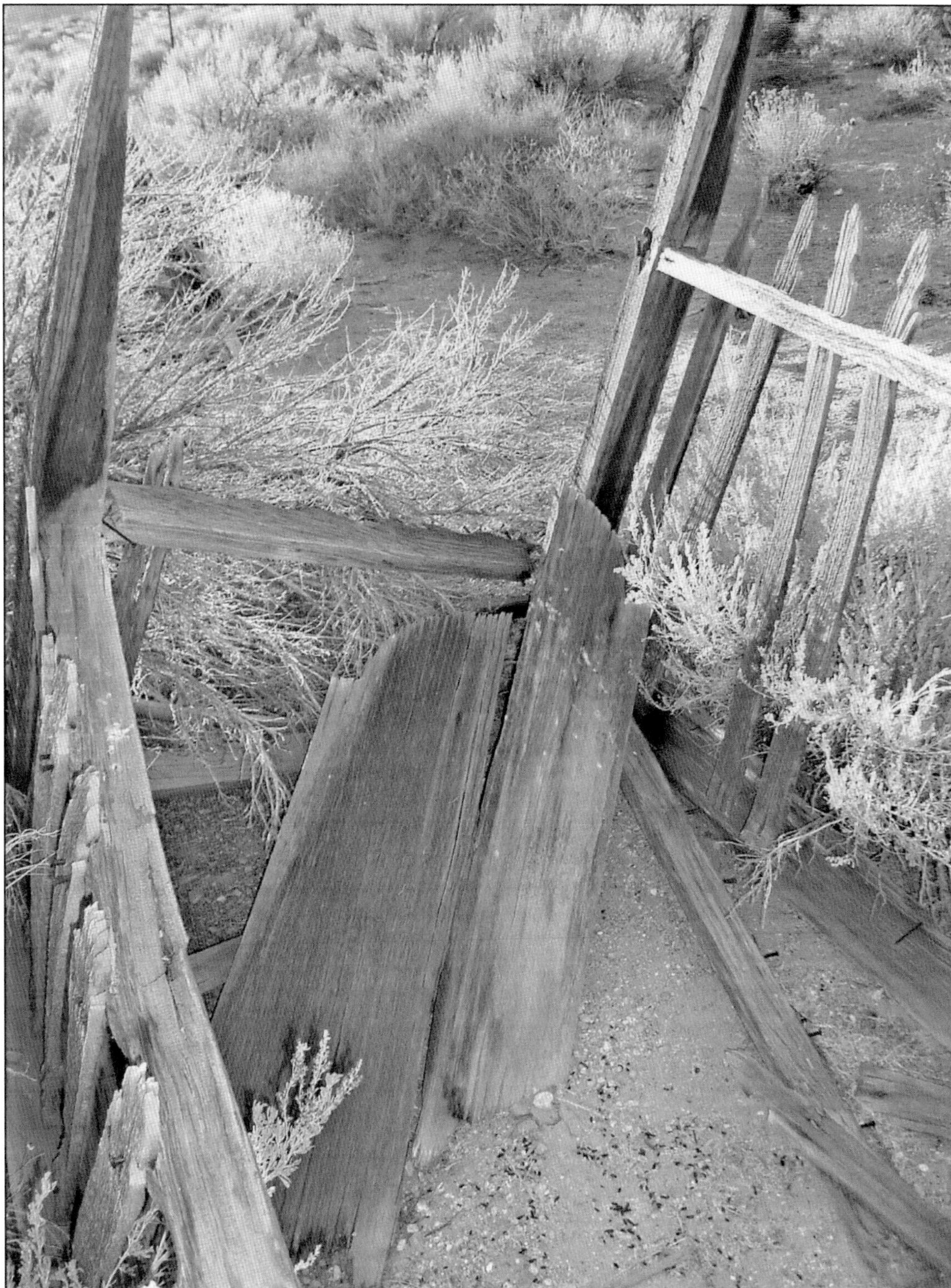

As in many old cemeteries, wooden markers do not stand the test of time and those buried with them are often forgotten. People whose markers have faded include Y. C. Benites, a Benton postmaster killed on March 15, 1880, by James Morrow. Dan Ashley died in January 1882; he had owned a livery stable and then a saloon. (Courtesy of Cat House.)

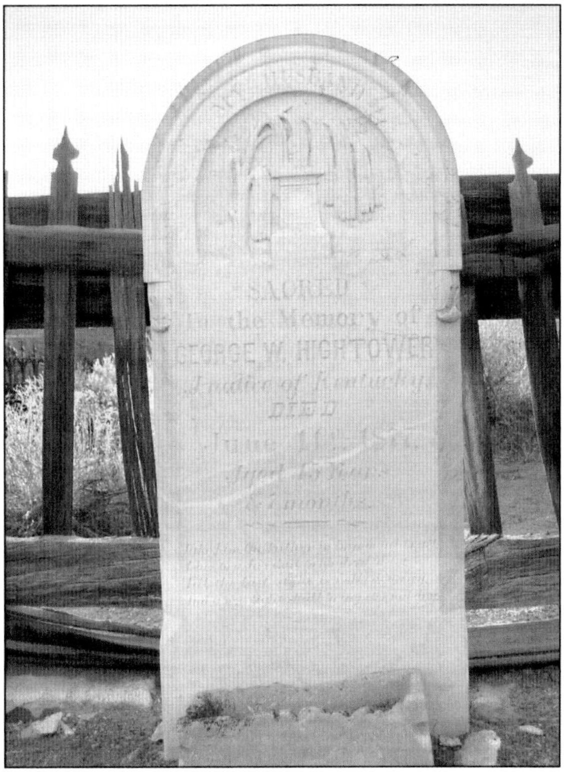

George Hightower, a native of Kentucky, was a blacksmith in Mono County. He died on June 11, 1877, at the young age of 45 years, leaving behind his wife, Martha, and his children, George and Sarah. On the top of his tombstone is written "My husband" along with the carved image of a weeping willow tree leaning over a headstone. The weeping willow was symbolic of grief and sorrow. (Courtesy of Cat House.)

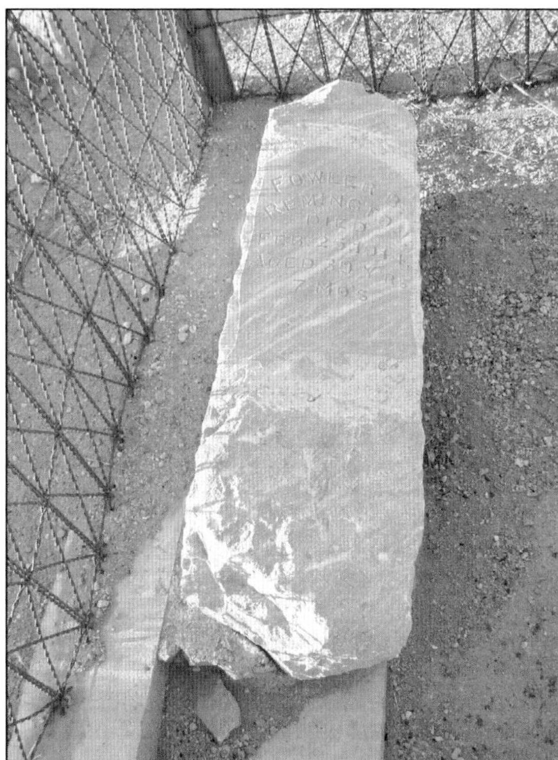

Fowler Remington and his wife and daughter, both named Gail, came to the Eastern Sierra sometime between 1900 and 1909 from Massachusetts, where he was a manager for a manufacturing company. By 1910, he was running a boardinghouse in Benton that employed a Japanese cook and waiter. (Courtesy of Cat House.)

In the Thousand Island Lake area near Mammoth lies a lone monument and grave for Conrad and Ann Rettenbacher. The Rettenbachers were hikers and members of the San Francisco German hiking group *Die Naturfreunde*. The Rettenbachers were hiking in this locality in August 1934 while on vacation from their work as domestics in the Hillsborough area home of Howard Parks. On August 5, 1934, when they did not return to their base camp, a massive search was conducted. Recovery efforts included park rangers and local guide Norman Clyde, who found the Rettenbachers' bodies. They had fallen more than 600 feet down a glacier to their deaths. Like many of those who die in remote areas where transporting a body can be near impossible, it was decided that the Rettenbachers would be buried near where they died. (Courtesy of Harv Galic.)

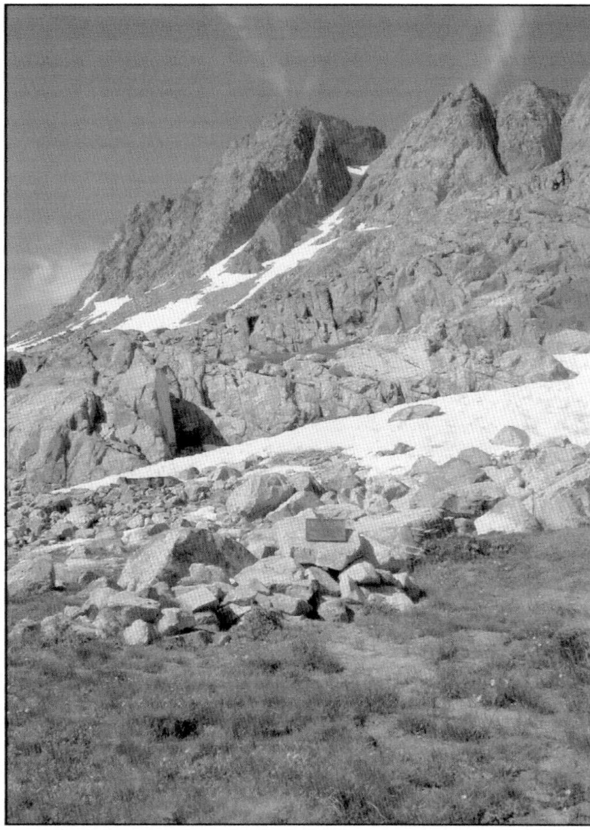

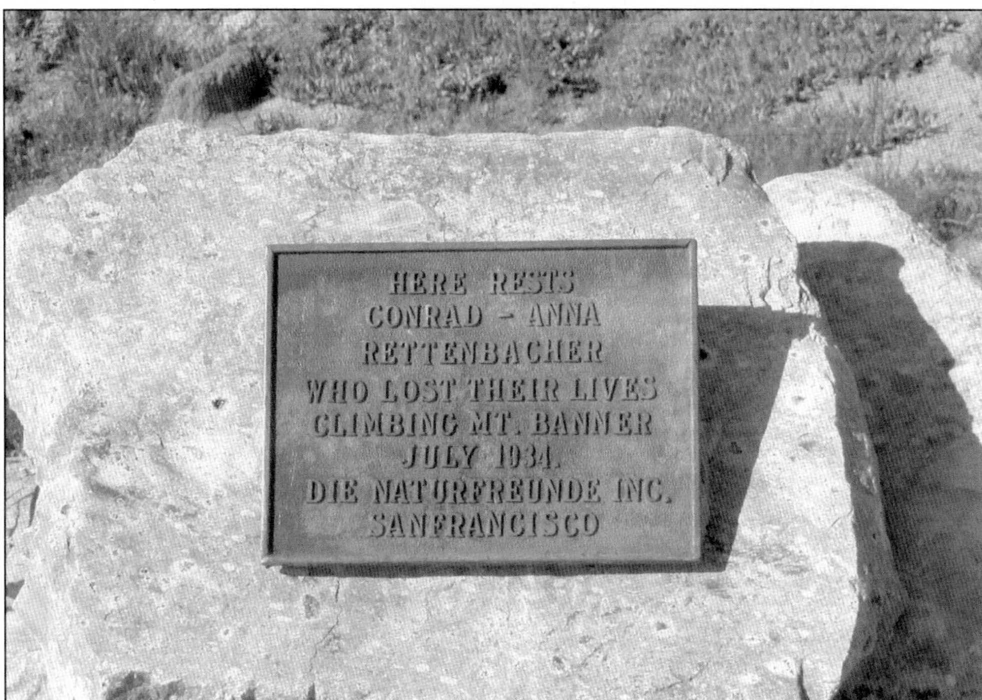

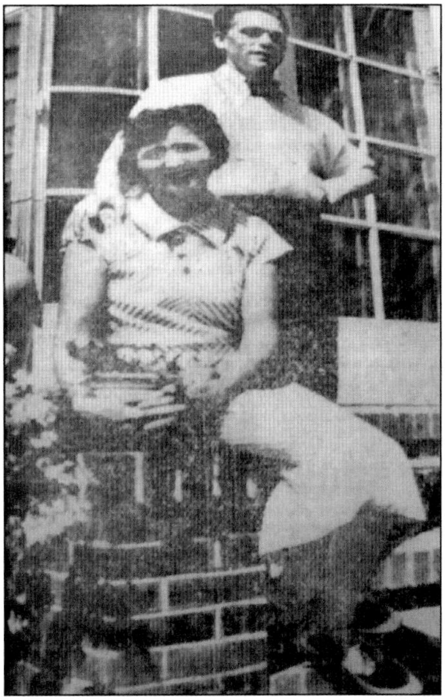

Little is known about Conrad and Anna Rettenbacher. They immigrated to the United States from Germany in 1926 and initially lived on the East Coast before moving west in the early 1930s. As members of a hiking group for German immigrants, they were most likely experienced hikers, but, like other accidents in the mountains, the cause of their deaths will remain a mystery. (Courtesy of the author.)

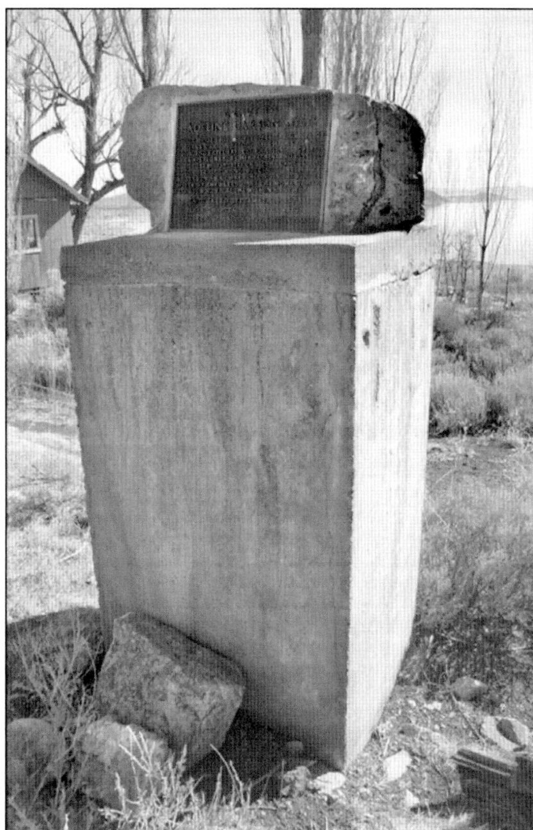

Adeline, also known as Prairie Flower, was the daughter of American frontiersmen Christopher "Kit" Carson and his Arapaho wife, Waanibe. Adeline's mother and sister died when she was young, and her father then took her to Missouri to be schooled. Adeline later came to the Mono County area with her husband, George Stilts. She died at the young age of 21. (Courtesy of Cat House.)

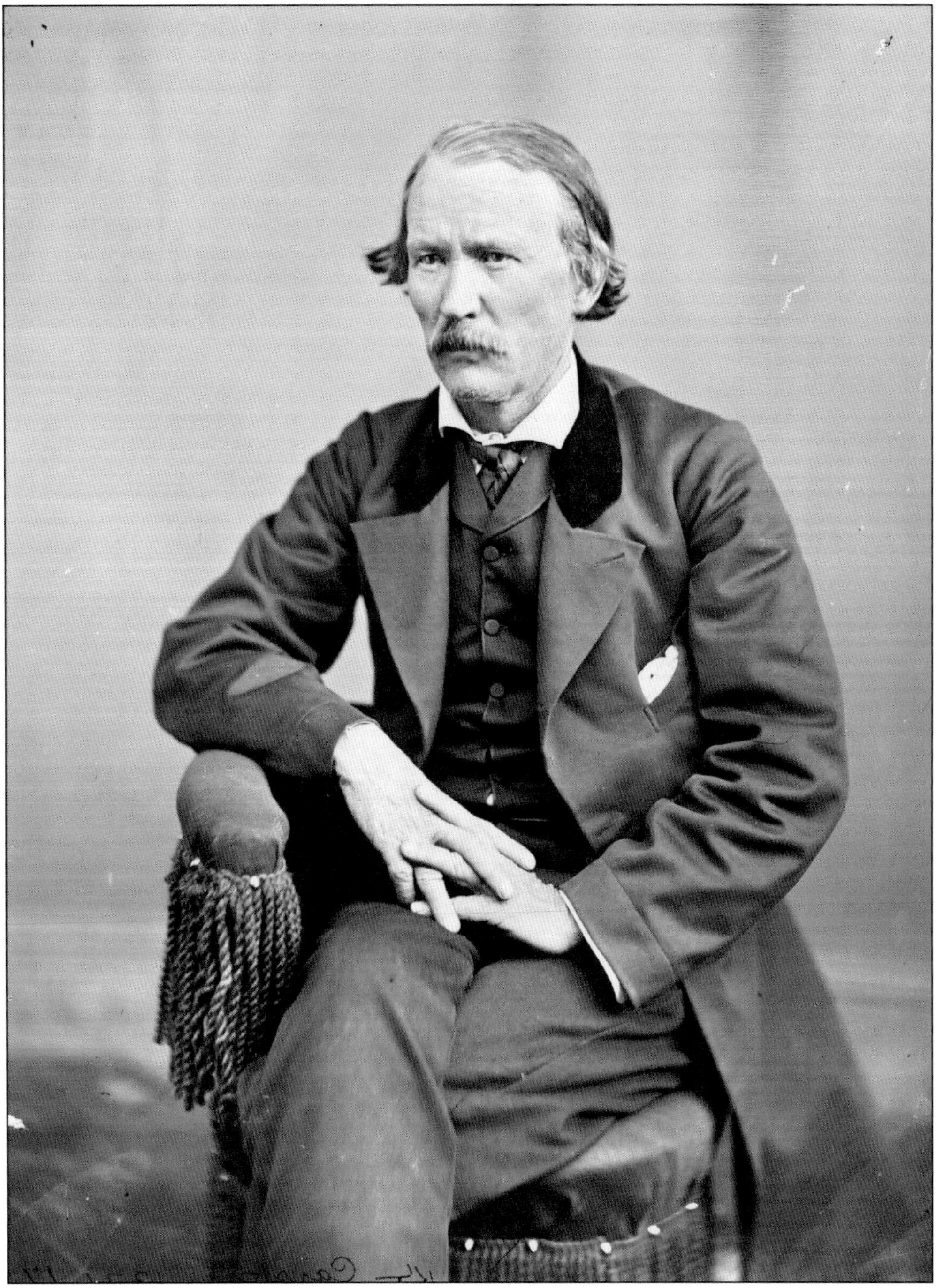

Born in 1809, Christopher "Kit" Carson was a trapper, scout, soldier, and Indian agent. While working as a trapper, he lived among the Native Americans and took two of them as wives. He was involved in the Bear Flag Rebellion in California and the Civil War. Although seemingly a friend to Native Americans, he was responsible for forcing 8,000 Navajo on the Long Walk from Arizona to New Mexico. (Courtesy of the Library of Congress, Prints and Photographs Division, LC-DIG-cwpbh-00514.)

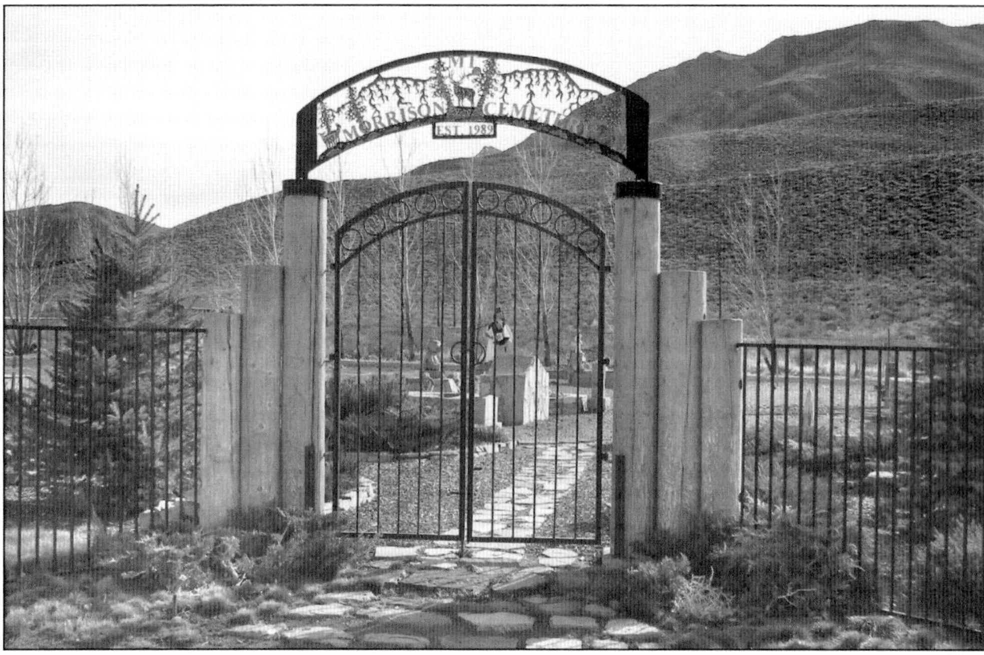

Established in 1989, the Mount Morrison Cemetery is located on Highway 395, near the junction with Highway 120. Mount Morrison, a 12,268-foot peak in the Sierra Nevada, was renamed after Robert Morrison, a Benton Wells Fargo agent who was killed in 1871 chasing down escaped prisoners. Morrison and his posse encountered the prisoners at the head of a lake, now called Convict Lake, where Morrison was killed. (Courtesy of David Ortega.)

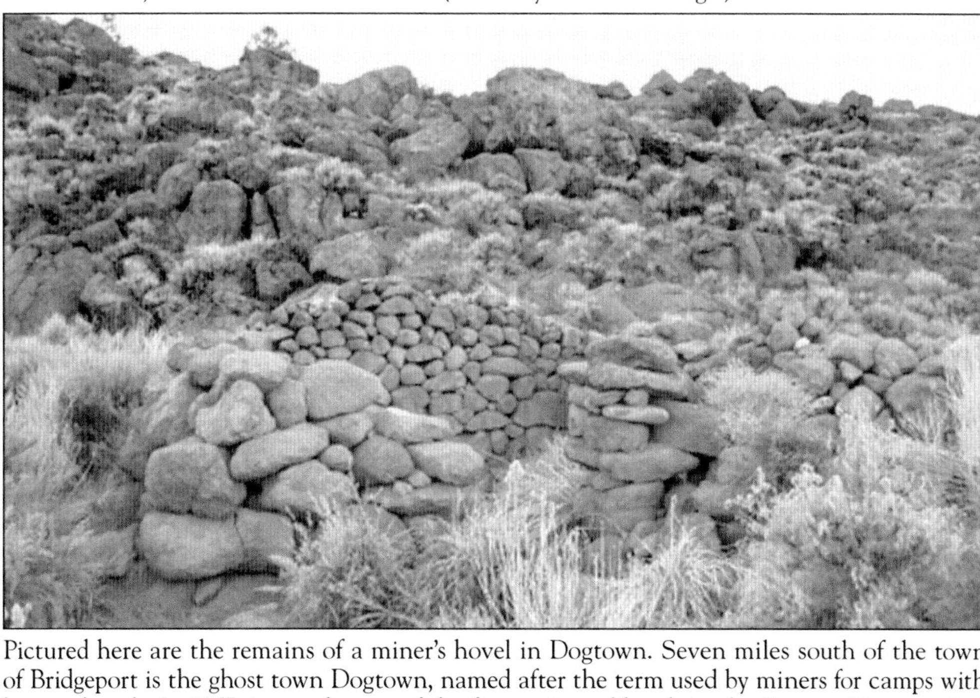

Pictured here are the remains of a miner's hovel in Dogtown. Seven miles south of the town of Bridgeport is the ghost town Dogtown, named after the term used by miners for camps with huts or hovels. In 1857, it was the site of the first major gold rush in the Eastern Sierra region. (Courtesy of Cat House.)

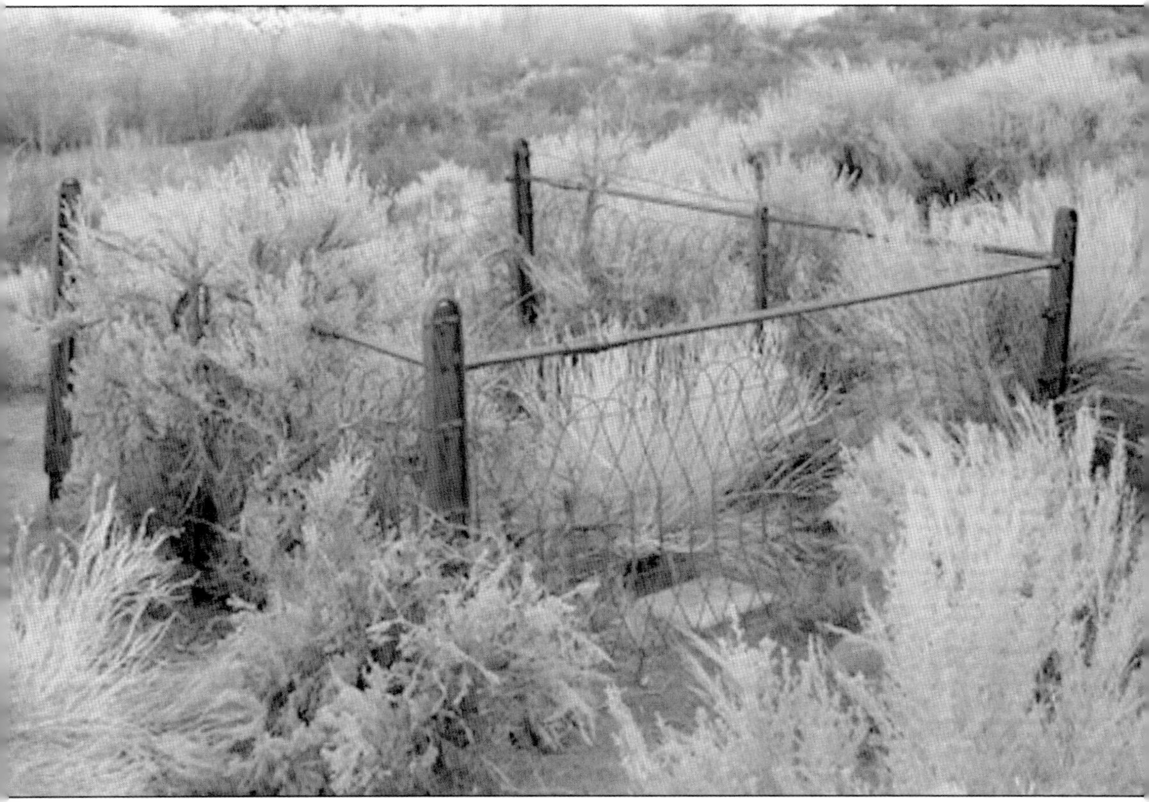

Only a few ruins are left at Dogtown. A lone grave contains the remains of a man named Anderson, about whom nothing is known, not even how he died. The headstone is now gone, and all that remains is a metal fence like those traditionally erected in old western cemeteries to keep out grazing cattle and other animals. (Courtesy of Cat House.)

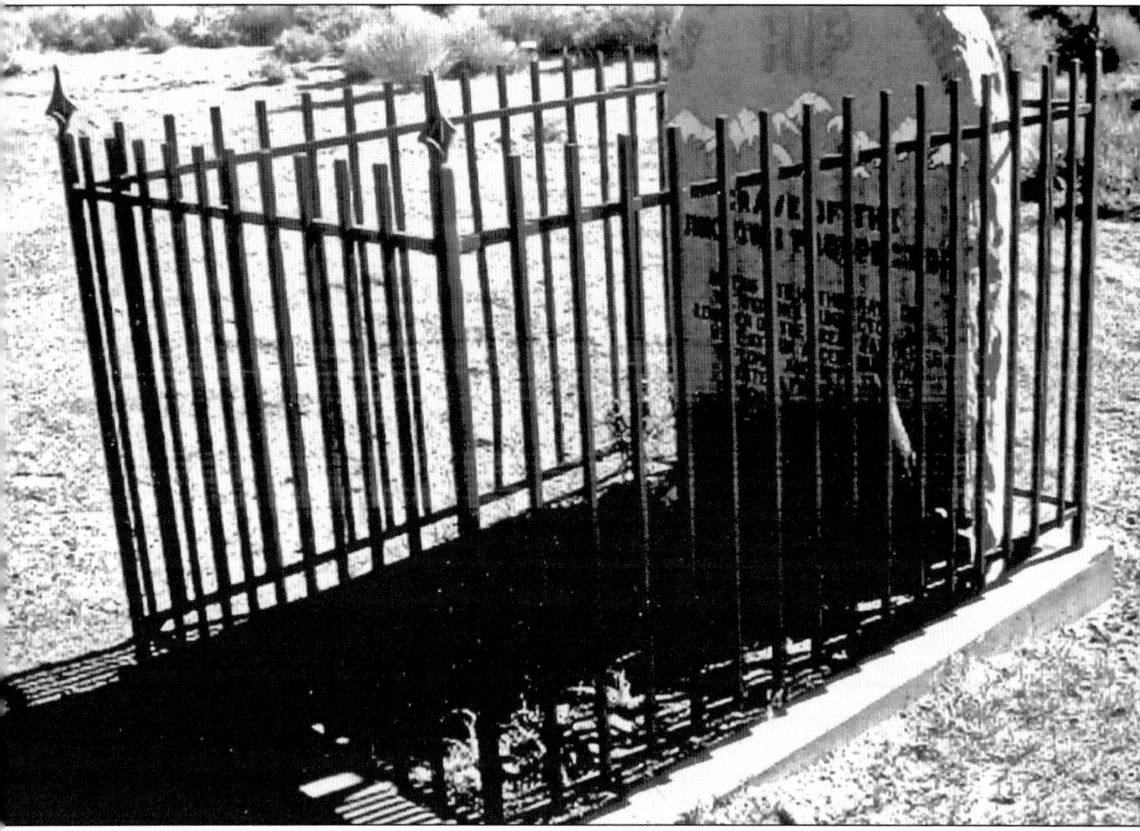

Located along Highway 395 near Highway 120 lies a solitary grave of an unknown prospector. His marker reads, "On this site is the grave of The Unknown Prospector. A reminder of the great sacrifices made by our ancestors who explored and settled the Western Frontier . . . especially to the memory of all of the pioneers of Mono County, whose resting place is known only to God." (Courtesy of Cat House.)

Four

Tragedies, Earthquakes, and Avalanches

There can be no doubt that life was difficult for pioneers. Disease, ignorance about hygiene, and an overall lack of knowledge about the world around them resulted in a high child mortality rate, epidemics, and death by accident and nature.

Children in earlier times were often short-term visitors. Infant mortality was high, and in an era where medicine was a new science, such basics as the importance of washing one's hands had not yet been discovered. Epidemics took their tolls on communities partly because of the lack of knowledge about disease epidemiology. Scarlet fever, a disease that took its toll on the children in the Owens Valley around 1875, typically affected children under the age of 10 years the hardest and was usually fatal prior to the introduction of antibiotics.

Disease was not the only killer of early settlers. The March 1872 earthquake centered in Lone Pine was the source of significant alterations in the landscape and deadly destruction, especially in Lone Pine. According to the U.S. Geological Survey, 52 out of 59 houses were destroyed and 27 people were killed in Lone Pine alone. The near-total destruction of Lone Pine was caused in part by the use of adobe as a building material for most houses and buildings.

This 7.4-magnitude earthquake woke people up as far south as San Diego and as far east as Elko, Nevada. Soldiers from Fort Independence were dispatched to help with digging for bodies. Naturalist John Muir describes feeling the earthquake: "At half-past two o'clock . . . I was awakened by a tremendous earthquake, and though I had never before enjoyed a storm of this sort, the strange thrilling motion could not be mistaken, and I ran out of my cabin, both glad and frightened, shouting, 'A noble earthquake! A noble earthquake!' feeling sure I was going to learn something."

On March 7, 1911, the Jordon Power Plant, located just outside of Lundy, was destroyed by an avalanche, and seven employees were killed. The Lundy area was no stranger to avalanches, which often caused death and destruction in the canyon.

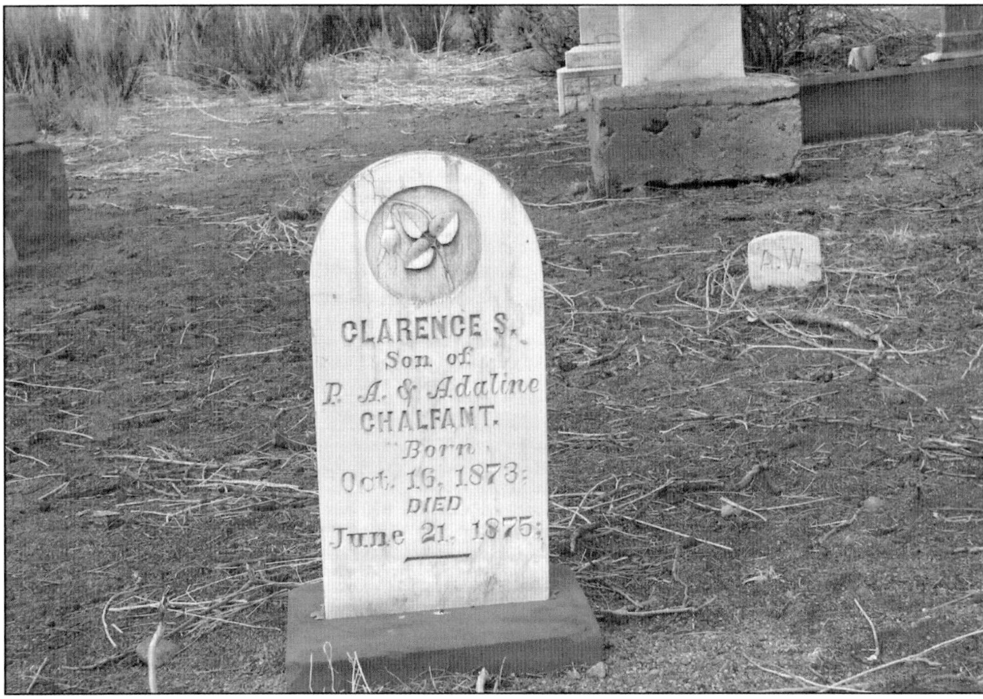

Pleasant Arthur Chalfant began publication of the *Inyo Independent* newspaper with his brother in 1870. He sold his share in the *Independent* a little over 10 years later, only to begin the *Inyo Register* in 1885 with his son Willie Arthur as full partner. P. A. and his wife, Adaline, were the parents of eight children, three of whom died as children: Clarence at 20 months and Maude at 4 years, both from scarlet fever, and son Adrian at about 1 year. Maude's grave contains a small line that reads, "I'se well now Mama." (Courtesy of David Ortega.)

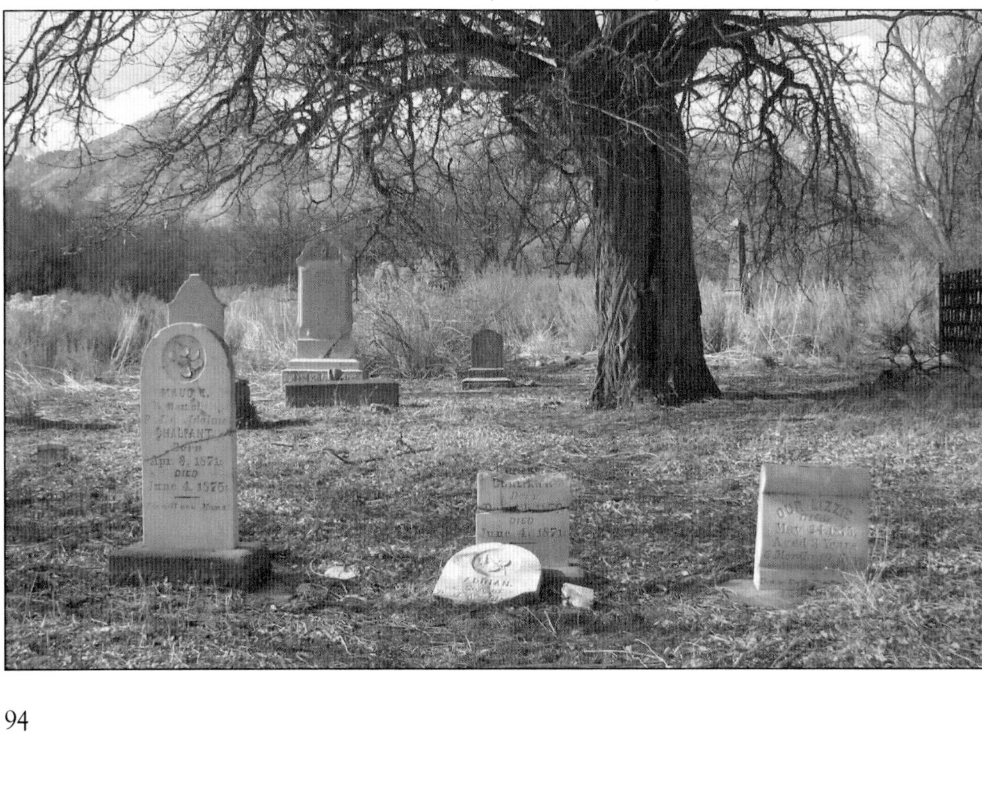

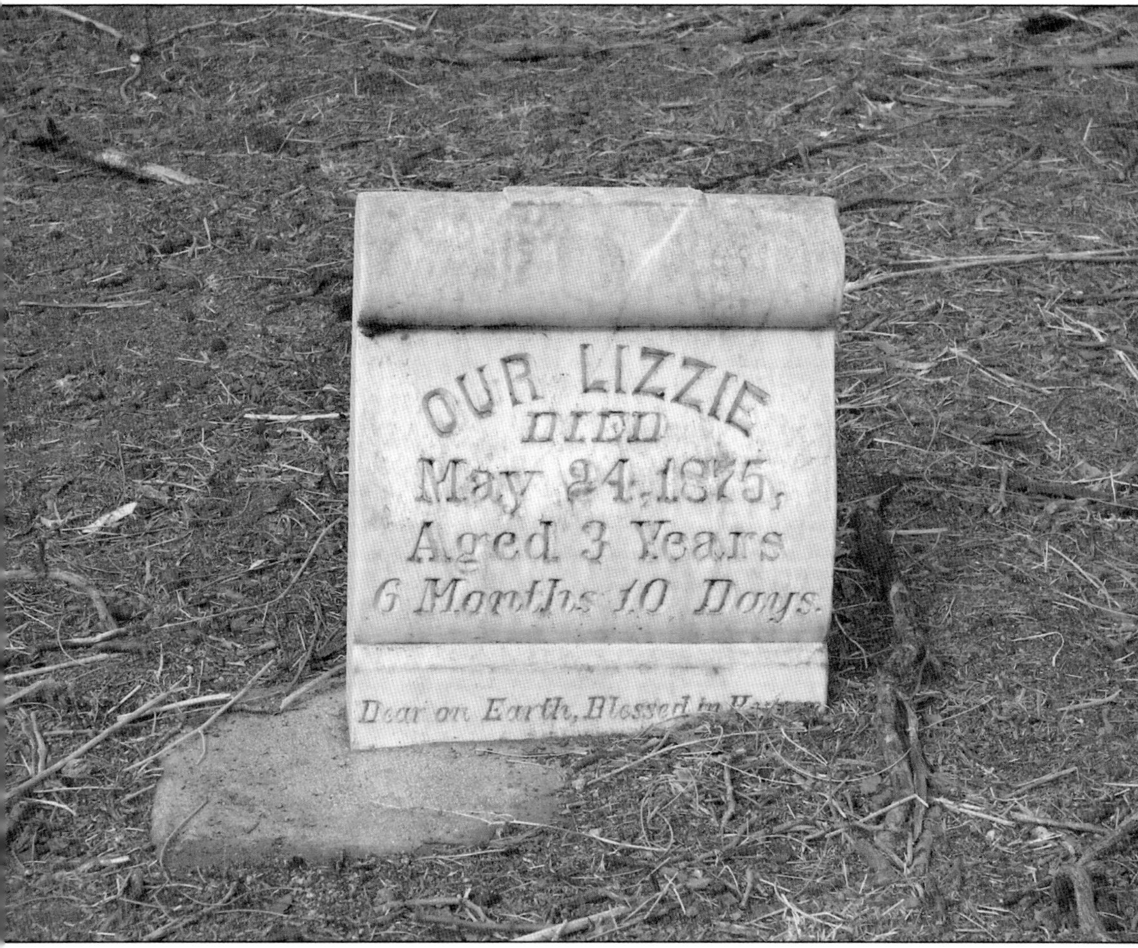

Buried next to the Chalfant children is Lizzie Thompson, daughter of Venes and Nettie Thompson. Her father was a local hotelkeeper in Independence. Like the Chalfant children, Lizzie was a victim of the 1875 scarlet fever epidemic. Her tombstone reads, "Dear on Earth, Blessed in Heaven." (Courtesy of David Ortega.)

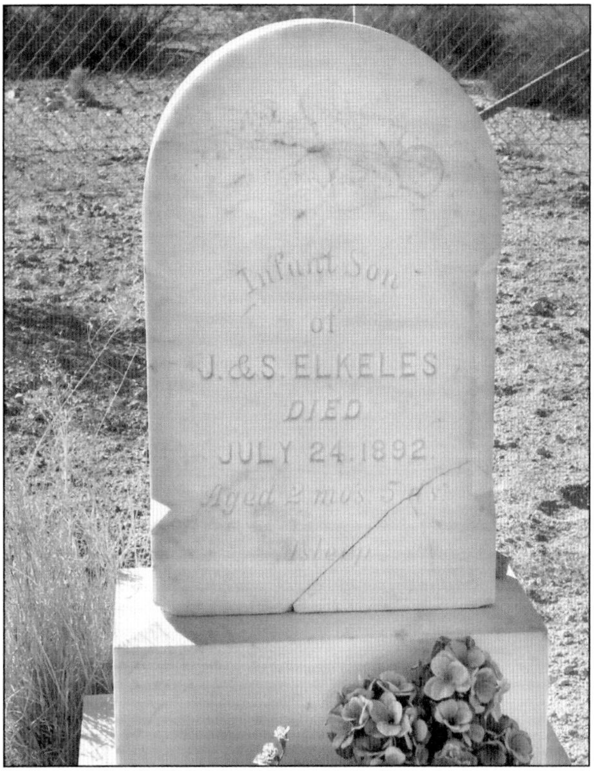

The unnamed son of Jacob and Sarah Cohn Elkeles rests in the Jewish Cemetery outside of Independence. Jacob Elkeles was a merchant in Bishop. Although no relation to the Levy family, several of whom are buried in this cemetery, his grave is here because there was no Jewish cemetery in Bishop where his parents lived. Baby Elkeles died at two months old. Six years later, the Elkeles moved to San Francisco. (Courtesy of David Ortega.)

Lorenza and Larkin McKellips died in 1876 during an illness, possibly the scarlet fever epidemic. They were buried near the home of their parents, Alonzo and Nancy McKellips, a way station called Orne's Station. The original wooden headstone is now gone, and in its place is a white cross placed there by community members. (Courtesy of David Ortega.)

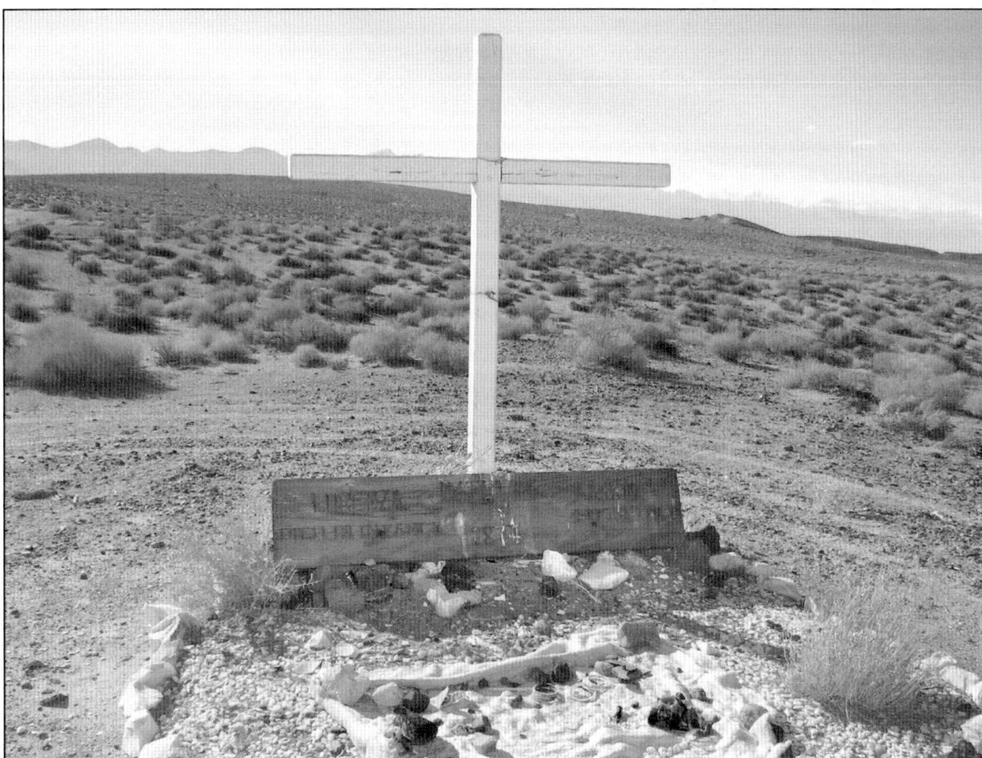

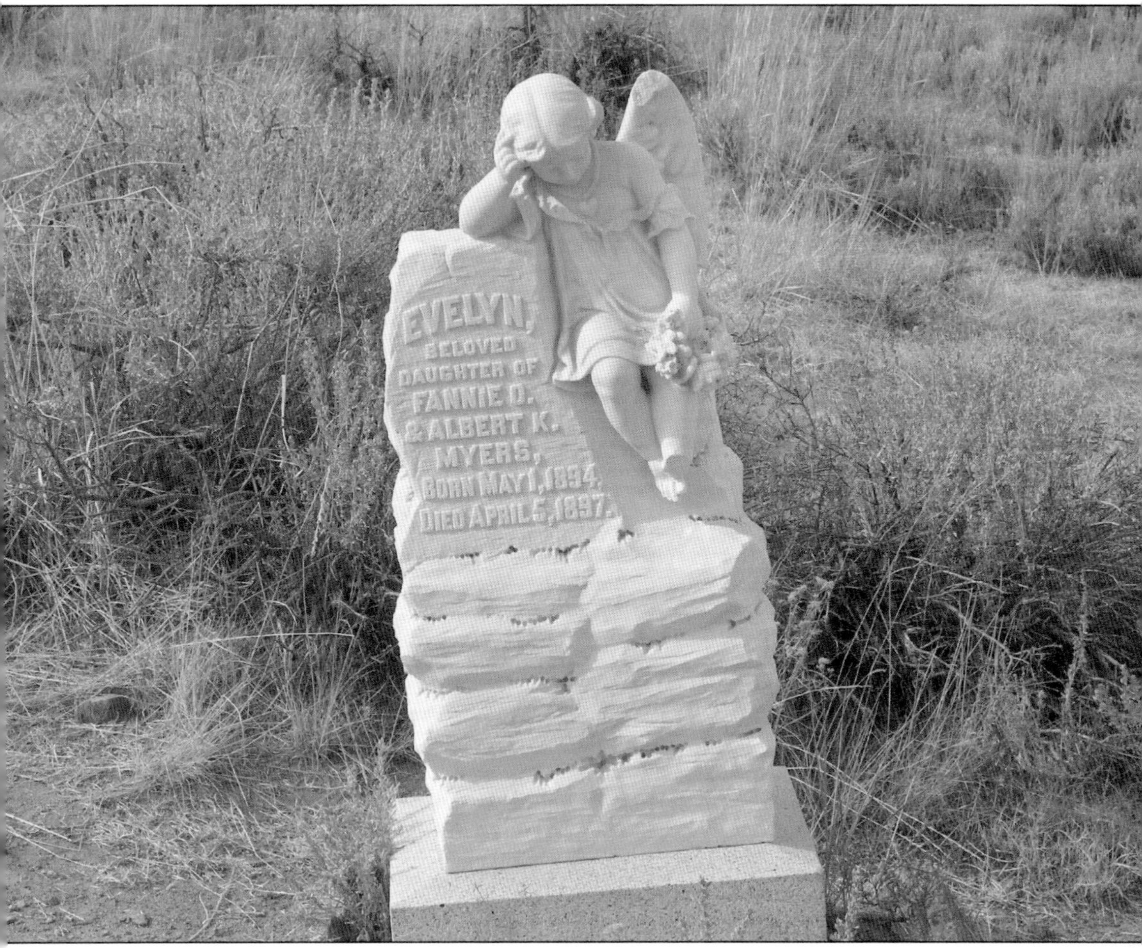

Evelyn Myers, the three-year-old daughter of Albert and Fannie Myers of Bodie, died when she was accidentally struck in the head with a pickax. Some stories claim that she was following a kindly miner whom she befriended when she got in the way and was accidentally hit. Some believe that her ghost can still be seen at Bodie. (Courtesy of David Ortega.)

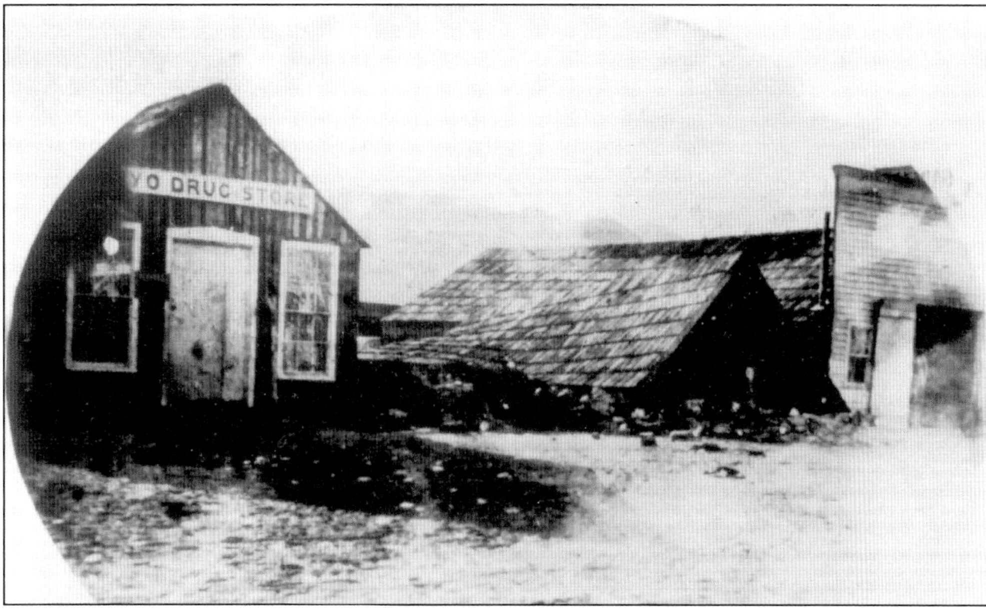

The *Inyo Independent* newspaper for March 30, 1872, summed up the feelings of the citizens of Owens Valley with its front-page multiple headline: "HORRORS!! Appalling Times! EARTHQUAKES. Awful Loss of Life! 24 People Killed! Earth Opens! Houses Prostrated." One of the quoted people in the newspaper story is quoted to have said to his wife during the earthquake, "Get up; hell's broke loose!" Thousands of aftershocks, some severe, continued to shake the Owens Valley. The 7.4 earthquake, in retrospect, could have resulted in more damage and loss of life if it had occurred in a more populated community. By contrast, the 1906 San Francisco earthquake was a 7.8 magnitude, but it and the resulting fires killed upwards of 3,000 people. (Courtesy of County of Inyo, Eastern California Museum.)

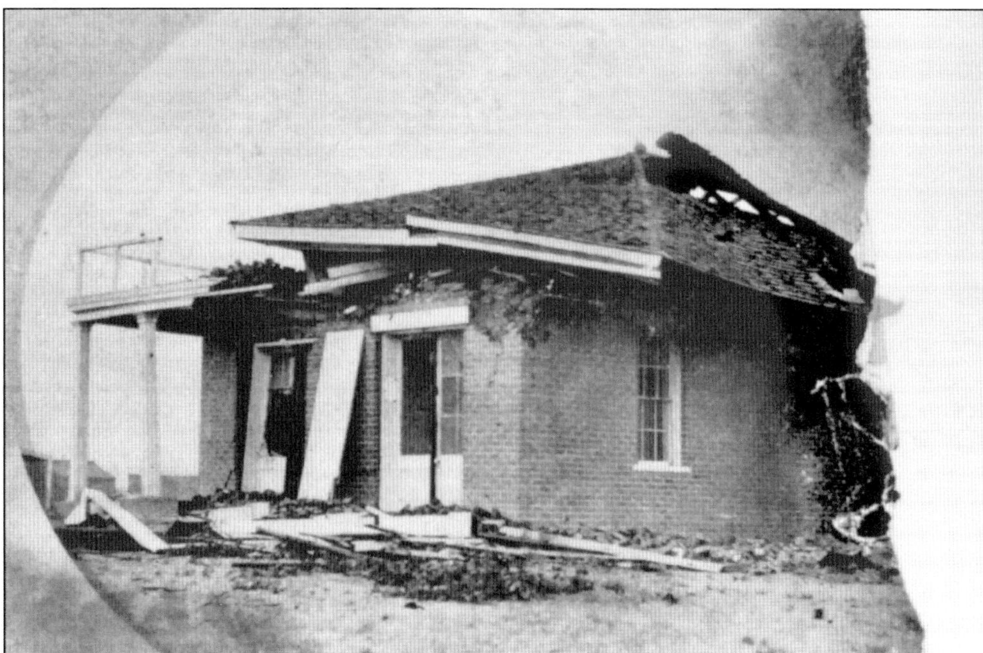

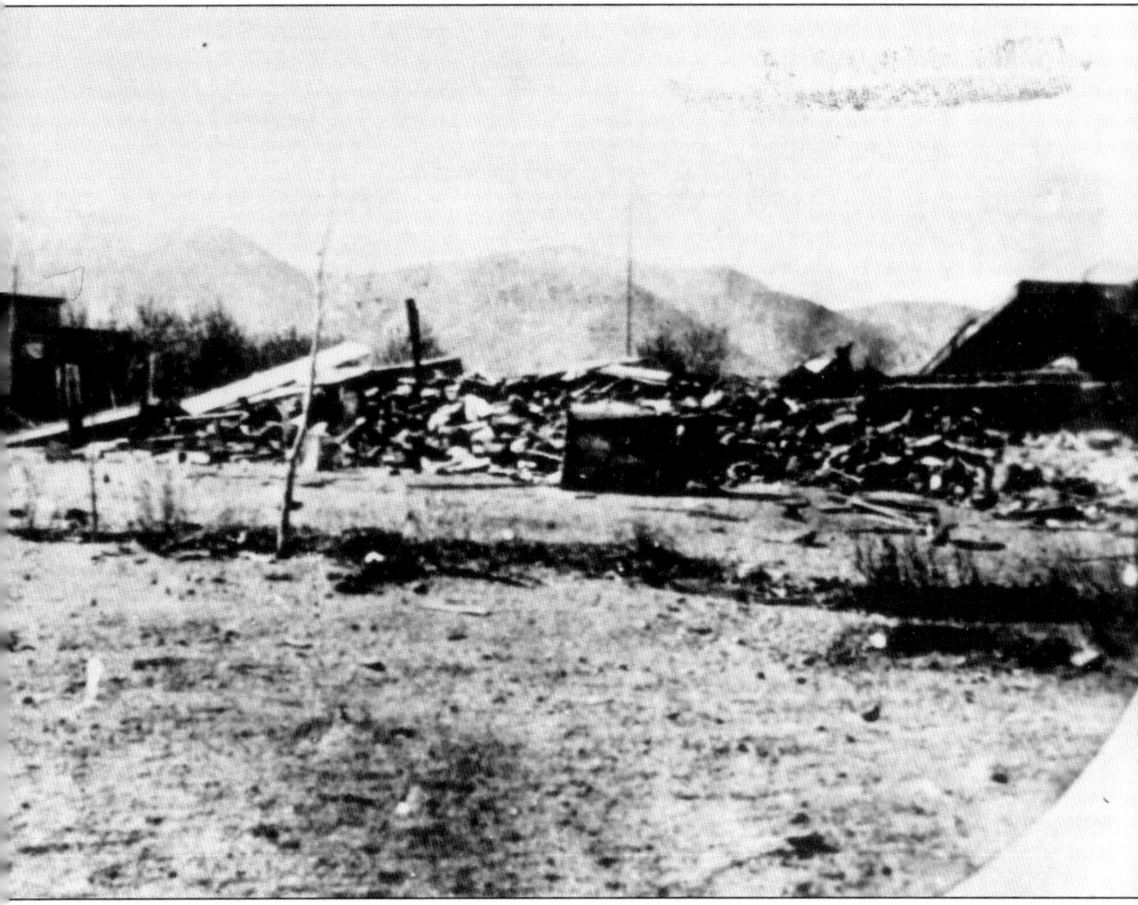

Meta Vagt was crushed by the adobe that fell on her and her parents at 2:30 a.m. on March 26, 1872, during the earthquake. While her father dug an airway, little Meta was not able to withstand the weight of a collapsed house. She was the only child killed in the Fort Independence area and is likely buried in the same plot as her parents, Henrietta and Jacob Vagt. (Courtesy of County of Inyo, Eastern California Museum.)

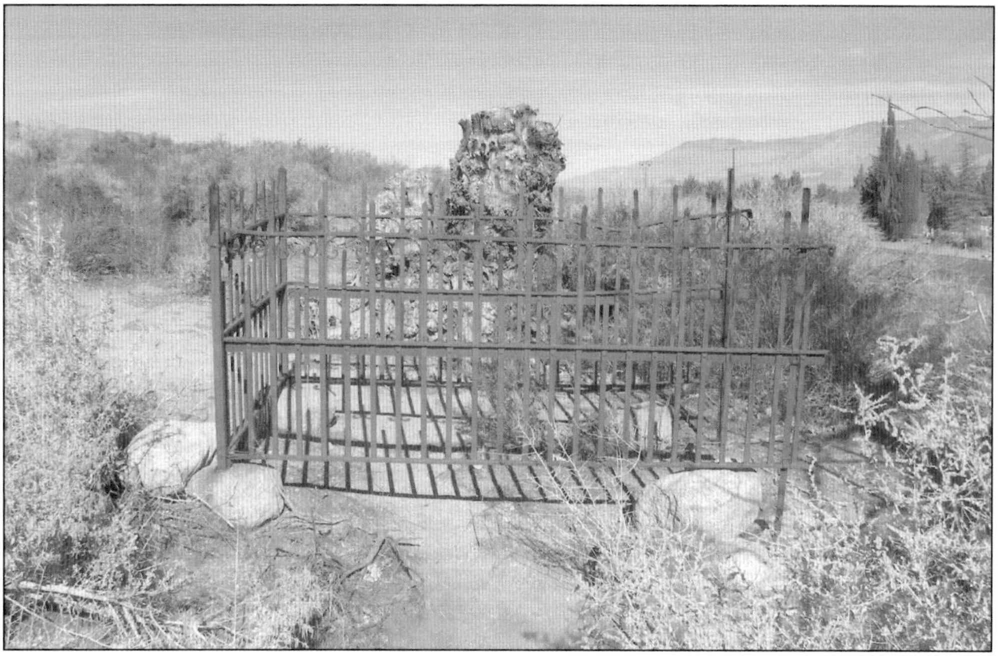

A newspaper report in the *Inyo Independent* explained that "a large grave was prepared on a little rise north of town. In this grave all of foreign birth were consigned the next day. Fifteen coffins numbered and containing sixteen bodies were all deposited in one huge grave." Those who were laid to rest in this common grave were from France, Ireland, Mexico, and Chile. Protestant and Catholic rites were said over the bodies. The remaining dead were claimed by their families for burial or were buried nearby. (Above, courtesy of David Ortega; below, courtesy of County of Inyo, Eastern California Museum.)

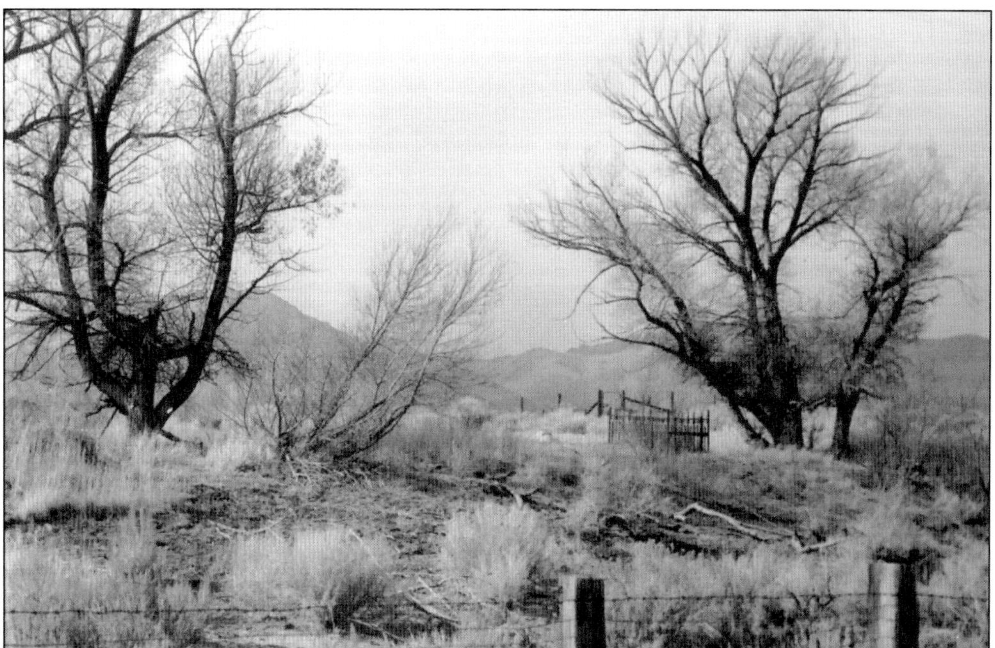

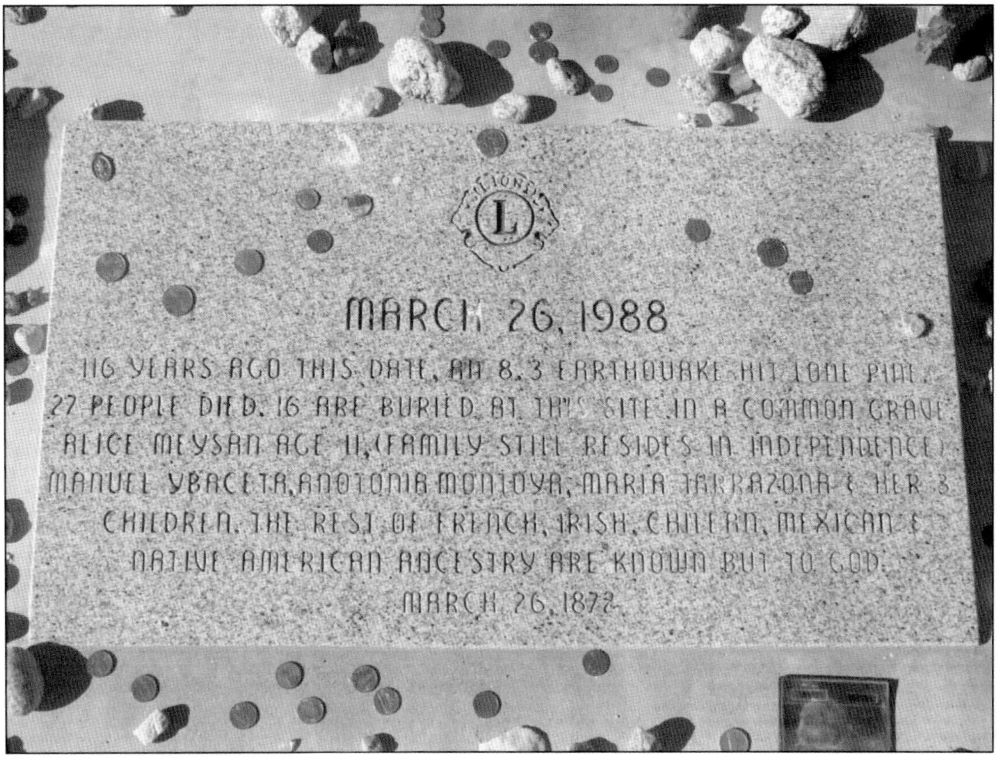

At the historical marker for the victims of the 1872 earthquake, there is a more modern monument and flagpole placed by the Lone Pine Lions Club. This marks the area where the solitary grave for the earthquake victims is. It also lists some of those who were interred here, including Alice Meysan, Manuel Yabaceta, and Maria Tarrazona and her three children. (Courtesy of David Ortega.)

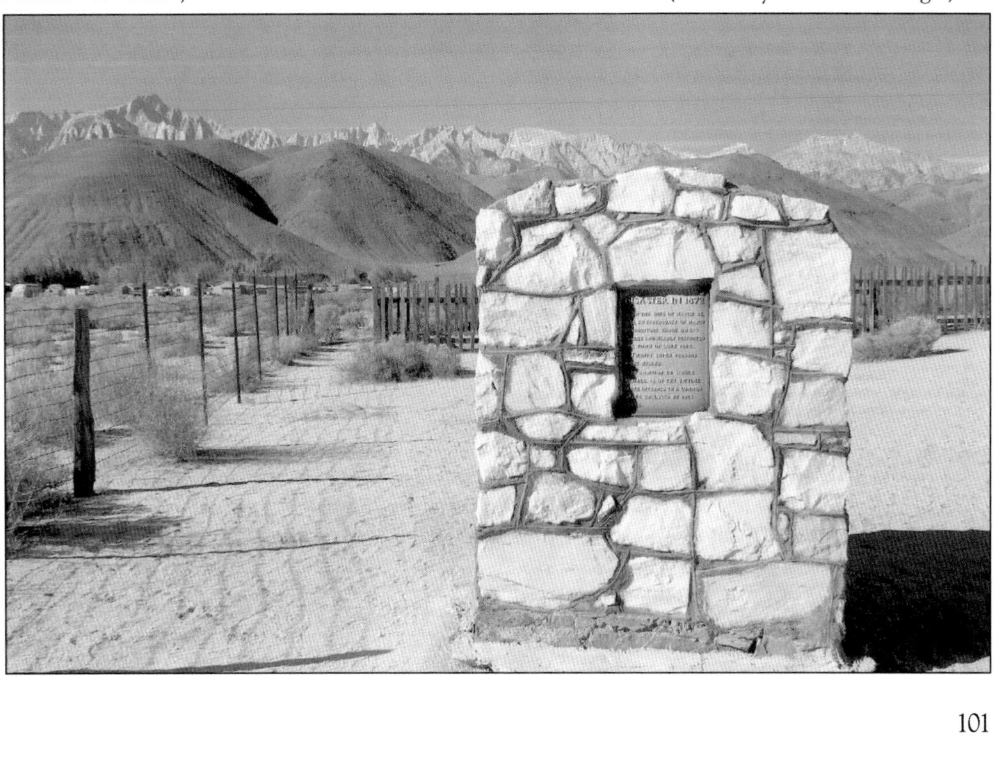

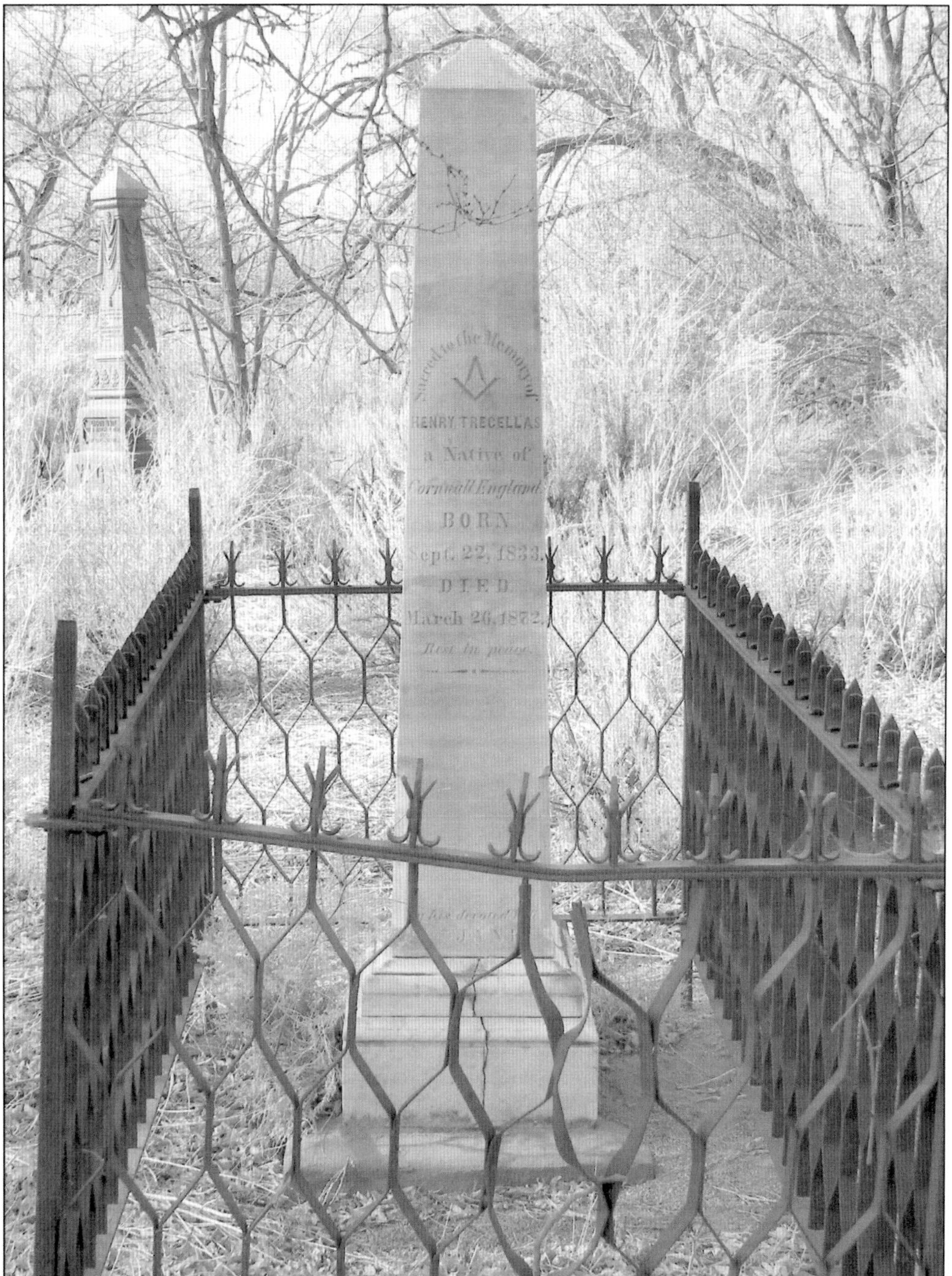

Henry Tregellas died during the Lone Pine earthquake. Tregellas, a superintendent of the Eclipse Mine near Independence, was found dead in what was left of his home. According to the local newspaper, his terrified employees found him with his arms locked around his injured wife. Tregellas was buried in the Camp Independence Cemetery. (Courtesy of David Ortega.)

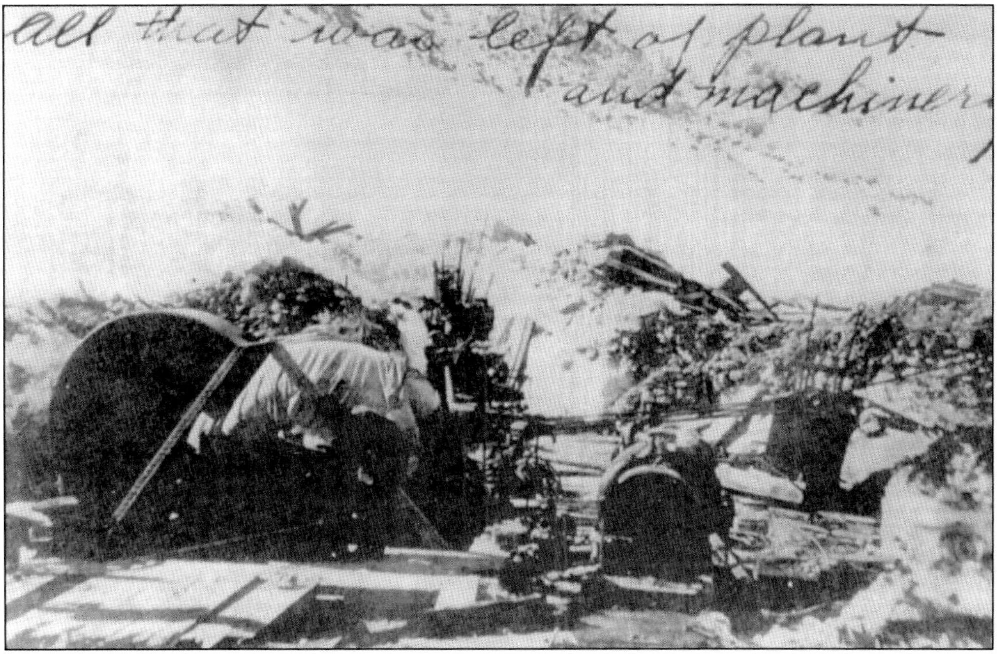

Originally called Copper Mountain, Jordan was the site of an avalanche on March 7, 1911. The snowslide was a mile long, half a mile wide, and up to 22 feet deep. The avalanche destroyed the Jordan Power Plant and all the surrounding buildings. Large trees were toppled in the avalanche's path. The electric transformer inside the power plant, weighing more than 20 tons, was carried over 300 feet by the force of the avalanche. (Courtesy of the Mono County Historical Society.)

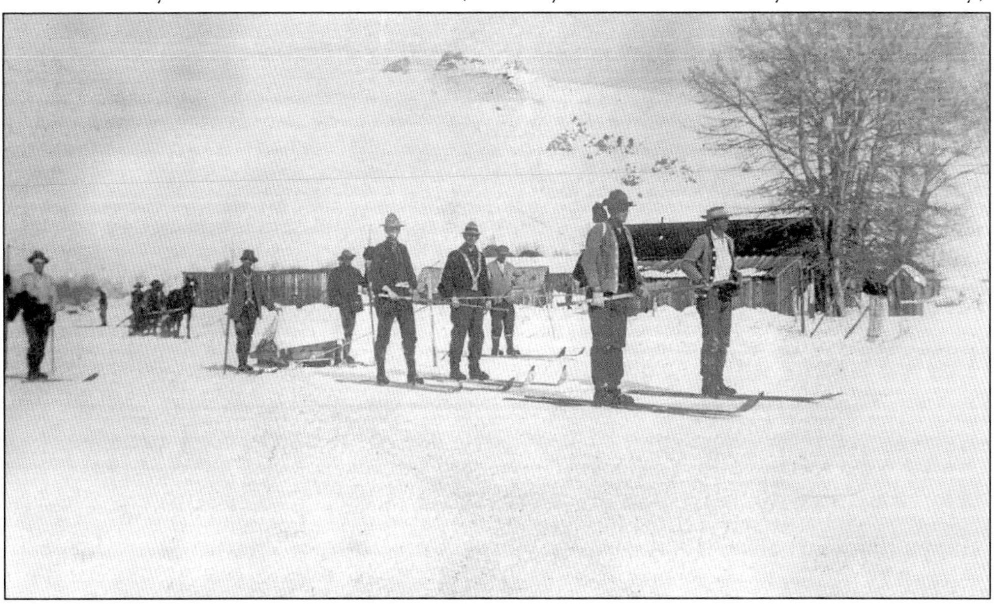

When electricity was cut off at midnight, in Bodie, two power company employees skied down from Bodie to Jordon to see what was wrong. When they reached the top of the ridge, all they could see was snow. Word was sent back to Bodie, and within an hour, men were skiing down to Jordon to perform a rescue for the seven men and one woman who were buried in the snow. (Courtesy of the Mono County Historical Society.)

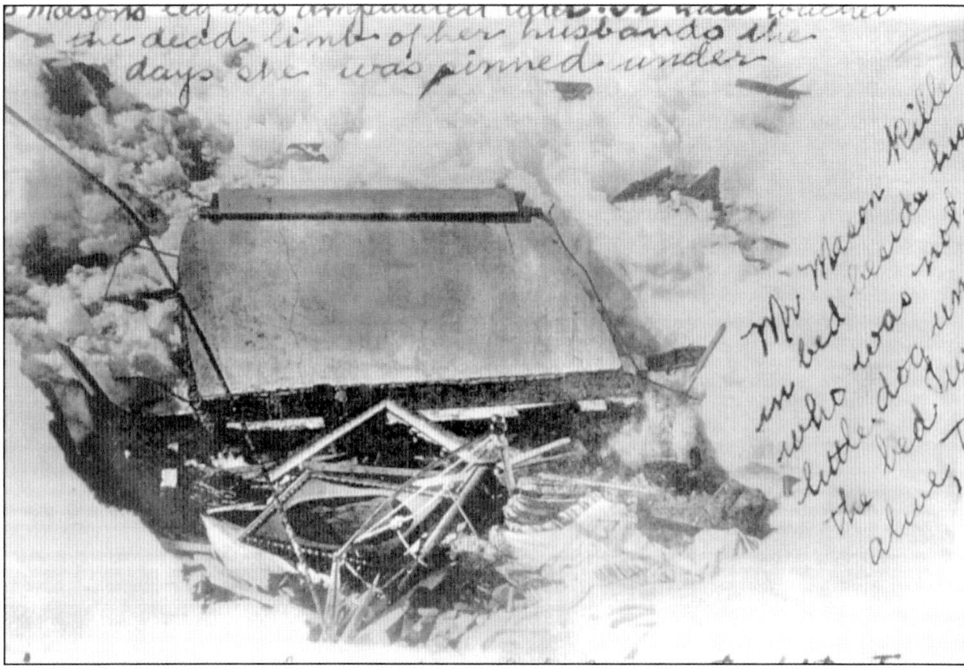

One of the employees of the Southern Sierra Power Company, R. H. Mason, and his wife, Agnes, were sleeping at the time of the avalanche and were buried. Rescue teams dug them out, but only Agnes survived. She had been buried in snow for over 62 hours when she was finally rescued. (Above, courtesy of the Mono County Historical Society; below, courtesy of David Ortega.)

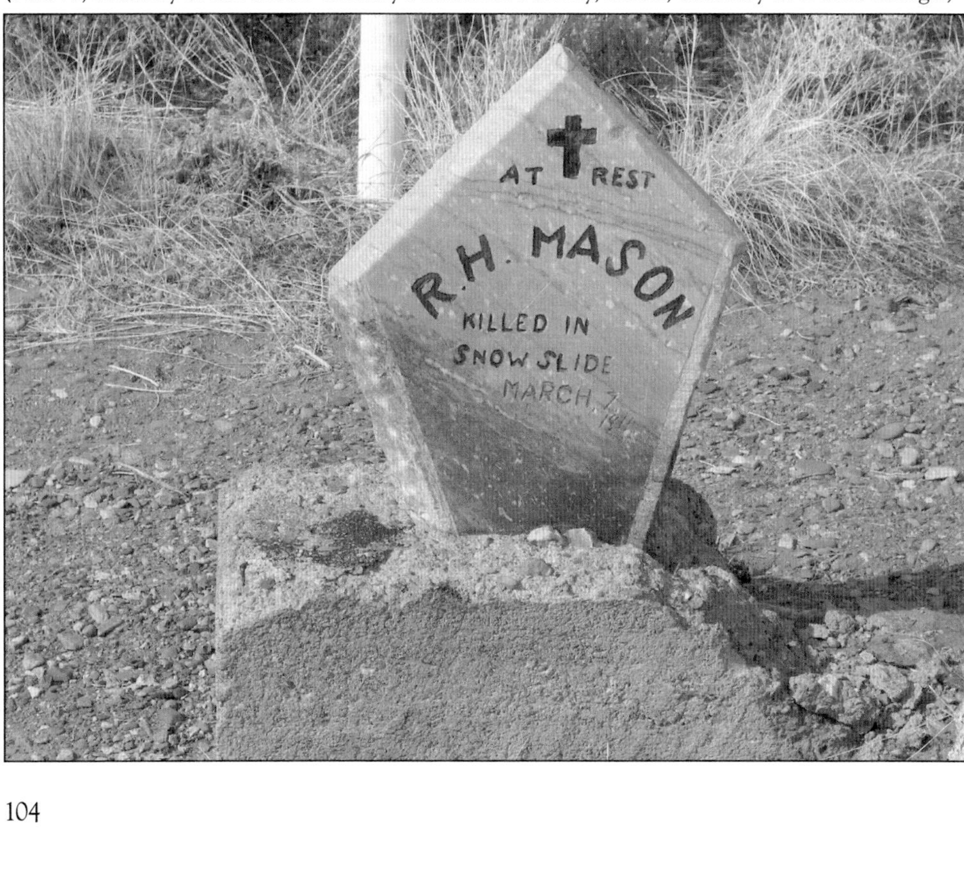

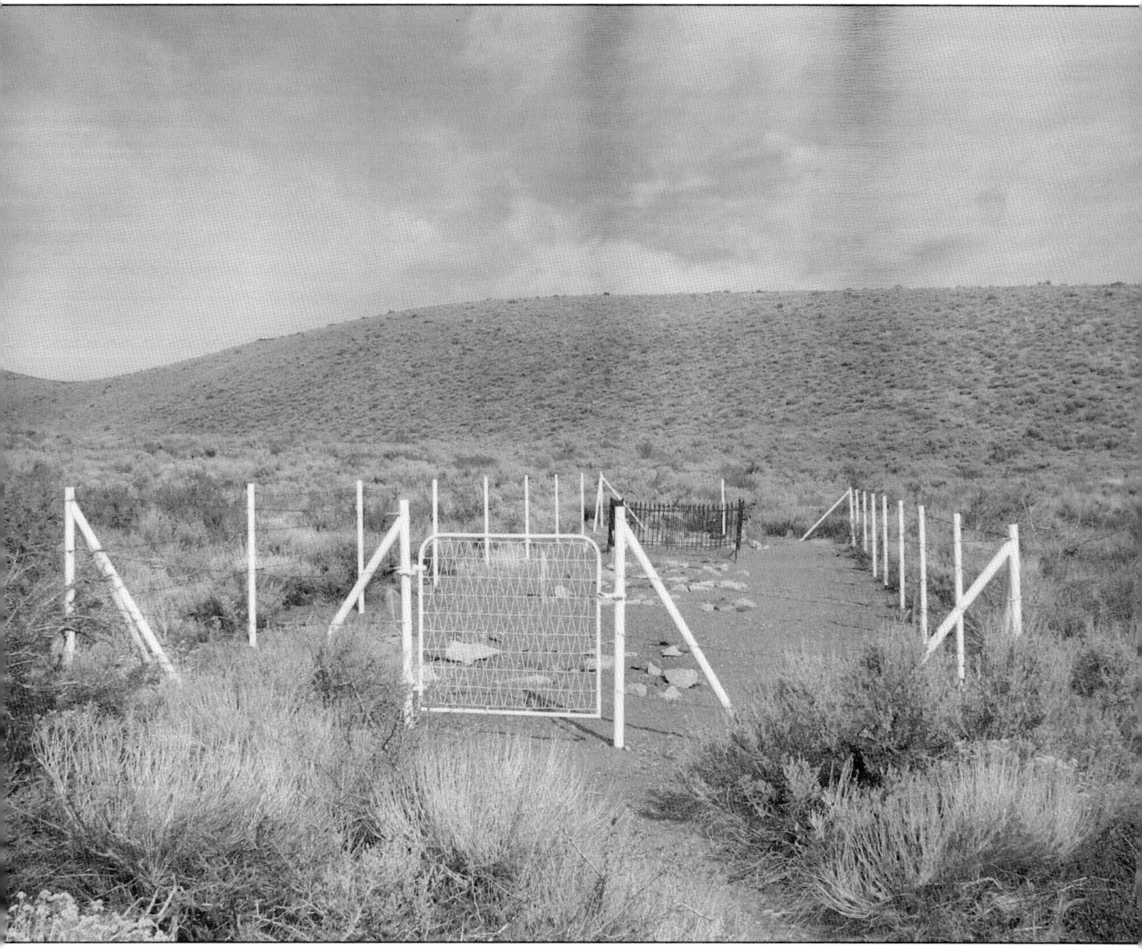

A small graveyard lies up on a hill above where the Jordon Power Plant avalanche occurred. Nine graves mark those who died on March 7, 1911. One of the young men killed was Patrik Stromblad from Sweden. Patrik and some companions came to Lundy about 1910. On March 7, 1911, he and several companions took shelter in the power plant. He was killed when the avalanche destroyed the power plant. (Courtesy of David Ortega.)

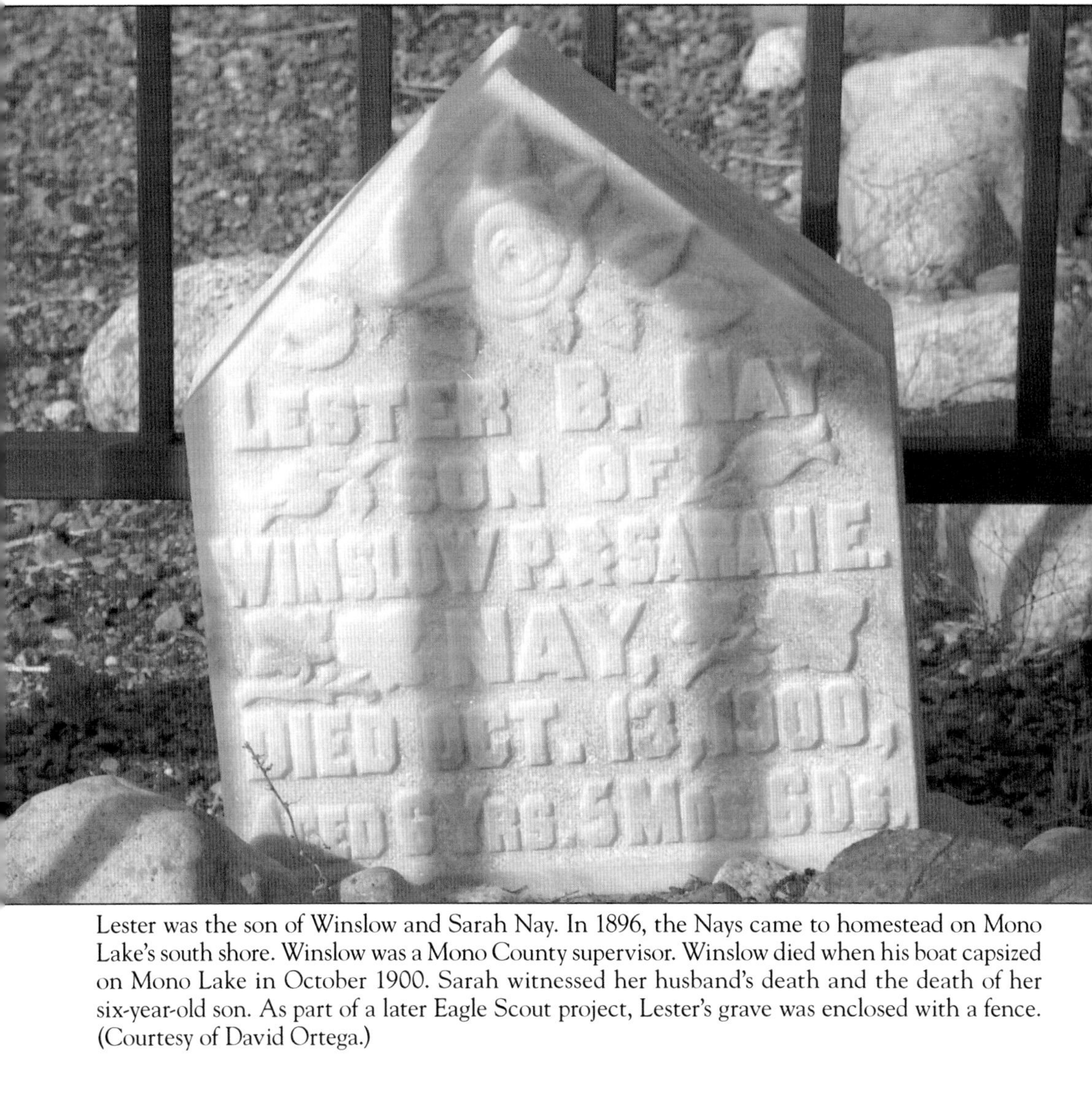

Lester was the son of Winslow and Sarah Nay. In 1896, the Nays came to homestead on Mono Lake's south shore. Winslow was a Mono County supervisor. Winslow died when his boat capsized on Mono Lake in October 1900. Sarah witnessed her husband's death and the death of her six-year-old son. As part of a later Eagle Scout project, Lester's grave was enclosed with a fence. (Courtesy of David Ortega.)

Five

The People of the Owens Valley

People have lived in the Owens Valley for over 10,000 years. In more recent times, the people known as Paiute and Shoshone Indians inhabited the area and lived in communities along the streams that flow out of the Sierra Nevada. White settlers came to the Owens Valley beginning in the 1860s as miners and ranchers. From the start, the Owens Valley was home to a virtual melting pot of people that included many cultures and ethnic groups. They included the Chinese, who came to work on the railroads and worked also in restaurants and laundries in the white towns. Living in "Chinatowns," they buried their dead in separate cemeteries, with the hope of eventually sending those who had passed on back to their homeland. One report states that in the 1940s, approximately 35 graves were located here. One woman described the Chinese Cemetery as being a part of the Independence Chinatown that was enclosed with a high fence.

Jewish families came to Inyo County as merchants and established stores and markets, some of which are still operating today. Like most immigrants, they were far from their homelands and traditional communities, and one can only imagine the loneliness they endured in the earliest days of settlement.

Mexicans and South Americans, too, came to the valley, first as miners and later to work on ranches, the railroad, and in the soda ash industry. Among them were the Diaz brothers from Chile, for whom a lake near Lone Pine is named.

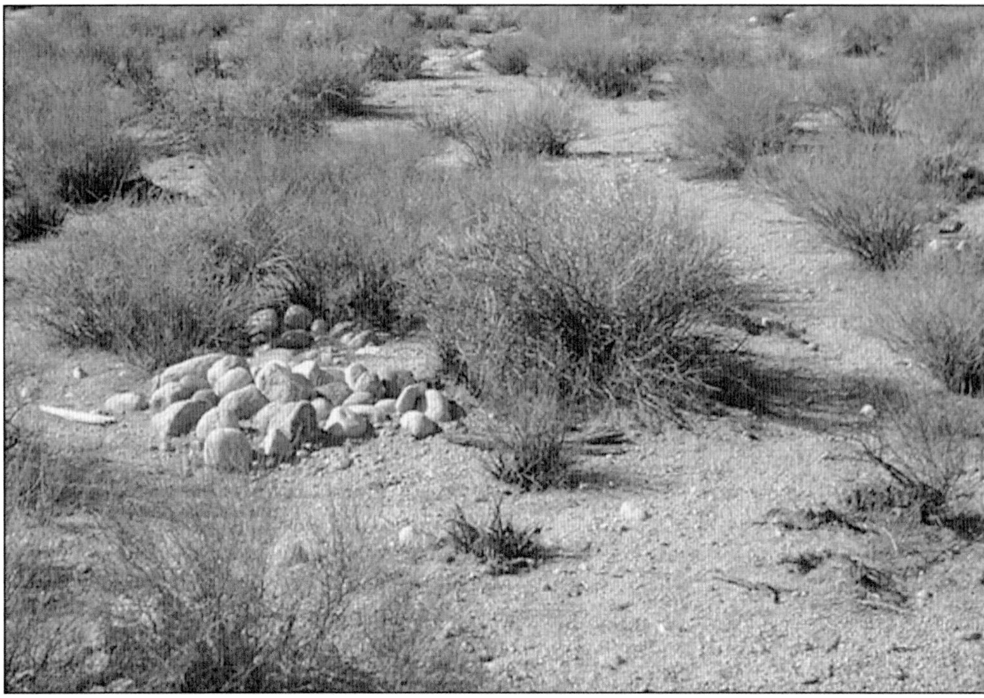

No history or records exist for this cemetery located south of Independence. It is believed to have been an abandoned graveyard taken over by the Chinese who lived in the town. One estimate places the number of graves at 35, including the possible grave of Mary Mallory Squire, an area resident. What we do know comes from local citizens who remember the little cemetery and can recall the Chinese funerals that took place there. (Courtesy of Jerry Eskew.)

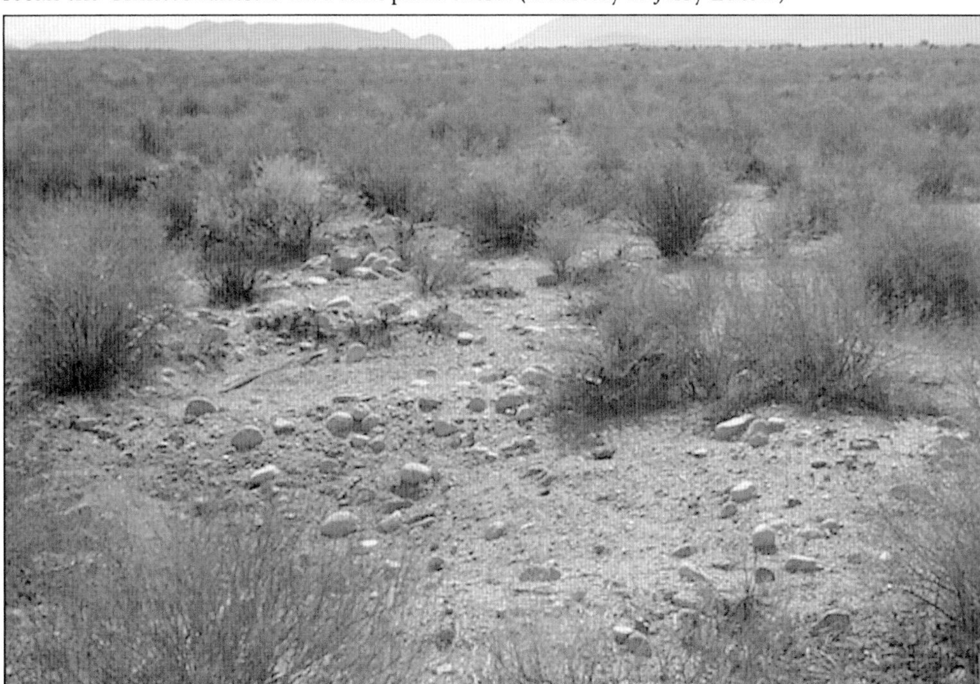

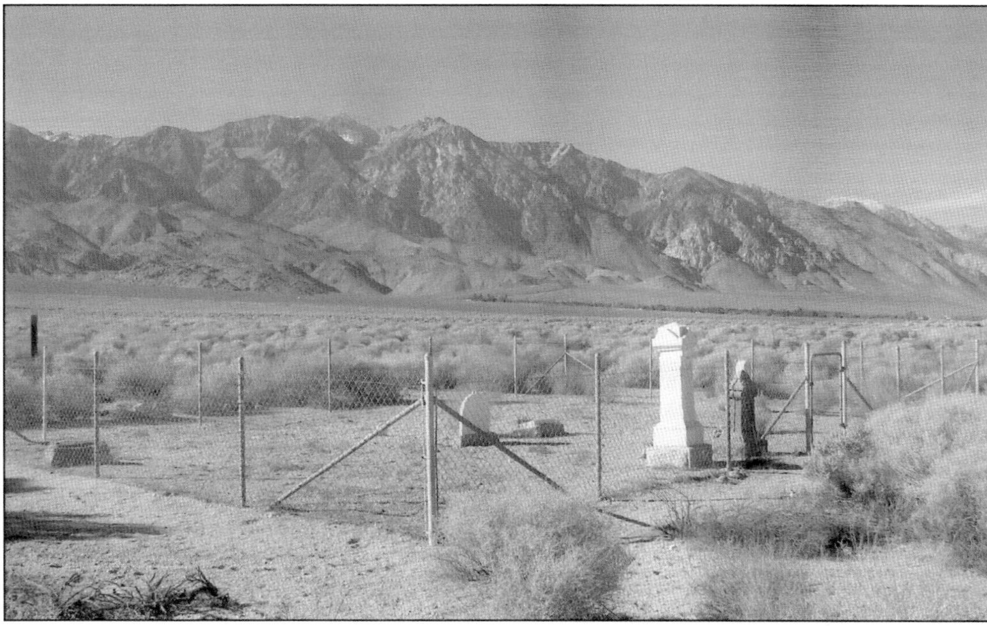

The only Jewish burial ground dating from pioneer times in the Eastern Sierra, the Jewish Cemetery, north of Independence, is the final resting place for four Levy family members and an infant Jewish boy from neighboring Bishop. While it is unknown when the cemetery was founded, Hulda Levy, who died in February 1876, is the first burial there. (Courtesy of David Ortega.)

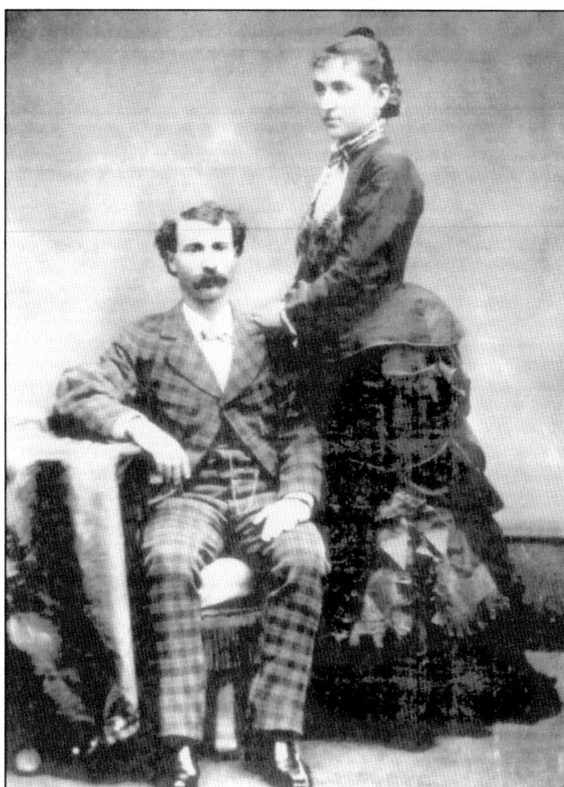

Henry and Mary Joseph Levy were married in the winter of 1876. Mary Joseph was just 16 years old and living in San Francisco when she married the widower Henry. They went on to have eight children. Two of their boys died before adulthood. The Levy family, who was Jewish, are an example of pioneers who left everything they knew and that was familiar to make a new life. (Courtesy of Arlene Brierly Pearce.)

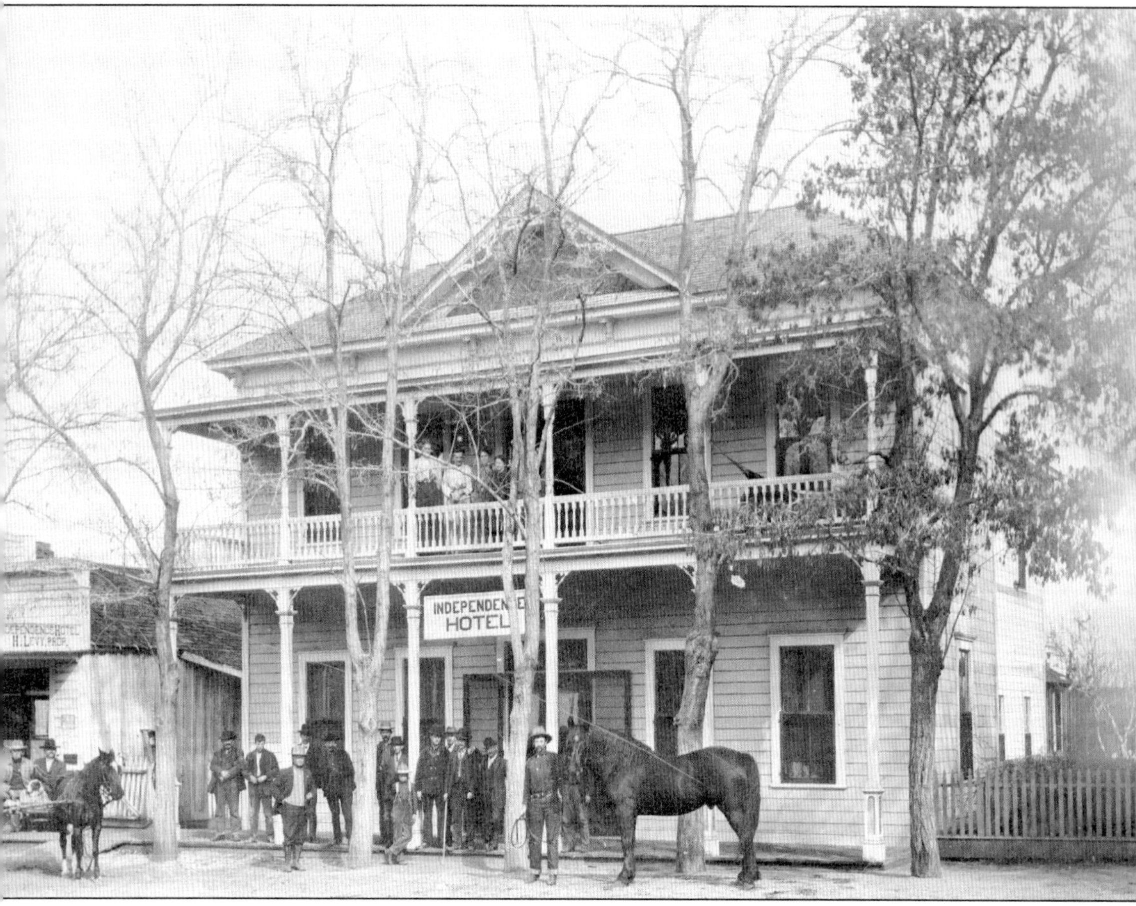

Henry Levy, the patriarch of the Owens Valley Levy family, was born in 1849 in Prussia. He owned the Independence Hotel, described as "cool and serene, with a double decked veranda beautifully shaped by magnificent locust trees." In later years, the hotel boasted a livery stable and an auto service that provided a "fine Buick car" for clients' needs. (Courtesy of University of Southern California, on behalf of the USC Specialized Libraries and Archival Collections.)

Henry Levy came to the United States from Golub, Prussia, when he was a teenager, first living in San Francisco and other nearby locales and eventually settling in Independence. Henry started out as a barber but quickly switched to the hotel business. In 1874, he built the Independence Hotel and restaurant. Henry retired from his business in 1920, but the hotel continued in operation under his wife and children. Mary Joseph Levy, Henry's second wife, is buried next to him in the Independence Cemetery. (At right, courtesy of County of Inyo, Eastern California Museum; below, courtesy of the author.)

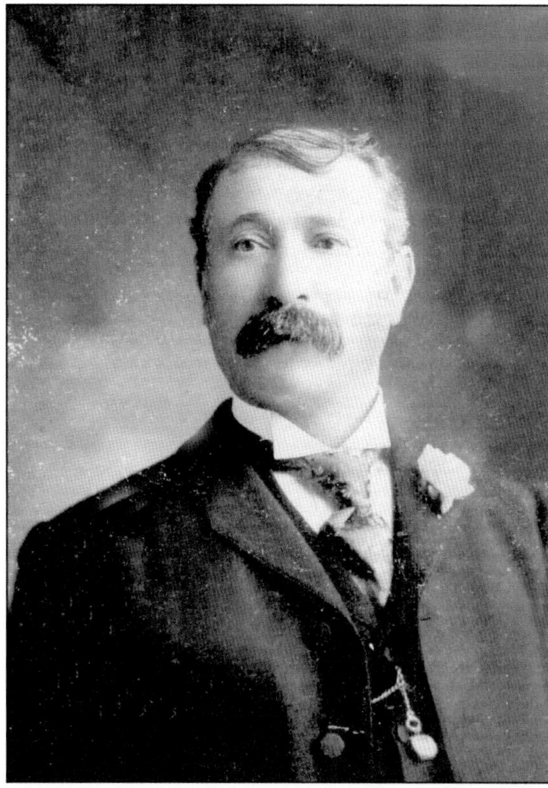

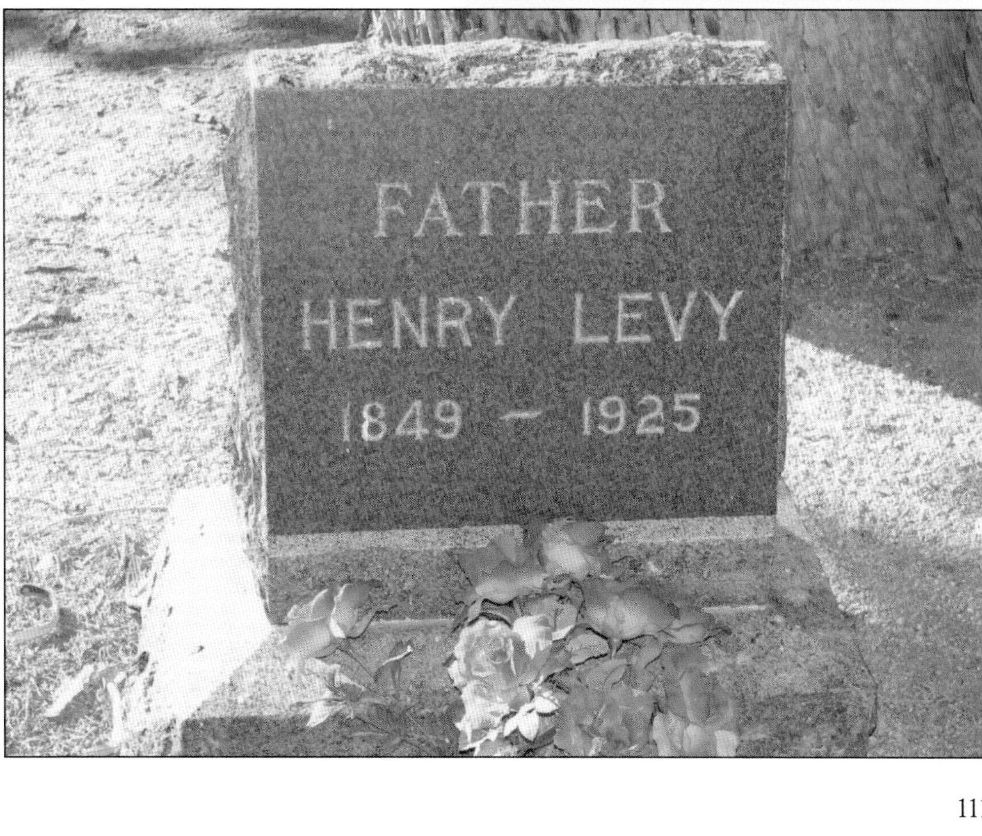

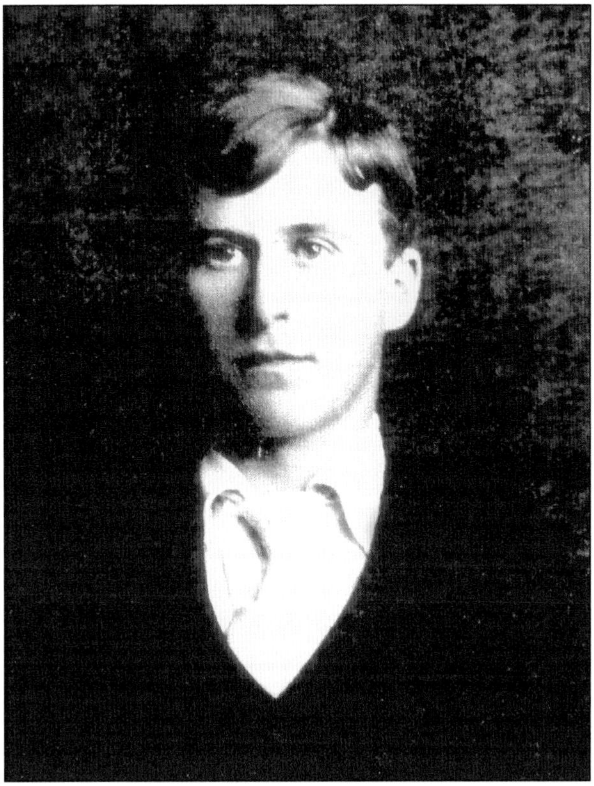

Joseph Levy, a son of Henry and Mary Levy, died from drowning in the Owens River. Joe Levy and a friend, Johnny Ruiz, were riding horses when Joe's horse turned over, throwing him into the river. After trying to save his friend, Johnny ran into town for help, but a search for Joseph turned up empty. The next morning, 40 people dragged the river and employed other techniques to find Joseph. Four days later, he was found dead in the river. His obituary noted that he was "a boy of gentle and amiable disposition and was loved by all." (Courtesy of Arlene Brierly Pearce.)

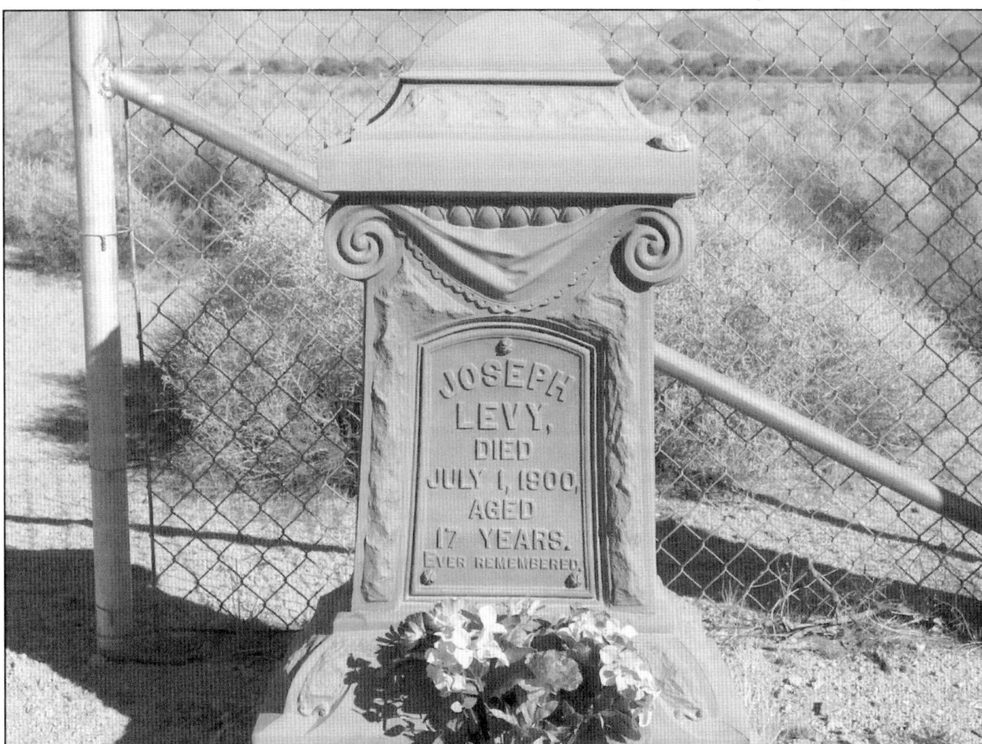

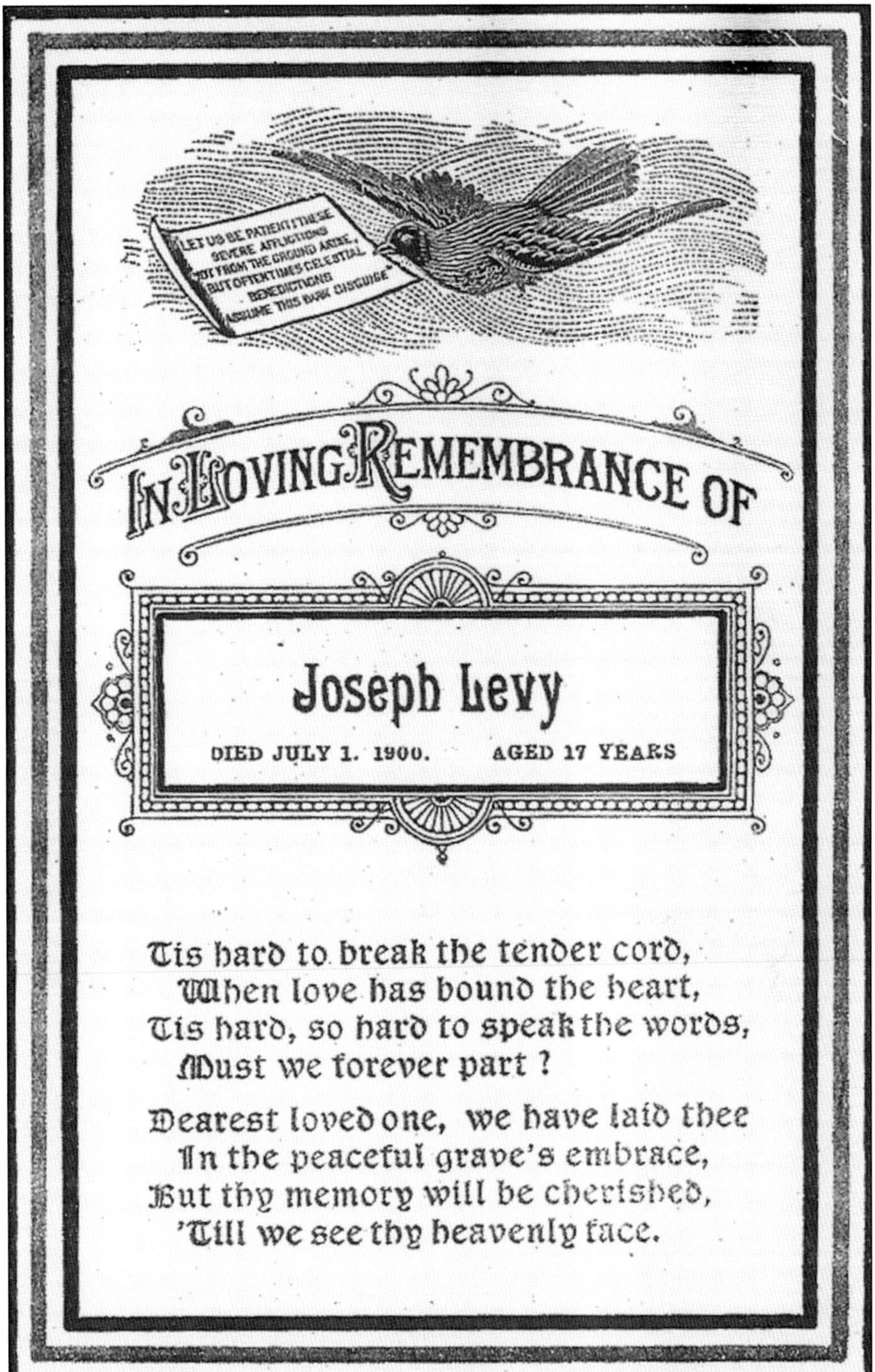

LET US BE PATIENT! THESE
SEVERE AFFLICTIONS
NOT FROM THE GROUND ARISE,
BUT OFTENTIMES CELESTIAL
BENEDICTIONS
ASSUME THIS DARK DISGUISE

IN LOVING REMEMBRANCE OF

Joseph Levy

DIED JULY 1. 1900. AGED 17 YEARS

Tis hard to break the tender cord,
When love has bound the heart,
Tis hard, so hard to speak the words,
Must we forever part ?

Dearest loved one, we have laid thee
In the peaceful grave's embrace,
But thy memory will be cherished,
'Till we see thy heavenly face.

Joseph Levy, who died at 17 years of age, was surely missed by the community of Independence. His obituary stated, "His sudden disappearance from the ranks of the living so unforeseen and unexpected stunned the hearts of his relatives almost past the realization of their loss and threw a gloom over the entire community that time alone can dispel." (Courtesy of Arlene Brierly Pearce.)

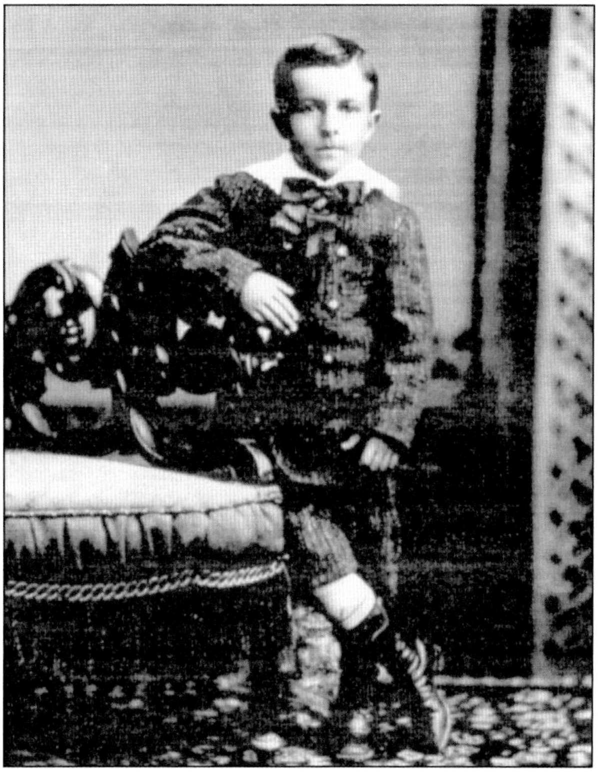

Mark Levy, the oldest son of Henry and Mary Levy, died at seven years of age from whooping cough, a highly contagious respiratory disease caused by bacterial infection. In the first half of the 20th century, it was the leading cause of childhood illness and death. (At left, courtesy of Arlene Brierly Pearce; below, courtesy of David Ortega.)

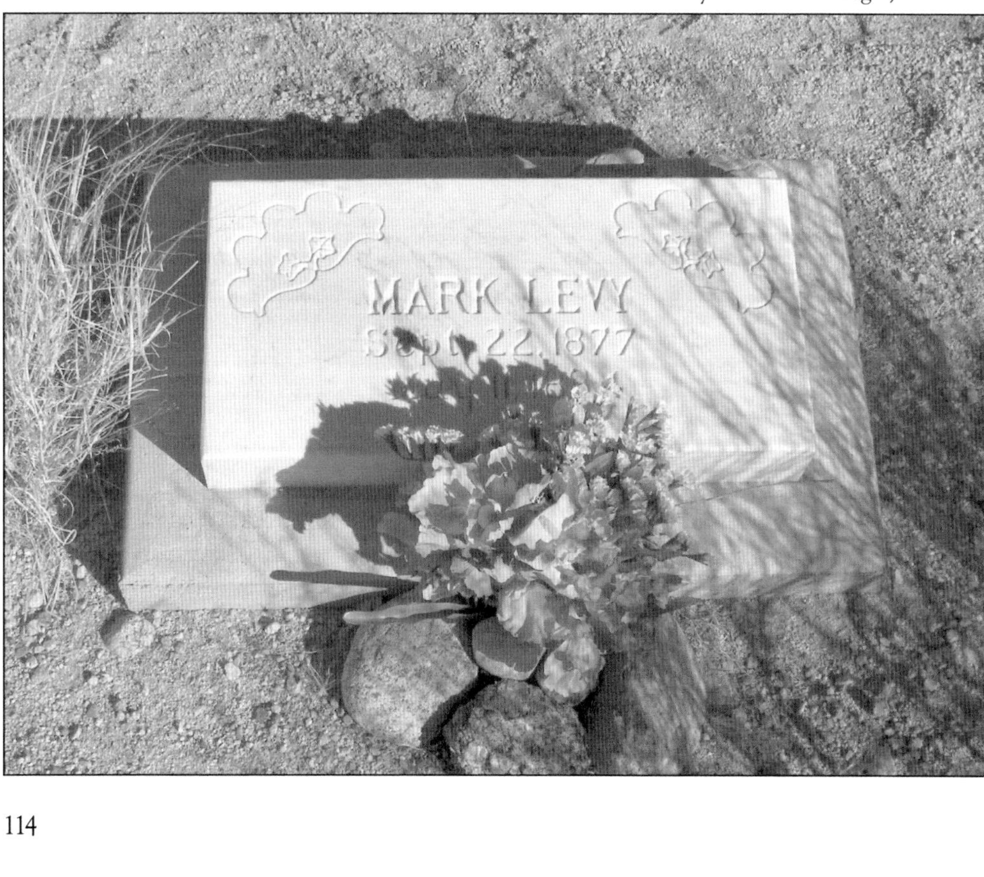

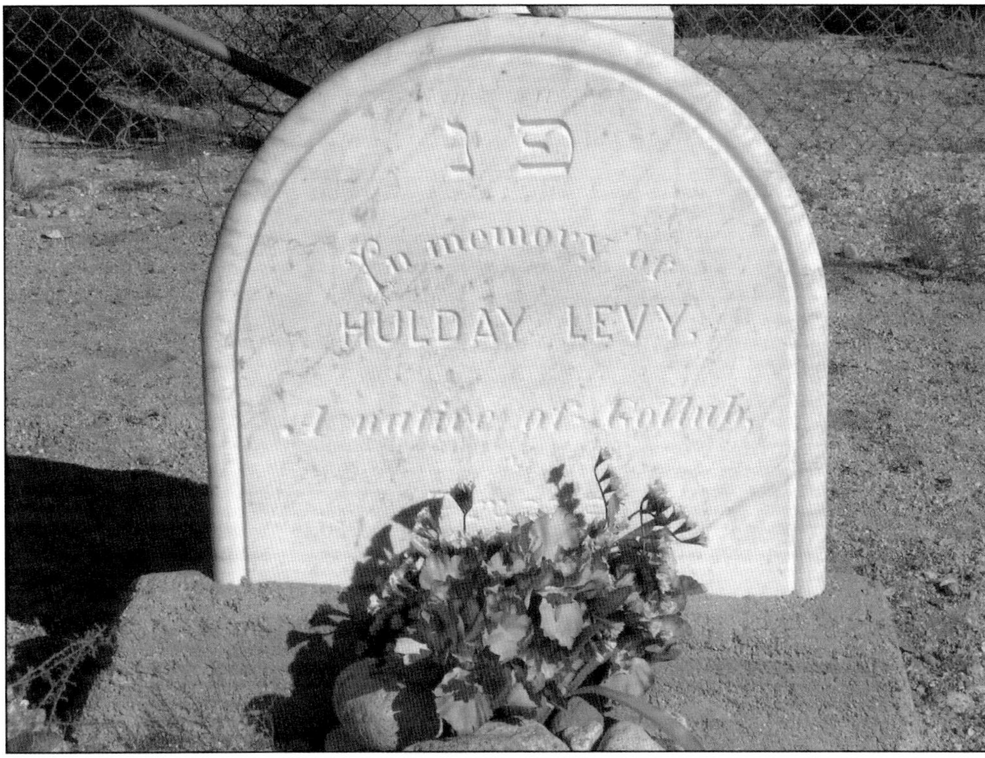

Hulda Sultan Levy, misspelled as Hulday on the tombstone, was the first wife of Henry Levy. She died in childbirth just 10 months after she arrived in Independence. Henry married Mary Joseph Levy less than a year after his first wife's death. Her sister Johanna Wood is also buried in the Jewish Cemetery. (Courtesy of David Ortega.)

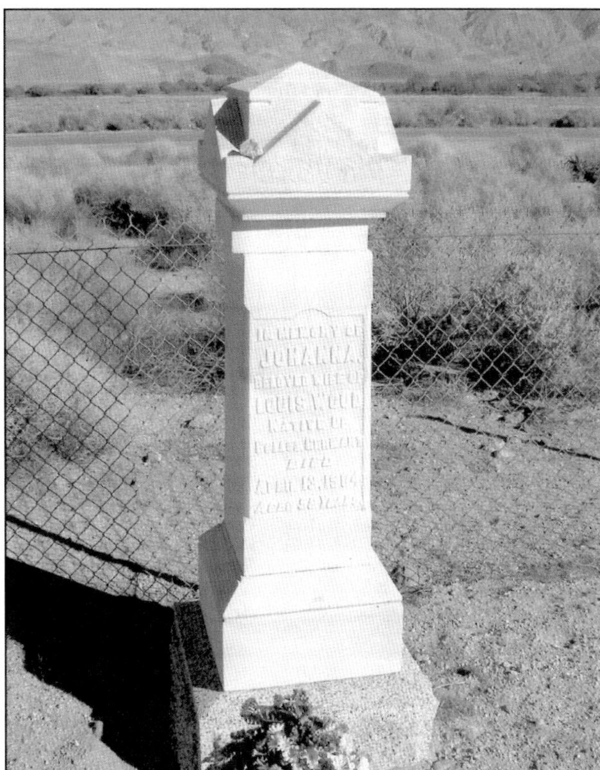

Johanna Sultan Wood, Hulda's sister, was the wife of Louis Wood, a merchant in Independence. She immigrated to the United States from Golub, Prussia, now a part of Poland. Her obituary in the April 15, 1904, issue of the *Inyo Independent* was written by Mary Austin, the California writer who went on to write about her life in the Owens Valley in the book *The Land of Little Rain*. (Courtesy of David Ortega.)

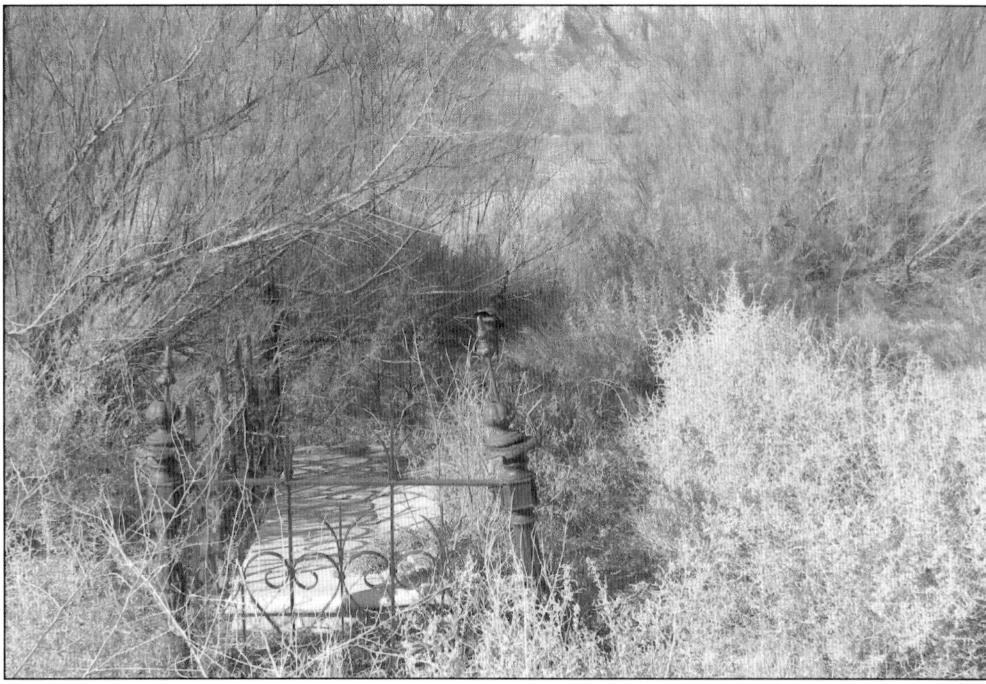

Rafael Diaz and his brother Eleuterio emigrated from Chile in the 1860s, working as miners in Santa Clara County in the 1870s prior to establishing themselves in the Lone Pine area. Their legacy lives on in the lake that is named for them. The brothers worked as butchers and owned their own cattle ranch. (Courtesy of David Ortega.)

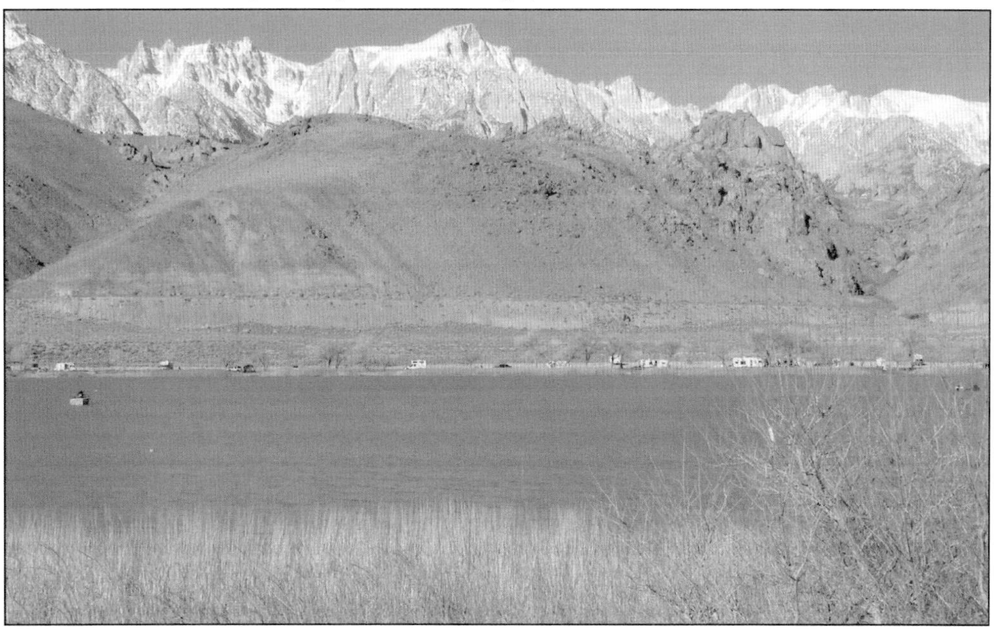

Diaz Lake, located just south of Lone Pine, is named after the Diaz brothers, Rafael and Eleuterio, who had a cattle ranch near here. Diaz Lake was formed when the Owens Valley earthquake fault dropped 20 feet during the 1872 earthquake. An underground spring opened and filled the area, creating Diaz Lake. (Courtesy of David Ortega.)

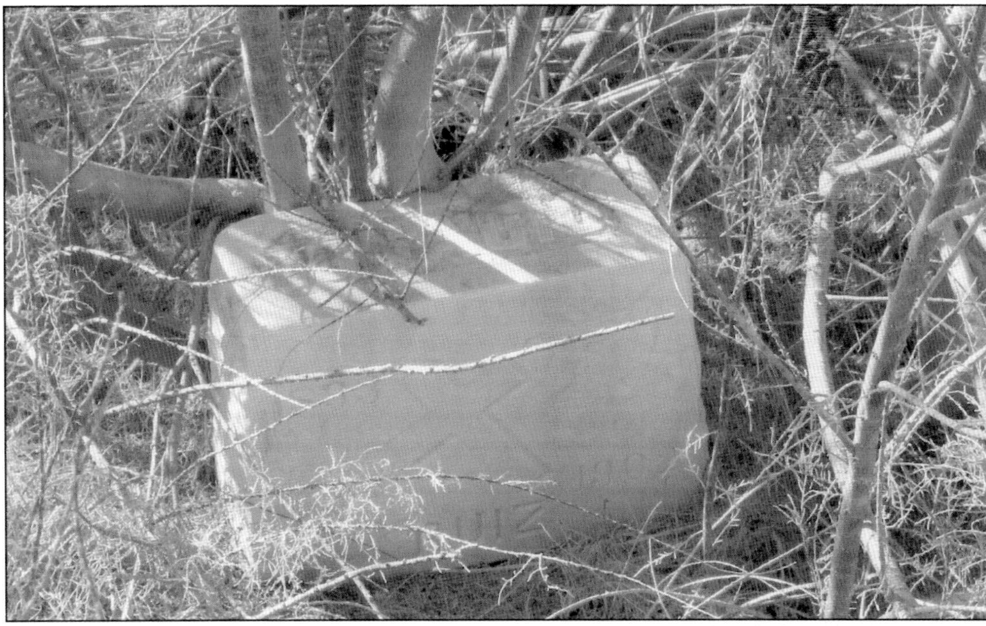

Ignacio Ruiz was most likely the nine-year-old son of Ignacio and Isabel Ruiz of Lone Pine. Ignacio Sr. was a gold ore miner who lived with his wife and eight children. He is buried at the Lone Pine cemetery, where recently his headstone was vandalized and moved a few feet from its original location. The vandals left the stone and the tool they used to move it. (Courtesy of David Ortega.)

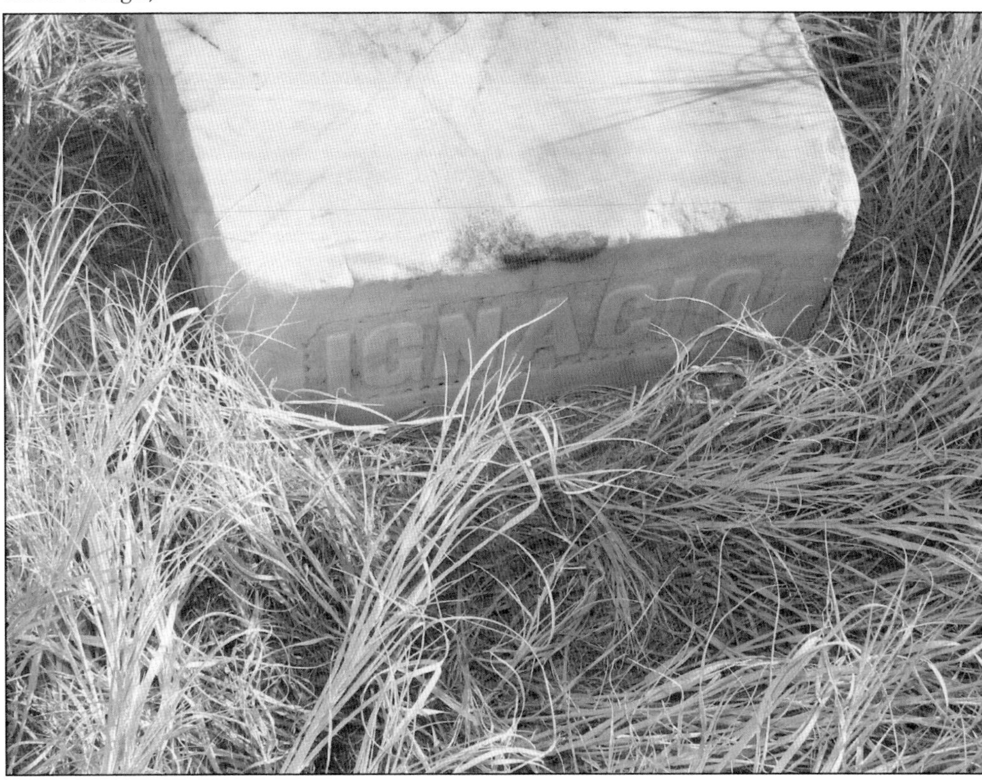

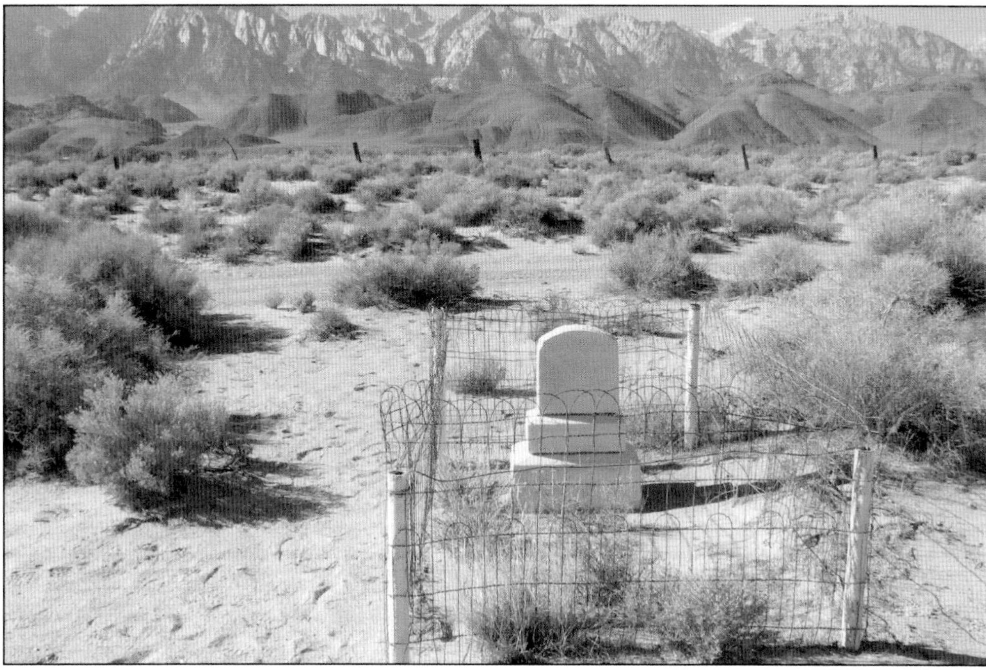

This cemetery near the road that leads to the old Southern Pacific railroad depot in Lone Pine currently includes markers for only about nine burials. Marked headstones range in date from 1892 to 1912. Most likely, there were more graves at this burial ground, but no early records exist describing the cemetery. (Courtesy of David Ortega.)

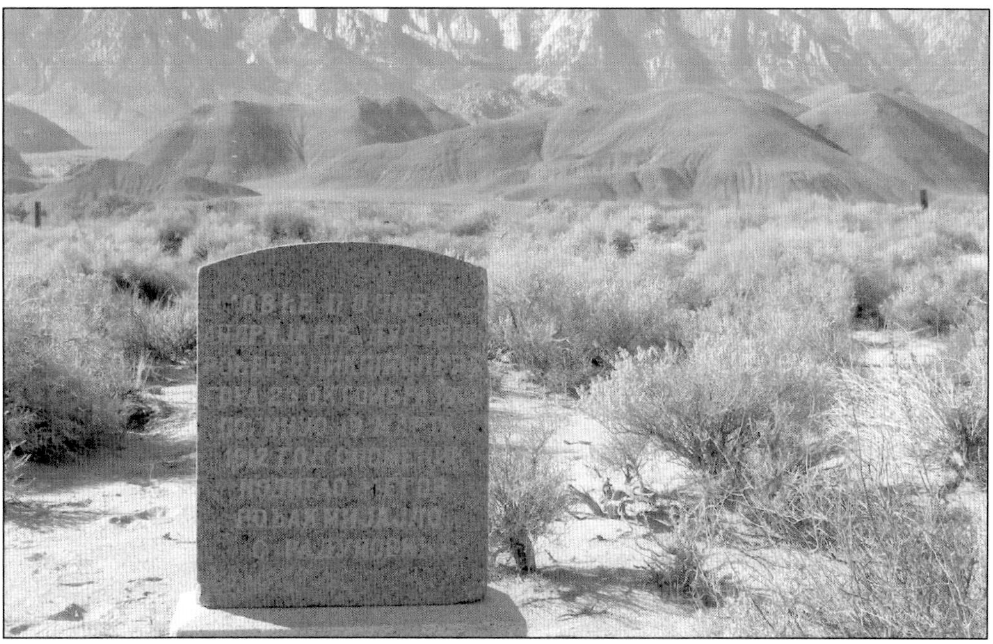

This grave marker located along the depot road in Lone Pine memorializes a 26 year old who died in 1912. Believed to be in Serbian or a Russian dialect, it is one of the many markers that honors immigrants who came to this valley in hopes of creating a better life. (Courtesy of David Ortega.)

Josefa de Alday's tombstone reads, "Your children wish to remember the proof of the great love they had for you." In 1880, Josefa was 40 years old and living in Inyo County with two children. The D. E. P. at the bottom of her stone means "rest in peace." (Courtesy of David Ortega.)

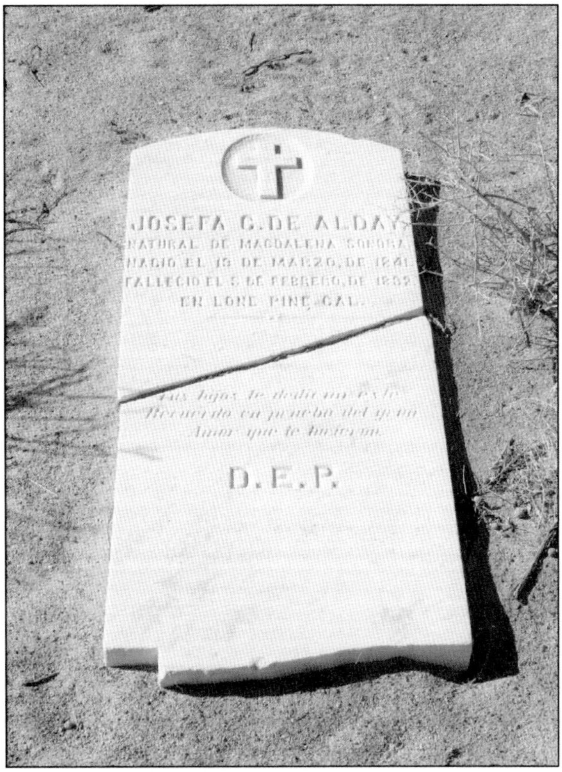

Ana V. deCastro, a Mexican immigrant, lived in the mining community of Cerro Gordo with her husband, Miguel. They lived in an area with other Mexican and Chilean immigrants. Her grave is in the town of Lone Pine near the old Lone Pine Depot. Her headstone is surrounded by a fence that could have been placed there originally to protect it from cattle and other animals. (Courtesy of David Ortega.)

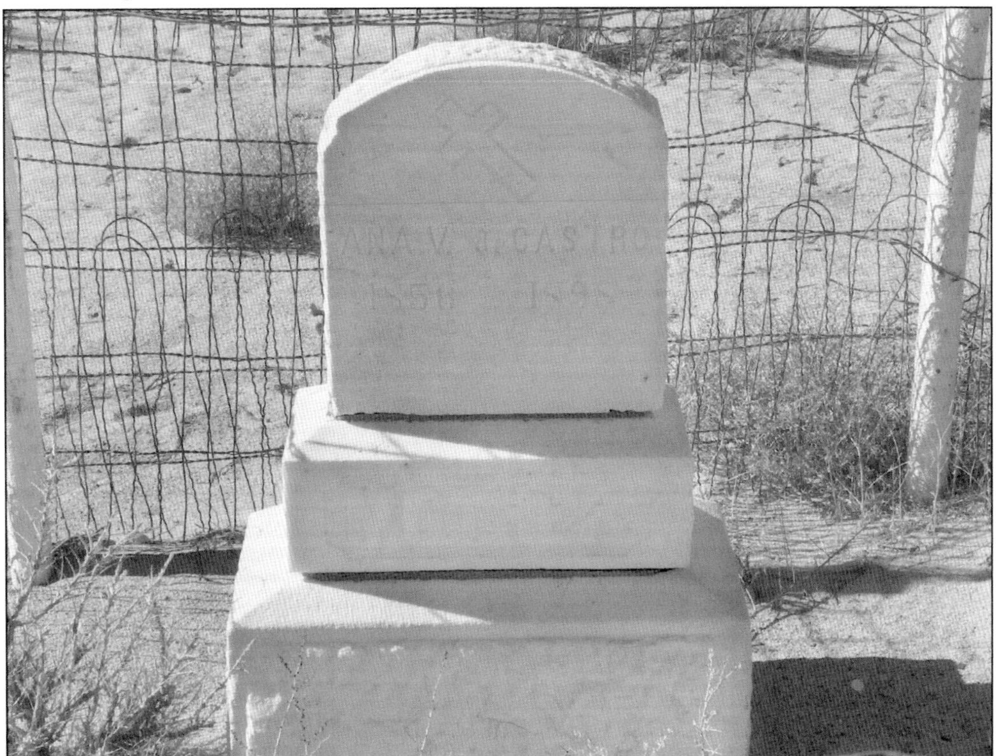

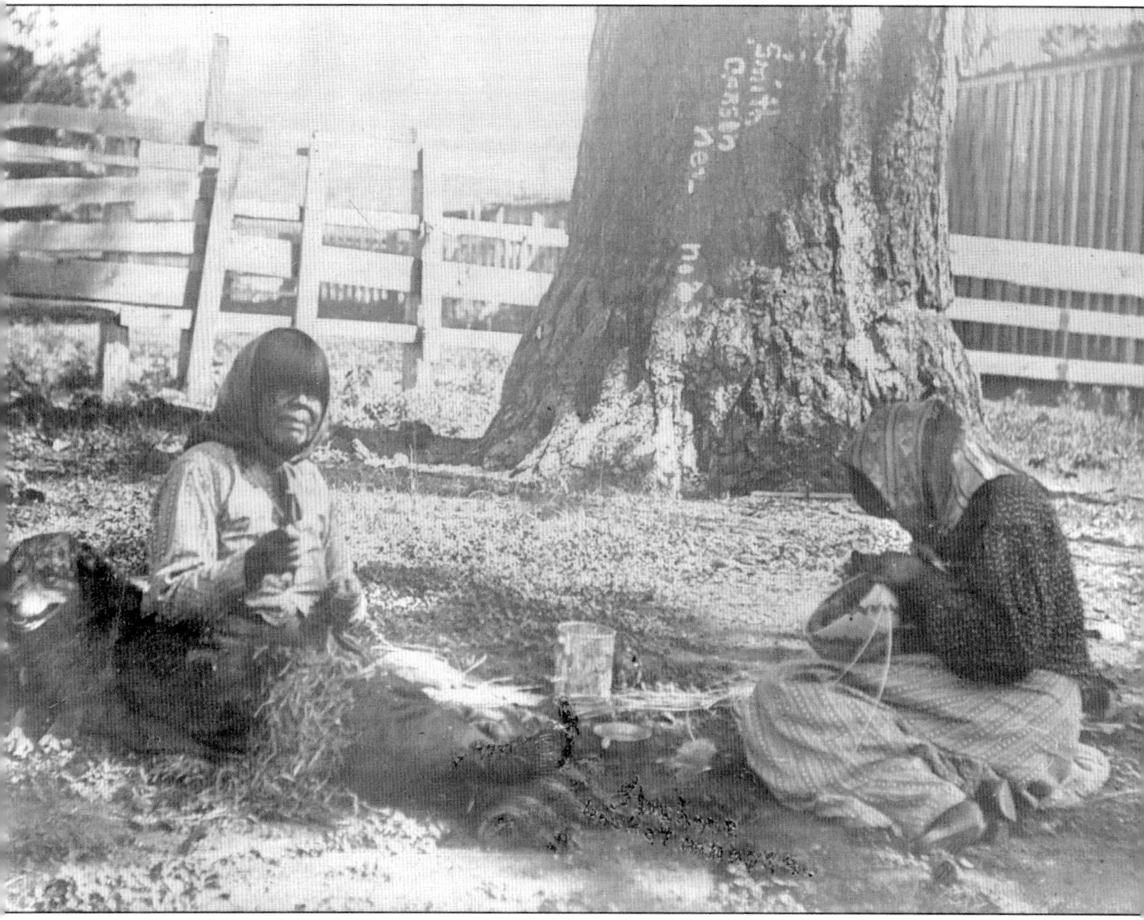

The Paiute and Shoshone people have lived in the Eastern Sierra for over 1,000 years. Originally the Paiute area extended from the northern Owens Valley to the state of Oregon, and the Shoshone lived in the southern Owens Valley and areas to the east. This photograph shows two Owens Valley Shoshone basket weavers c. 1910. (Courtesy of University of Southern California, on behalf of the USC Specialized Libraries and Archival Collections.)

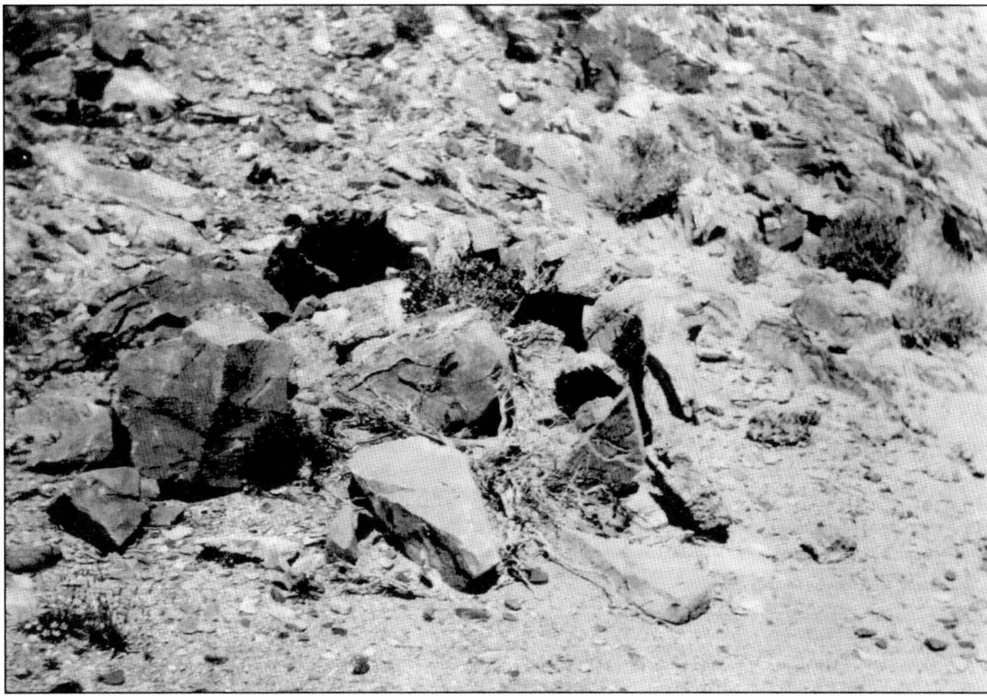

Named after a town in South Wales and founded in the late 1860s, Swansea is located at the northern end of Owens Lake at the base of the Inyo Mountains and north of the mining town of Keeler. This photograph shows a Native American grave in Swansea. A storm in 1874 turned Swansea into a ghost town. (Courtesy of County of Inyo, Eastern California Museum.)

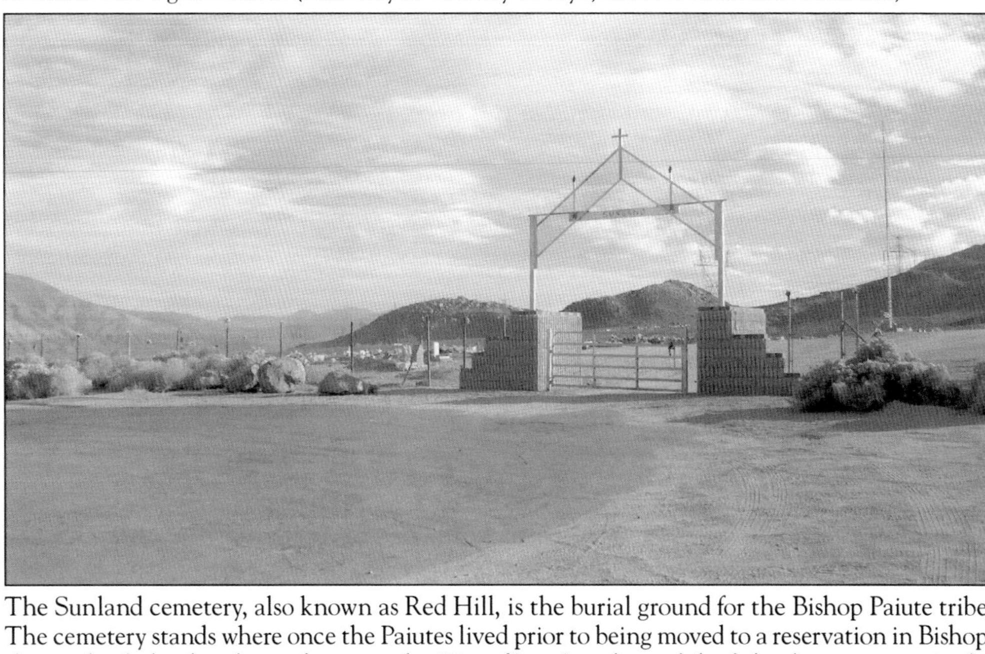

The Sunland cemetery, also known as Red Hill, is the burial ground for the Bishop Paiute tribe. The cemetery stands where once the Paiutes lived prior to being moved to a reservation in Bishop, the result of a land exchange between the City of Los Angeles and the federal government in the 1930s. In the shadow of the Eastern Sierra, the cemetery includes recent burials as well as older burials simply marked with wooden crosses. (Courtesy of David Ortega.)

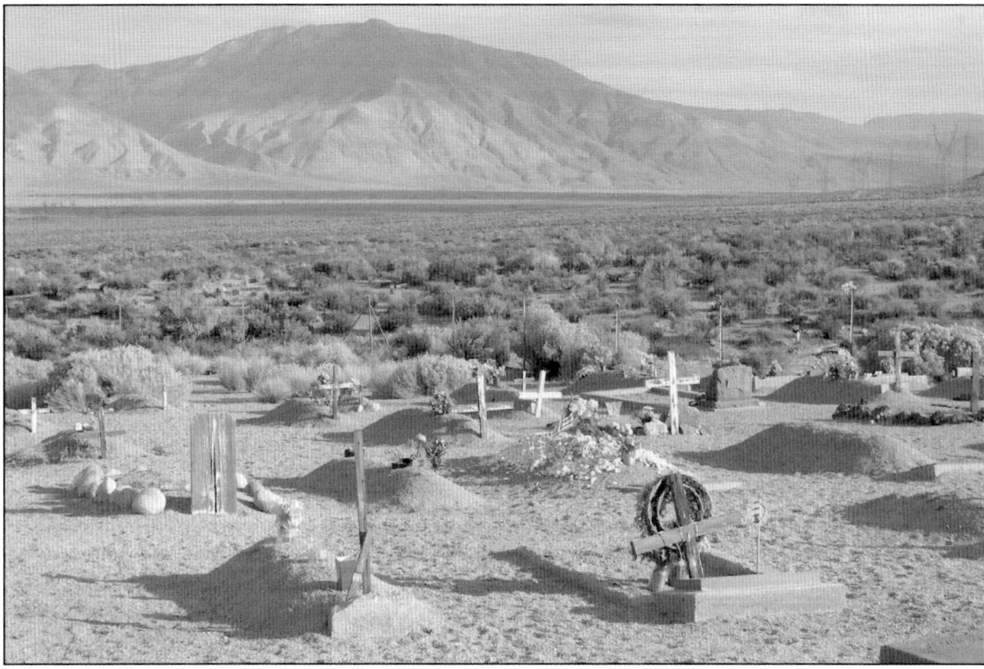

Death and the costs associated with it were expensive in the late 19th century and early 20th century, much as they are now. Tombstones engraved with names, imagery, and poetic verse were a costly indulgence. It was easier for most families to just erect their own memorial, sometimes a wooden cross or simple headstone. Unfortunately, with time, wood decays and names become impossible to read. (Courtesy of David Ortega.)

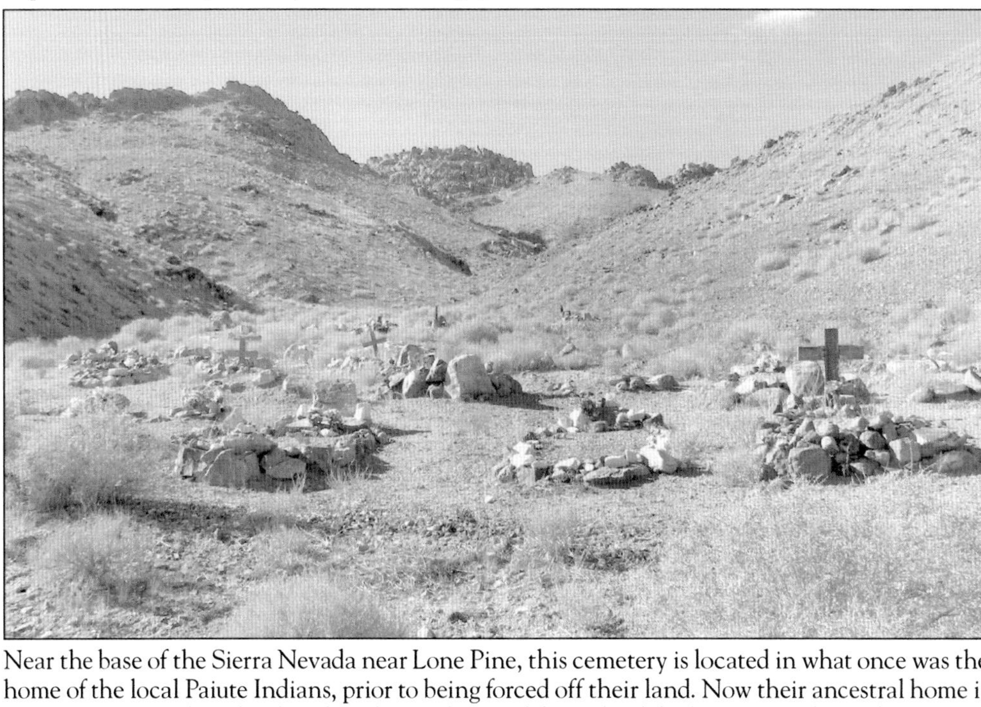

Near the base of the Sierra Nevada near Lone Pine, this cemetery is located in what once was the home of the local Paiute Indians, prior to being forced off their land. Now their ancestral home is the final resting place for their loved ones departed from this life. (Courtesy of David Ortega.)

Long before thousands of Japanese heritage were relocated to Manzanar during World War II, a single Japanese individual died in the Owens Valley. A small grave sits alone in the first section of the West Line cemetery in Bishop with the English words, "A Japanese, Died Oct 30, 1909." (Courtesy of David Ortega.)

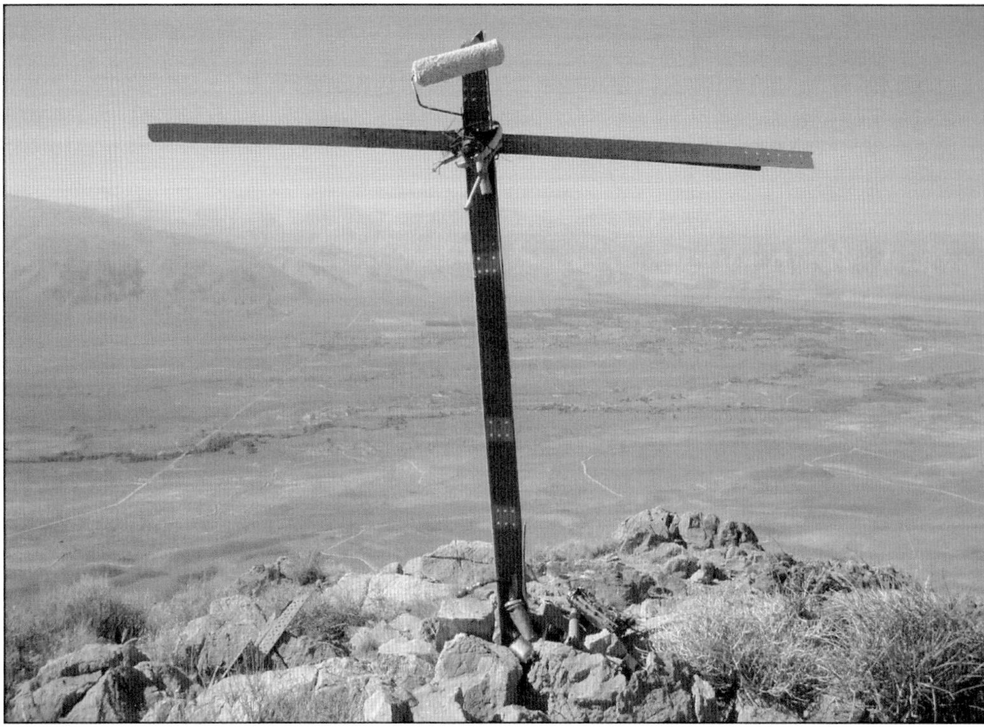

This Bishop memorial honors victims of one of the many plane crashes to occur in the Owens Valley. One Eastern Sierra plane crash survivor, Lauren Elder, wrote a book about her experience. A 1941 movie called *Three Secrets* depicts a plane crash in the area. The worst aviation disaster in Inyo County history was the 1974 accident involving actor Janos Prohaska and the cast and crew of *The Ascent of Man*. (Courtesy of Cat House.)

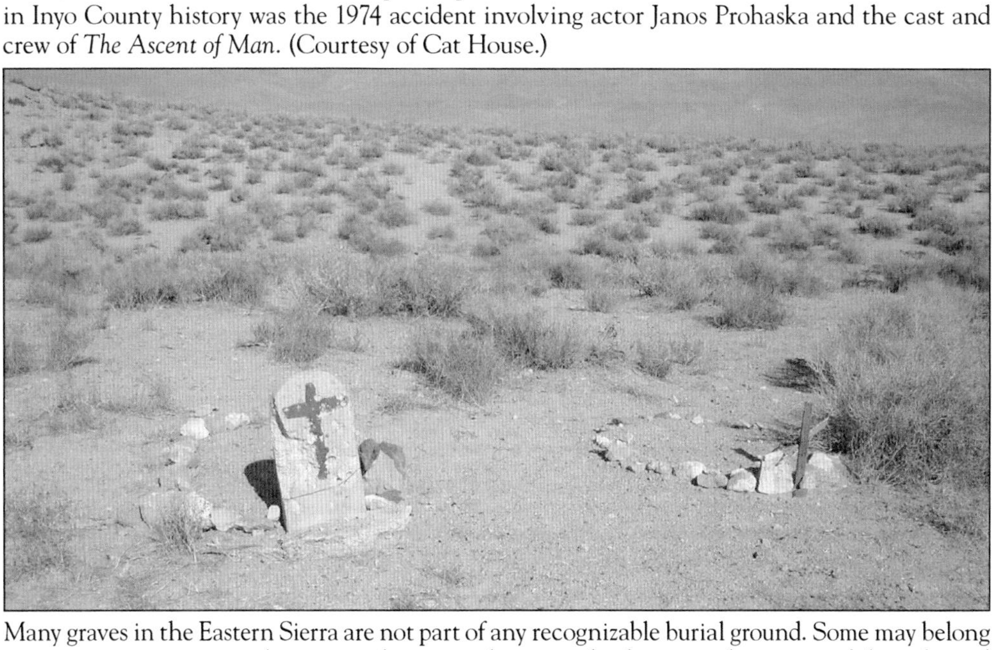

Many graves in the Eastern Sierra are not part of any recognizable burial ground. Some may belong to a pioneer cemetery unknown to those now living and others may be graves of those buried where they died. Still others are buried in open areas for reasons only known to those who buried them. These two lone graves are located in Bishop, California. (Courtesy of Cat House.)

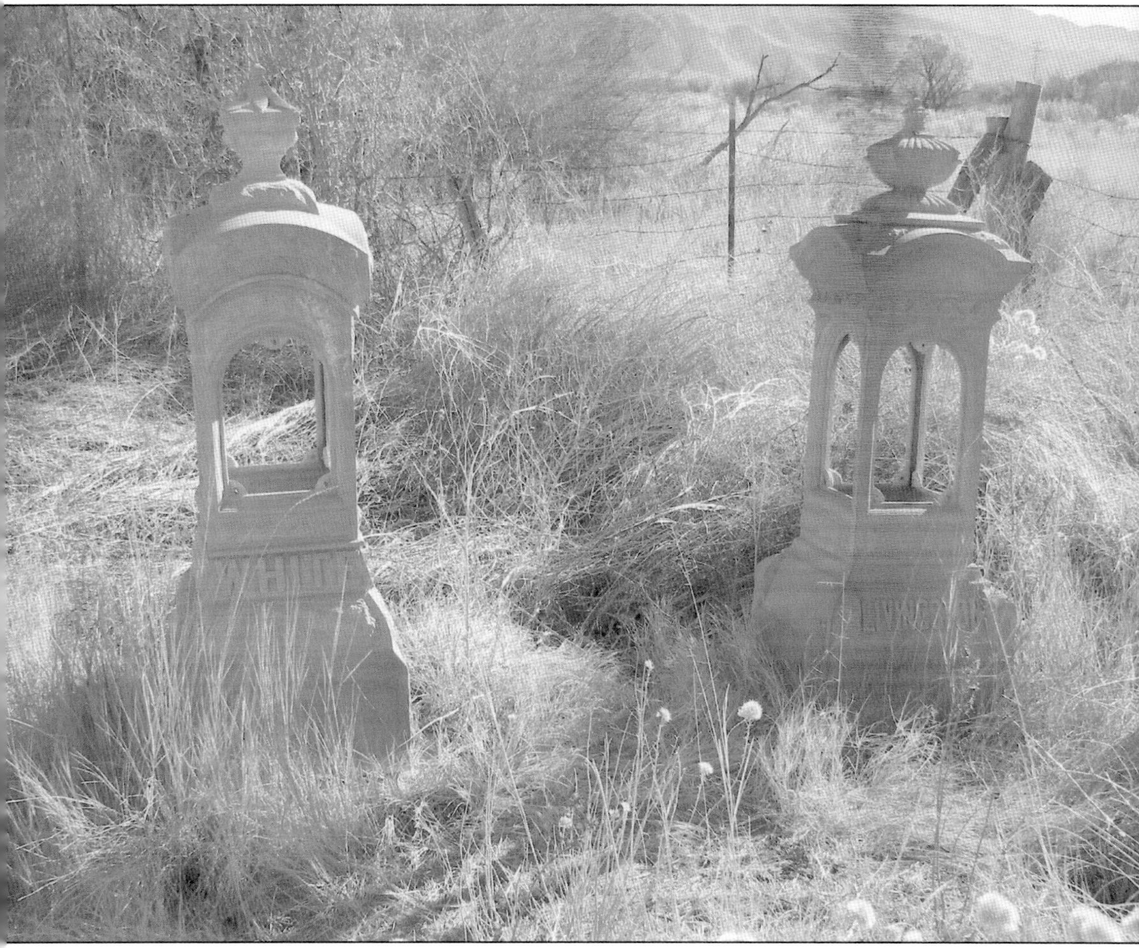

These two metal markers demonstrate just one type of vandalism that old cemeteries are prone to. These headstones, now simply labeled with the surnames White and Livingston, at one time included inserts that would have given the person's name, birth and death information, and other details that the family would have chosen. Each headstone could be a memorial for more than one person. (Courtesy of David Ortega.)

Bibliography

Austin, Mary. *The Land of Little Rain*. New York: Penguin Books, 1997.

Billeb, Emil W. *Mining Camp Days*. Las Vegas, NV: Nevada Publications, 1986.

Busby, Joan. *The Other Side of the Fence*. Concord, CA: Mustard Seed Press, 2005.

Cain, Ella M. *The Story of Early Mono County*. San Francisco, CA: Fearon Publishers, 1961.

Calhoun, Margaret. *Pioneers of Mono Basin*. Lee Vining, CA: R. C. Calhoun and Artemisia Press, 1984.

Chalfant, W. A. *The Story of Inyo*. rev. ed. Bishop, CA: Community Printing and Publishing, 1975.

Cragen, Dorothy Clora. *The Boys in the Sky-Blue Pants: The Union Troops at Camp Independence Preserved Peace in the Owens Valley-Nevada-Utah 1862–1877*. Fresno, CA: Pioneer Publishing Company, 1975.

Doyle, Helen MacKnight. *A Child Went Forth: The Autobiography of Helen MacKnight Doyle*. New York: Gotham House, 1934.

La Barque, Lilly Mathieu. *Man from Mono*. Self published, 1984.

Likes, Robert C. and Glenn R. Fay. *From this Mountain—Cerro Gordo*. Bishop, CA: Community Printing and Publishing, 1975.

Reed, Adele. *Old Mammoth*. Mammoth Lakes, CA: Genny Smith Books, 1994.

Southern Inyo American Association of Retired Persons. *Saga of Inyo County*. Covina, CA: Taylor Publishing, 1977.

Walton, John. *Western Times and Water Wars. State, Culture, and Rebellion in California*. Berkeley, CA: University of California Press, 1992.

Wehrey, Jane. *Voices from this Long Brown Land. Oral Recollections of Owens Valley Lives and Manzanar Pasts*. New York: Palgrave Macmillan, 2006.

INDEX